# Effective Stillwater Fly Fishing

# Effective Stillwater Fly Fishing

An analytical approach to help you catch more fish

MICHAEL GORMAN

HEADWATER BOOKS

STACKPOLE BOOKS

Joann Severson, ace fly angler
and World's Best Sister

*No one on Planet Earth gives me greater pleasure when playing a worthy fish than my sister Joann. And very few people are as appreciative of my guiding efforts as she is. Her fly-fishing focus, her patience with her big brother's casting and fishing instructions, and her relentless joy make Joann my all-time favorite fishing guest. Besides excelling at trout fishing in lakes and streams, she is an excellent steelhead fly fisher.*



Published by
STACKPOLE BOOKS
5067 Ritter Road
Mechanicsburg, PA 17055
www.stackpolebooks.com



Printed in the United States of America

10 9 8 7 6 5 4 3 2 1

First edition
Cover photo: Michael Gorman and Lesley Arle
Cover design: Caroline Stover

**Library of Congress Cataloging-in-Publication Data**

Gorman, Michael, 1950–
Effective stillwater fly fishing : an analytical approach to help you catch more fish / Michael Gorman. — First edition.
pages cm
ISBN 978-0-8117-1301-6
1. Trout fishing—Handbooks, manuals, etc. 2. Fly fishing—Handbooks, manuals, etc. I. Title. II. Title: Effective still water fly fishing, an analytical approach to help you catch more fish.
SH687.G67 2014
799.12'4—dc23

2013033841

# CONTENTS

# INTRODUCTION

More fish, bigger fish, and plenty of elbow room to catch them: these are the things that learning to successfully pursue fish in lakes and ponds will offer the resourceful fly angler. Sounds good, but . . .

I have some angling friends who have excellent fly-fishing skills, but they absolutely refuse to fish lakes or ponds. It's mostly pride, I think. They have a low threshold for the pain of a humility injury. Because lake fish have not always come easily to these folks, they wade and boat only streams and rivers where fish—mostly trout out here in the Pacific Northwest—are more easily located and caught. For them, lakes are too demanding, with too many puzzles to solve, and their fish-catching egos might be bruised.

It is true: all good lake fishermen know defeat, as measured in fish-landed success. It's part of the learning process. So why fish lakes? When my students in Oregon State University's fly-fishing and fly-tying classes pose this logical question, I reply with the three good reasons I gave in my opening sentence: elbow room, lots of fish, and the possibility of BIG fish. I'll expand briefly.

**Elbow room:** River fishermen have their favorite spots. I am no exception. Stream fish hold in very specific, sometimes small, areas. That can be a big downside to moving waters: when the fishing is good and the weather is nice, other anglers may commandeer every single place I want to fish. Grrrr!

**Lots of fish:** River fish concentrate in relatively tiny zones for the combination of food, safety, and comfort. "Small" neighborhoods that meet all three criteria limit the number of fish in most streams, as compared to the prime habitat and food production broadly available in quality ponds and lakes. So angler

A floating craft is a necessary tool to be consistently successful on most stillwaters.

crowding on stillwaters is usually not to the same degree as that found on streams. With more food available in more areas in quality lakes, there are simply more fish per square surface acre.

**Big fish:** If a fisherman wants to try for a truly large resident, non-migratory trout, or a lunker bass, the best chances will be found in productive stillwaters.

These three considerations make it rationally desirable for fly anglers to learn how to effectively fish lakes and ponds. However, reason can fly out the window when frustration and its related emotions come into play in the fisherman's psyche.

Sometimes even a mediocre fly angler can put up All-Star statistics on lakes. The fish seem to be everywhere he casts his fly, and the pattern and method are not important to success. It is days like these that can create a false confidence in the fly fisherman, whereby he believes he actually knows the basics—even the skilled nuances—of catching worthwhile trout in stillwaters. Rude surprises and frustration are only one fishing trip away for delicate egos.

Even the best stillwater anglers I know in my large circle of angling friends and acquaintances meet total defeat now and then. Me, too. There seem to be two camps of emotional reaction to being humbled on stillwaters: 1) resignation to only fish rivers and streams or 2) embracing the challenge with a determination to figure out the puzzle next time. My hope is that after reading this book you will always be in the camp with those who are inspired by a beating on a lake to turn it into a positive determination to learn more, discover more solutions to fishing challenges, and take pleasure in future fish-catching successes when you can correctly arrange all the puzzle pieces on a lake when others cannot.

The chapters that follow are replete with many of my personal experiences so that you may learn from my challenges and my solutions, and understand the outlook that drives me to always want to learn more about fly-fishing stillwaters, and, as a result, catch more fish on a consistent basis. Besides conveying effective fish-catching tools, skills, and knowledge, this book is intended to give—as best it can—the healthy psyche-preserving mental approach to successfully catching stillwater fish. It is for those who want to overcome the psychological defeat that we all inevitably deal with when fly fishing lakes.

Before I sat down to write this introduction, I read a magazine article about fly fishing lakes. The author presented his views on necessary fly lines, trick techniques, where the trout will likely be in the lake at any given point during the fishing day, and some fly recommendations. This was all well and good for a brief, no frills article. However, I found myself saying to the author, *Tell me a situation where you would truly need a Type VI sinking line, where a Type III or IV would not do the*

The author in his classroom discussing fly fishing with students at Oregon State University. The university offers four different credit classes on fly fishing and fly tying.

*same job. Tell me a story to illustrate, so that I might believe.* Or, *Why is this particular damsel nymph you have suggested superior to the other damsel patterns available on the market? Tell me a story about the day it produced for you when others would not. Convince me why I should use your methods, your tackle, your fly recommendations. Tell me about lake fishing puzzles you encountered and solved with your techniques, your special equipment, and your special flies. Make me believe you really know what you are writing about.*

This is more than a sterile fishing cookbook containing only the same old hackneyed recipes on how, where, when, and what. As I did in my first book, *Steelhead Fly Angling: Guerilla Fly-Rod Tactics*, I have filled this book with stories of victory and defeat, elation and frustration, to illustrate lessons I have discovered to be key in successfully fishing lakes.

Owning a fly-fishing shop (The Scarlet Ibis in Corvallis, OR) for twenty years, I had to know how to catch fish in lakes. Simply, it was a matter of good business: I had to be the local expert. People came to me for fly-fishing advice and products. If I could enable them to be successful in catching fish with the equipment and flies they purchased from me, I had happy customers who patronized my business and told their friends. To do this, I had to learn not only how to fish rivers, but lakes, too.

If you welcome the challenge of puzzle-solving, as I do, stillwater fly fishing has much to offer. For me, each lake or pond is the next Sudoku challenge in a book with endless pages. Some days the solutions are easily figured out; on others—those where there is an opportunity to learn something new—I have to be clever, experimental, and resourceful. A "hard," "challenger," or even "diabolical" puzzle definitely has the potential for the highest level of satisfaction when a solution is discovered. Successful puzzle-solving builds confidence and determination to overwhelm the frustration which will inevitably greet lake and pond anglers in their fishing journeys.

Later in the book, one of the stories I'll relate is about fishing famous Roche Lake, near Kamloops, British Columbia. Though the conditions were good on June 10, 2010, and lots of rainbow trout were present, I, along with scores of other fishermen, had no fish-catching success. This was a real head scratcher. Like any good magician, I had a lot of tricks, but nothing that fooled the audience. Instead of leaving in tears, though, or vowing never to return for a future thrashing at the hands (fins) of these heartless trout, I was excited and intrigued to return to Roche. I did so the following year, when I had some modicum of success, hooking (and even landing!) some memorable fish. My experiences with this lake taught me new things, gave me fresh insights, and reminded me of lessons I had forgotten or ignored.

Elbow room and serenity are commonplace on lakes and ponds. Edith Lake, BC.

Stories like this are representative of what you may encounter in fly-fishing stillwaters. I hope in sharing my experiences, I'll inspire you to solve your own fishing puzzles, to earn the satisfaction of successfully using your wit and your resourcefulness to catch stillwater fish when others cannot. Most importantly, I want you to be determined and excited—not frustrated—to return to those waters where the fishing results challenged you and success was minimal, with the anticipation that you *will* catch fish there on future trips.

CHAPTER 1

# Fear of Lakes, and Overcoming It

Josh Cuperus battles a large cutthroat trout on Henry's Lake in Idaho.

In my line of work, I meet a plethora of excellent stream anglers. To qualify as "excellent," this particular group of fly fishermen (and women) share common traits: good casting skills; a fair to good knowledge of aquatic entomology; the ability to locate fish; effectiveness in fishing dry flies, wet flies, and nymphs; and the resourcefulness to successfully think through challenging fishing situations. What they don't share is the ability to successfully fish lakes. In fact, a significant number of this moving-water brotherhood seem to actually fear the challenges of stillwaters, having been too often defeated by the puzzles presented by locating and catching fish in lakes. Having reveled in many memorable days of big numbers and big fish in rivers and streams, it's a hard kidney punch to the ego when a proud angler has humble pie for breakfast, lunch, and dinner on a lake.

Fish in streams and rivers are definitely easier to locate compared to the constant nomadic movements of those in stillwater. Most fly anglers in the typical trout stream can quickly learn to find fish. In the freestone streams of the American West, take into consideration these factors: current velocity, depth, and structure. I tell my Oregon State University (OSU) students they can most easily find catchable trout in:

- 3 to 7 feet of water
- walking speed current
- structure in the form of boulders, ledges, pockets, and channels
- transition zones where shallow water slopes into deeper water

Large stillwaters, such as Oregon's Davis Lake, add to the angler's challenge of discovering where the fish are at any given time.

Yes, fish can be found in shallower/deeper areas, with faster/slower current velocities, sometimes devoid of discernible structure. But when fish are not obviously in other locations, focus on seeking out the water types described above. With a little practice and experience, stream fish can be located and caught. By focusing on moving water where trout likely hold, you have solved the cornerstone challenge of all successful fly fishing: you are precisely where the fish are. Then it's a matter of selecting the right fly, with the right technique, fished at the appropriate depth.

In lakes (and rivers) it does not matter that you are fishing the right fly with the right retrieve at the correct depth if there are no fish in your immediate area. And, even when you successfully locate lake fish—even catching some—the fish may move out of your area as sunlight intensity changes, water temperatures rise or decrease, insects stop hatching, or fishing activity intensifies. Successful anglers move when the fish vacate the area. If the fish are not rising to surface insects or cruising in the shallows where you can see them, it may not be easy to find the fish again. You must learn how to do so. Often, the bigger the lake, the bigger the challenge: the larger the haystack in which to find the needle.

So, how does an angler develop the inner strength and determination to become an excellent and resourceful lake fisherman? Their best hope, I think, is twofold: 1) make a commitment to persevere at lake fishing, embracing its challenges, and 2) broaden and increase experience.

## Committing to Win

It is not in everyone's emotional composition to make the necessary commitment to learning effective stillwater fishing. The occasional fly angler may want to spend minimal effort and not do too much puzzle-solving to catch a reasonable number of fish for his efforts. Because he does not fish very often, he is content to wade in familiar, approachable, and productive areas of rivers he can easily read, catching fish he knows are there and willing to bite his fly. If for no other reason, the time required to learn about lake fishing usually prevents the occasional fly angler from becoming consistently proficient in stillwaters.

Then there is the fisherman who is content to catch fish in streams and rivers because he enjoys the moving water environment: the feel of the currents flowing around his legs, reading the water, watching the flies and line carried in the flow, and anticipating the strike he hopes will come. This type of setting and its fish speak to him. With thousands of streams and rivers in America and Canada, the dedicated river angler will always have one more stream to fish. He is perfectly satisfied to explore and fish moving waters until he makes his last cast.

Some anglers fish lakes often and dedicate a lot of time to their fishing. However, they fish only one or a few lakes. They may become good at catching fish in the tiny number of waters they know intimately but may adapt poorly to a new lake and its idiosyncrasies. Their experience base is too narrow.

The broader and more varied an angler's fishing experiences, the larger the skill set he or she has to draw on when fishing is difficult. The most resourceful and competent lake anglers have fished many different lakes successfully, under a variety of conditions, for a variety of fish species. Commitment, devotion of time to the cause, and the ability to learn from and rely on a broad base of lake fishing experiences are the factors that combine to create a lake fly fisherman who has the very best chance of catching fish in stillwaters. For some of us, this is the ultimate test of skills, experience, and resourcefulness.

As already mentioned, there are times on lakes when minimal skill and experience are needed to catch fish. Fly pattern, retrieve, depth, and location may not matter. The fish are suicidal. Everyone is catching fish. There is no intrigue, no challenge. If you are new to fly fishing, this can be great fun; it may even inspire you to persist at fishing lakes. However, for experienced fly fishermen seeking a challenge, suicidal fish can be fun for a brief while—maybe longer if the fish are BIG—but interest soon wanes.

It is my opinion that suicidal fish have very little to teach an experienced, hungry-to-learn-more lake angler. It is not merely the number of lake fish landed in a day that give the sense of success, but the number of *challenging* fish that are caught. If you can catch fish when others cannot—and do this on a somewhat consistent basis—you have confirmation that you have truly solved some of the mysteries of lake fishing.

At this point, pride will color your thoughts, guaranteed. Your head can swell with your success. Be careful. Know that a hard lesson will follow, and you *will* eat crow for lunch in your future. Maybe not tomorrow, or the next day, but sometime . . . your Roche Lake will find you.

## Roche Lake, British Columbia

Despite more than forty years' experience fishing lakes, I have an occasional day when I am skunked—even on a very good, highly productive lake. Though these days are rare at this point in my fishing life, there was one I can't forget in the not-too-distant past: June 12, 2010. Though I was fishless, it was an excellent

Unusual color combinations for standard fly patterns, like the Woolly Bugger, may sometimes entice reluctant fish to bite.

day for me. It had been a very long time—years—since I had been so soundly thrashed on a lake when conditions appeared to be good, and numerous fish were definitely in my vicinity. Just the day before, I had been the high rod on a new lake I fished for the first time. As far as I could discern from the anglers I watched and spoke with on my high rod day, everyone there was a local Canadian, familiar with Edith Lake and its fish—and I'd outfished them all. This success added an extra sting to my shut-out performance at the famous Roche Lake the following day.

Prior to this trip, it had been more than a dozen years since I'd fished lakes in British Columbia. In the late winter of 2010, I started collecting information on the lake-fishing possibilities in and around the city of Kamloops. Over several months, I narrowed to five the number of waters to be fished during my week's stay. One of the five was Roche Lake, a productive lake within thirty minutes of Kamloops. It is easily accessed and very popular. To keep the fishing masses happy, British Columbia Fisheries plants many, many rainbow trout here. I had high hopes for lots of trout-catching photos and stories of glory during my day at Roche Lake.

When fishing a lake for the first time, it is helpful to watch other anglers to get some clues about where and how to fish. On Roche Lake that day, there was no shortage of fishermen to observe. Float tubes, pontoon boats, rafts, canoes, and powerboats were everywhere. I expected a lot of people; people go where the fish are, especially if it's not difficult to get there. And, there were, indeed, many fish in this food-rich environment.

To begin exploring a new lake, I attach my depth finder unit to my float tube or pontoon boat. As I kicked away from the launch site, I immediately had fish readings on the screen of my finder—so many readings, in fact, that there was no time in the first thirty minutes on the lake that I was not getting multiple images of trout swimming under and around me. I imagined that John Gorman, my cousin and fishing companion on this trip, and I were going to have not just a good day, but a stellar day on Roche. With so many sightings on my radar, I was not prompted in any way to remember that pride often comes before a fall. Not today, for sure; too many fish and too much experience. Moreover, I was fully prepared, carrying three fly rods on my craft, with boxes of killer flies to fish the top, middle, and bottom of the water column. Those fish did not have a chance!

For the first hour, I bobbed and weaved through several dozen anglers anchored or kicking around in the bay where we had launched. I watched and listened as I mindlessly trolled leeches, scuds, chironomids, and my dependable Beadhead Prince among and over the trout that seemed to be everywhere. In that first sixty minutes I saw a grand total of two fish hooked among a group of no fewer than twenty anglers who appeared to know what they were doing. I suspected that the majority were local regulars familiar with Roche Lake and its idiosyncrasies; however, they weren't offering any help. I was going to have to figure it out on my own, since no one else around me seemed to be having much luck catching anything.

Seven hours later, the expert from Oregon had landed not a single fish! Ouch! I moved constantly, experimenting with flies and retrieves at a variety of depths. I continued to watch and listen, but to no avail. I could not remember a day in recent years when I had been as soundly thrashed by trout in a lake, especially one that had so many fish in it. My only consolation was that there were many other anglers, including skilled locals, who recorded a goose egg on Roche Lake that June day.

However, my experience was not a total loss; there were adjustments I realized needed to be made for my next trip to

There are times it may make sense to hire a local fly-fishing guide to familiarize you with a particular lake you wish to learn.

Stillwater fish come in all sizes. Every angler loves to catch big fish, but don't overlook the spirit and aesthetics of small fish, too.

this lake. Some of the changes to be made came from hours of reflection on my fishing day; others came from talking to several semi-successful anglers with whom I spoke on the lake during the day. I knew with certainty that there was an answer to that lake's riddle.

There was at least one angler—apparently a guide—who knew exactly where to park his boat, the correct fly to use, and the retrieve that got results. He also knew when to pick up the anchor and move. I found him and his guest at the farthest range of my travels on the lake in late afternoon. The guest was doing most of the fishing and catching, while the boatman guide gave directions, pointed to where to make the next series of casts, and tied on new flies. Occasionally, he would pick up a rod and catch a fish, too. I circled in my pontoon boat at a courteous distance, watching and listening. Through triangulation, I tried to pinpoint their position as best I could so that I might examine the area where they were anchored.

When they left their initial spot, I moved in to the kill zone, trying to discover if there was an obvious underwater feature—a channel, spring hole, drop off, or weed line—where the trout had concentrated. My electronic device revealed nothing obvious. Unable to discern the magnet that had drawn the fishermen and fish to that exact location, I eventually kicked my boat nearer to the next anchoring point of that same guide. He and his guest were again catching fish at their new location. I had watched from a distance as the boatman had zigged and zagged the new area with his boat, all the time staring at his electronic depth finder. He was scouting for something quite specific before he finally dropped his anchor. From the fish-catching results, he had found it.

Though I eventually traveled in, around, and through the second location after the guide boat left, I failed to discover any obvious features he had apparently sought out. Whatever drew his attention and guided his decision to drop anchor was too subtle for me to discern. However, the most important thing to me for a future trip here was the fact that there was, indeed, a solution: these fish could be caught.

My first inclination was to return to Roche Lake the next day to redeem myself. I had a revised game plan to implement: earlier arrival, a few different flies, and a more exploratory, stay-on-the-move approach to locate willing, feeding fish. But our schedule was tight, and my top priority was to explore different lakes during our short stay.

Even though my ego was pummeled, I knew I would be coming back to Roche Lake to make adjustments and finally fool those wily trout that refused to bite for the vast majority of fishermen on my day there. Instead of resigned defeat, I was inspired to try again and again until I found the solution to the puzzle.

If I had caught many fish in all the British Columbia lakes we fished, I would not be anxious to return. I went, saw, and conquered; it was time for a new quest. However, having failed, I know I must go back. Roche Lake will not beat me again. Even if it should, this will not instill a sense of defeat in me. Instead, my attitude will be one of determination, with a hint of anger in response to my stung pride. I will go back as long as it takes to crack the code.

I know there is never just one answer to challenging lake fishing. One revelation about location, fly pattern, or method may suffice for an hour or a day, but conditions and the fish in stillwaters can change constantly. It is best to assume that you will always face multiple challenges in a lake.

For instance, not only do fish relocate often during the fishing day, but also their food preferences can change hourly as well, as can the effective retrieve of the fly, the fly pattern itself, or the depth at which the angler finds willing fish. Changing weather, moon phase, and the angling activities of fishermen crowded into a small area can all affect angling success. Sometimes, the fish refuse to bite a fly no matter what is done. One of our challenges, then, is to discern whether the fish are truly "off the bite," or if they can be tempted when the necessary adjustments are made.

To be a successful lake fly fisher, you must embrace these challenges. You must enjoy puzzle solving. And you must cultivate a determined attitude to win tomorrow after being defeated today. There will be tough days, but on most, the fish can be caught. After all, they must eat, just like you and me. Vow that if anyone can catch a fish today, it will be you. Success begins with that decision.

# CHAPTER 2

# Stillwater Entomology

*Callibaetis* mayflies are a prevalent food source for stillwater fish in spring and summer.

Almost every child knows about the life stages of moths and butterflies: egg, caterpillar (larva), chrysalis (pupa), and adult. Aquatic insects, too, go through a distinct life cycle. With the exception of the miniscule egg stage, lake anglers who want to maximize their fishing success learn the importance of imitating and fishing each of the life stages of aquatic insects.

There are two distinct life cycle paths, referred to as *complete metamorphosis* and *incomplete metamorphosis*. Metamorphosis literally means "change in shape or form; transformation."

Insects such as caddisflies and midges move through complete metamorphosis, from egg to larva to pupa to adult. Insects that go through incomplete metamorphosis—including mayflies, damselflies, and dragonflies—transform from egg to nymph to adult.

## Caddisflies

### Adults

In their adult form, caddisflies look like moths at first glance. They are identified by their wings, which are longer than the body and are held tent-like over the body at rest. Upon close inspection with a magnifier, it is evident that the wings are covered with tiny hairs. The caddisfly has no tail but is equipped with long antennae, sometimes longer than the body.

Look for caddisflies to be hatching and most active during the warmer months of the year, April through October. During a caddis hatch, the adults will be in evidence fluttering and skating on the water's surface, particularly over the littoral zone of the lake or pond, where the water is shallow enough for sunlight

A Stimulator is an excellent artificial imitation of the caddisfly adult, a moth-like aquatic insect characterized by tent-like wings, no tail, and long antennae.

Hungry fish may swallow a caddisfly larva, case and all. The digestive juices break down the larva in the case and the nutritional substance of the insect is then available to the fish. The empty caddis case is eventually expelled.

to penetrate and the caddisflies have good habitat in which to live and grow. In deep lakes, the shallows along the shorelines are where the floating and fluttering adults will be concentrated. If conditions are windy, look for many of the pupae and adults to be pushed to the downwind end of the lake—a good area, obviously, to focus fishing efforts. When rising trout are feeding on adult caddisflies, cast a Parachute Adams, Elk Hair Caddis, or Stimulator in the vicinity of the risers. Let the fly sit. Strikes may be triggered if little twitches are imparted to the fly. If you should encounter caddisflies like the famous Canadian Running Caddis, lift your rod tip high and attempt to skate or skitter the fly across the surface. A skated fly can create a lot of miscues by the fish. Try to relax and enjoy the show as they swirl and splash, even when many strikes are missed. Hookups will come.

## Larvae

Because caddisflies have a four-stage life cycle, the lake angler needs to carry flies that imitate the larval and pupal forms of these insects. The caddis larva of main concern in stillwaters builds a tube-like case. The larva lives inside the hollow tube, which it constructs by cementing items like fir needles, leaf bits, small stones, and assorted chunks of vegetation from its environment. These construction items are bound into a traveling living space by secretions from the insect. In times of danger, the larva quickly retracts its legs and head into the case, just as a turtle ducks inside its shell. As caddis larvae crawl and make feeble attempts at swimming as they go about their daily activities along the bottom or amidst the vegetation in lakes and ponds, fish seek them out to eat, case and all.

To best determine the size and color of the caddis case and the larva inside, I try to capture a live specimen. I use a contrived tool that has a small aquarium net solidly taped to a broken fly rod. In shallow water, I can run the net along the bottom and through vegetation to see what I can discover. Early on, if I catch a fish, I will pump its stomach to check the contents for clues. And I am always on the lookout for pupae and adults in or on the water, or on the shoreline vegetation.

As for flies, the Peeking Caddis, Stimulator, and a skinny Woolly in a variety of colors and sizes 12 through 6 will catch fish. To effectively fish an imitation of the caddisfly larva, the angler should cast his fly into likely locations and allow the fly to sink near the bottom. The specific fly line used will depend on the depth. A floating line is best for casting a slightly weighted pattern into 6 feet of water or less. For deeper water, an intermediate or the clear, slow-sinking line is my preference. Once settled on or very near the bottom, a slow hand-twist retrieve, interspersed with a few slow, short strips and pauses, will do the trick if the fish are interested. A slow troll will also work. I cannot emphasize enough that these little creatures move painfully slowly. Your retrieve or troll must be the same. Creep the fly.

## Pupae

In preparation for the transformation into the adult stage, the caddis larvae in lakes seal off the openings of their cases. Over the next one week to almost two months (depending on the caddis family), the insects pupate, and major bodily changes occur. When the transformation is complete, the caddis pupa frees itself from its tube and swims to the surface, or crawls out on exposed vegetation or shoreline stones. Once there, the pupa splits its skin. Out of the pupal skin emerges the winged adult. When its wings are unfolded and dry, the newly hatched adult flies to safety in the nearby vegetation or shoreline. Over the next one to three weeks, it will seek a mate, do the dance of life, and die. Females drop their fertilized eggs into the water, and the cycle begins again. The eggs descend through the water of the lake or pond, where it becomes a game of numbers as to

When the caddisfly pupa swims to the surface, where it will transform into the adult, fish will feast on it. Because the pupa is more easily captured than the fluttering adult, fish feeding the surface may choose the helpless emerging adult.

When caddisflies are hatching, a pupal imitation, such as this Tied-Down Caddis, may out-produce the dry fly because the pupae are more easily captured by the fish.

which will land in a suitable growing environment and which will be lost.

Since some caddisfly pupae crawl toward safety and adulthood while others swim up through the water column, you must be prepared to simulate both types of locomotion until you discover the better of the two. In the case of the crawlers, fish the fly as I described for the larvae. To simulate pupae ascending vertically to the surface, it all starts with allowing the fly to sink to the bottom. Then slowly raise the rod tip, causing the fly to rise. From its raised position, the rod tip must be lowered to the surface again in preparation for another lift. While lowering the tip, strip in the slack line that was created by the lift. Patiently wait for the fly to sink before raising the rod tip once again to simulate a pupa swimming for the surface. Slow lift, slow drop, and gather the slack. Repeat. Use a floating line for shallow water and the clear line for deeper.

Assorted soft-hackles with silver beadheads and the Tied-Down Caddis are among my favorite emerging pupae patterns (see page 181), sizes 8 through 14.

Once a caddis pupa reaches the surface, it may linger for a few seconds, a minute, or forever. It is here that the swimming pupa will struggle mightily to free itself from its straightjacket skin, emerge, and fly away before being eaten. Some unfortunates will not successfully exit, remaining trapped until they are eaten or dying encased in their pupal skin tombs. At this point in the emergence, I fish a MijCadMay Emerger of appropriate size and color on the surface or in the surface film, just like a dry fly. In fact, my ideal two-fly setup matches this emerger on the point with a dry fly as the dropper. Let the flies sit for twenty or thirty seconds, then give them a twitch or short strip. Also, occasionally lift the rod tip to skitter or skate the flies.

## Midges

In spite of their small size, midges are one food source available to stillwater fish year-round. As fish forage for something to eat in the cold months when other insects are inactive and largely unavailable, hardy midges can be found hatching in any waters that are not ice-bound. Knowledge of these insects and fishing their imitations is imperative to the success of any serious lake fly angler, no matter the time of year.

Adult midges can be identified by two wings that are held in a delta-wing configuration when at rest and are shorter than the body of the fly. There are no tails, and the antennae of the males look like miniature plumes. Common colors include tan, gray, black, olive, bright green, and brick.

Let's briefly examine a little taxonomy. Within the class Insecta (insects, duh) is the order of insects Diptera (two-winged flies). Within the order Diptera is the family Chironomidae, or midges. Throughout this text, the terms midge and chironomid will be used interchangeably.

### Larvae

Like the caddisflies, midges pass through a four-stage life cycle: egg, larva, pupa, and adult. Depending on the environment and water temperature, midges may have one to several generations in a year. The larvae are simple, worm-like creatures living in

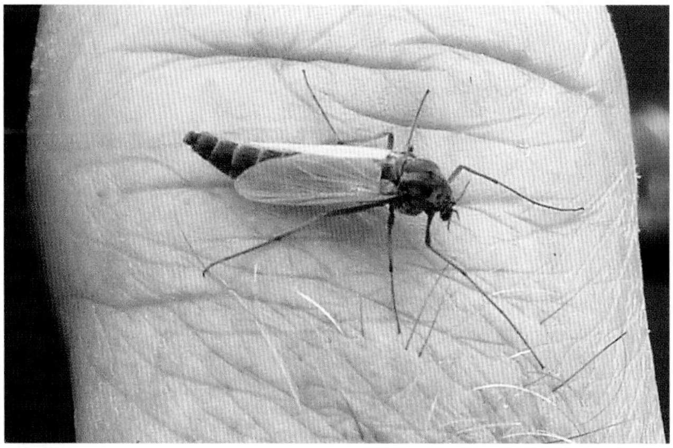

Though midges are small, they are abundant food sources available year-round.

or on the lake bottom, with some living in the dense jungle of bottom vegetation. Some chironomid larvae are free roaming wanderers, while others live in tubes or burrows in the mud. These "skinny worms" may be cream-colored or shades of brown or green. A striking red variety has a hemoglobin-like substance in its body that enhances the ability of the insect to extract oxygen from water where the oxygen levels can be extremely low. Feeding fish readily recognize the "bloodworm" as a desirable snack.

#### *Fishing the Midge Larva*

Midge larvae may be found in water up to 30 or 40 feet deep; they can also be found in the shallows along the shoreline. Depending on the depth the angler is exploring for fish, a floating line may be best, or a fast-sinking Type VI may be needed.

Whatever the line, once the fly is on or near the bottom, a very slow retrieve with occasional pauses can fool the fish. There are times I will suspend a V-Rib Larva pattern under an indicator, letting the fly sit stationary barely off the bottom. Occasionally, I will lift the rod tip very slowly to move the fly a few inches to a new location. My V-Rib Larvae are tied in sizes 18 through 12 in red, green, and brown.

### Pupae

Compared to the lengthier transition time of some stillwater caddisflies, midges pupate quickly, in about a week. When their time comes, the pupae float and wriggle excruciatingly slowly toward the surface, making them very easy for hungry fish to intercept. If they are lucky enough to reach the surface, the pupae must penetrate the surface tension barrier, sometimes a Herculean task for a tiny bug. They wriggle just below the surface, held there by an invisible ceiling, at least momentarily until their pupal skins split, enabling the pupae to break through the tension barrier.

#### *Fishing the Midge Pupa*

While the midge pupa fly can be cast and slowly retrieved using a variety of lines, many good anglers will use a floating fly line, an intermediate model, or a slow sinker. However, the most popular way to fish ascending pupae is suspended underneath an indicator cast with a floating line. Experimentation is needed to discover the exact depth, even when an electronic depth finder is used. It is usually best to have the flies situated barely off the bottom. Fishing two flies allows me to experiment with different sizes and colors. I may fish a larval pattern

Midge pupae are a food staple for fish year-round. The photo is of a stomach sample from a rainbow trout caught in Diamond Lake, OR.

A high-visibility floating fly line points the way to the indicator, under which hang chironomid pupae and larvae flies. Other fly patterns can be fixed the same way.

Though many species are small, midge adults can provide memorable surface fishing with the right artificial imitation.

on the point and a pupal pattern a couple feet above it on a short dropper line.

Effective chironomid pupae fly patterns usually have a number of characteristics in common including a thin abdomen with a distinctly larger head and thorax region, and obvious segmentation. There are many different combinations of body color and ribbing color segmentations, such as olive, green, brown, pearl, black, and red bodies, paired with a rib of gold, white, pearl, silver, gray, and red, in sizes 18 through 10.

## Chironomid Adults

Once the pupa breaks through the surface film and the skin is split, the adult quickly emerges and flies for the safety of shoreline vegetation. On colder days, the emergence takes longer and the adults linger longer before taking flight. When the air is calm, the males—characterized by their tiny bottlebrush antennae—gather in a large mating swarm. These swarms can be large enough so that the "hum" of thousands of tiny beating wings can be heard. When their eggs have matured, the females fly into the swarm of males and mating takes place. The fertilized eggs are eventually deposited into the water, and the cycle is complete.

### Fishing Chironomid Adults and Emergers

While fishing a dry fly to specifically imitate the winged midge adult can catch fish, it is often more productive to fish the struggling emerging stage of the insect. I may tie an adult imitation, such as Parachute Midge or Griffith's Gnat, on the dropper and my MijCadMay Emerger or Marabou Cripple as the point fly, always trying to match the size and color of the hatching insects. Casting the flies into a likely area, I let them sit. Occasionally, the rod tip is slowly lifted, or I pull the line a few inches, then allow the flies to remain stationary for another thirty to sixty seconds. Fly sizes range from 20 to 14.

## Mayflies

If there is a classic, prototypical aquatic insect in fly-fishing writing, photography, and art, it is the mayfly. With their delicate wings held high as they sit on the surface of a lake or stream, they appear as little sailboats adrift on a breeze, riding quietly on the currents or the wind.

With eighteen families of mayflies in North America, represented by numerous genera split into hundreds of species and

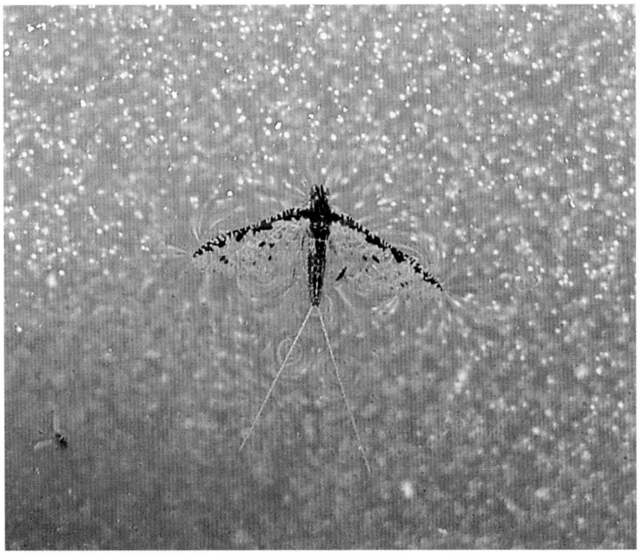

In spring and summer you can find an abundance of mayflies on stillwaters. Cruising fish will enthusiastically seek them out.

subspecies, mayflies abound in many non-polluted freshwater environments. For our discussion of stillwater mayflies, four families have members than can be of importance to the fly angler. Of these members, the genus *Callibaetis* mayfly of the family Baetidae garners the most attention of fish and anglers, especially in the American West.

Mayflies have an incomplete metamorphosis, with three life stages: egg, nymph, and adult. The adult stage has two phases. The newly hatched adult is referred to as the dun, or more technically, the subimago. A day or two after its emergence, the dun molts into the sexually mature spinner, or imago. The spinners have wings that are markedly clearer, more transparent than those of the dun stage. After mating in the next several hours or days, the females deposit their fertilized eggs on the water, dying soon afterward. Dead mayfly spinners lie on the water's surface, wings fallen to the sides of the insect. Fish will often feed heavily on the "spinner fall," quietly rising to prey that has no chance of—or need to—escape.

Adult mayflies can be identified by wings held upright when the insect is at rest. A tiny second set of wings may be seen at the base of the larger pair. Look for two or three long, slender tails extending behind a pronouncedly segmented body. The underside of the insect's body is often a lighter color than the dorsal side, an important difference for fly tiers and fishermen looking to match the exact color of the insect; the fish see the underside of the mayfly adult, not the top of the body that may be darker.

*Callibaetis* nymphs are most vulnerable as they swim for the surface, where they will split their nymphal skin to emerge into the adult stage.

## Nymphs

A single wing pad (a bulging area where the wings develop and grow) on the top of the thorax characterizes mayfly nymphs. Just as in the adult, there are two or three tails on an obviously segmented body, and gills are present on the abdomen of the insect. With a magnifying lens, you can observe a single hook or claw at the end of each leg.

The nymph of the Gray Drake mayfly, genus *Siphlonurus* of the family Siphlonuridae, is an energetic swimmer. With three hairy tails that can be interlocked for enhanced swimming capability, this insect darts around in the shallow weedy margins of a lake or pond in search of food. Because the nymph emerges by crawling out of the water onto exposed structures around and in lakes and ponds, the fish rarely get a chance to feed on the Gray Drake duns. The spent spinners provide food and are important to fly anglers.

The nymph of the huge *Hexagenia* mayfly (family Ephemeridae), or Big Yellow May, can measure up to 35 mm, just a little less than 1½ inches. Because they burrow into and live in the silt of the lake bottom, the nymphs are usually not available as fish food. Just prior to their transition into the adult phase, the nymphs are exposed for a short time as they crawl from their burrows in preparation for the swim to the surface.

Because of their tiny size and the fact that they are usually hidden in the vegetation and silt along the shallow margins of lakes and ponds, the nymphs of *Tricorythodes* mayflies (family Tricorythodidae) are of little importance to fly fishers. However, the duns and spinners will get the attention of fish.

Like the darting, swimming Gray Drake nymphs, the nymphs of the *Callibaetis* mayfly are excellent swimmers, making their daily rounds in search of water plants that hold the algae patches on which the insects dine. Besides gills that are a bit less prominent and tails that are not quite as hairy as those of the Gray Drake nymphs, the *Callibaetis* can be distinguished by longer antennae, which are about three to four times the length of the nymph's head. Because of their abundance, availability as food, and the emergence of several generations over a period of many months, spring into fall, lake anglers must take special note of the *Callibaetis* nymph; the fish certainly do.

### *Fishing Mayfly Nymphs*

Because the nymphs of the Gray Drake and the *Callibaetis* mayflies are the two of most concern to the fish, these are the ones to emphasize. To make matters even simpler, the nymphs of both are similar in appearance, live in similar habitats, and are both darting swimmers. Generally, to imitate and fish one is to imitate and fish the other. To fine-tune the fly pattern, it is always best to capture a natural or steal one from a fish's stomach for examination. It is then that size, color, and shape can be more accurately represented if the fish are being picky.

Cast the fly into weedy domains, allowing it to settle near the bottom, using the type of fly line appropriate for the depth. Strip the fly with short, quick bursts, interspersed with pauses. Experiment with the speed and length of the strips.

For flies, I like Hare's Ear, Pheasant Tail, and the Epoxy Back Callibaetis nymphs, sizes 12 through 18. Successive gen-

A Flashback Hare's Ear is an excellent mayfly nymph imitation.

erations of *Callibaetis* nymphs within a single year get successively smaller due to a shorter growing time before subsequent hatches occur.

## Mayfly Adults

The duns of the *Callibaetis* (Speckle-Wing Quill), *Hexagenia* (Big Yellow May), and the small *Tricorythodes* (Trico) are all fed upon by stillwater fish. Noting the exact timing of the Big Yellow May emergence is important. Whereas the *Callibaetis* and Tricos typically emerge during reasonable daylight hours, the Hex hatch begins at nightfall. To find lake fish seeking to feed on these large insects, anglers need to be ready to fish very late in the day and plan to stay until they can no longer see. The fish may dine equally on both the partially hatched emerger and the fully upright dun.

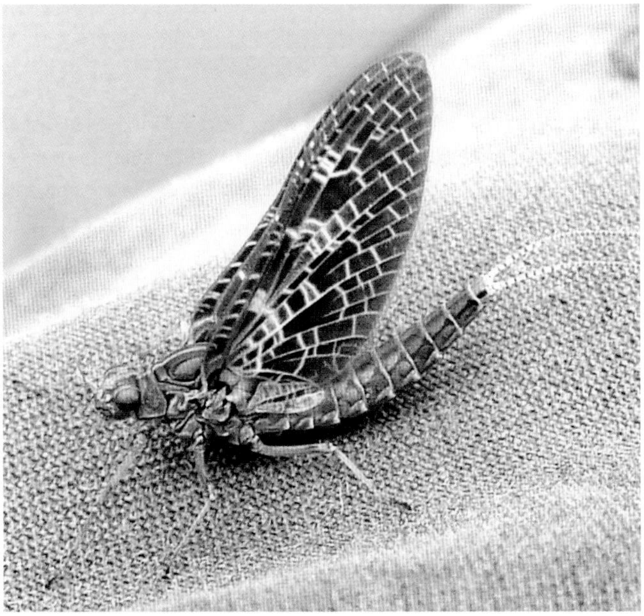

Even when newly hatched mayfly adults are prevalent on the surface, it is usually a good strategy to pair the adult imitation with an emerger pattern on the leader. Give the fish a choice.

The Trico genders hatch separately. The males emerge at night or in early morning, while the females dutifully follow in early morning through late morning. The male duns typically have dark brown bodies; the females are olive. Fish can dine on the emerging and resting duns and get a second shot at the females when they return to lay their eggs. Trico spinner falls can blanket the water, making fishing difficult, as an artificial fly must be selected by a feeding fish from among thousands of real insects.

During a hatch of *Callibaetis*, the struggling emergence of the wet and wrinkled adult as it escapes its nymphal skin is prime food and important for the fly angler to specifically imitate. Though they certainly eat the duns too, smart fish learn that it is much easier to capture a relatively stationary and helpless insect than one with wings, which might fly away just before being eaten. And, like the other lake and pond mayflies, the spinners of the Speckle-Wing Quills can cause a feeding frenzy when the females return to the water for egg laying and die on the surface.

The nymph of the Gray Drake crawls ashore to emerge and hatch, so the emergent form and duns of this bug are not available to the fish. There is little need to dedicate room in the fly box to these. It is the egg-laying female spinners of this insect that are of interest to fish and fishermen.

### *Fishing Mayfly Duns, Emergers, and Spinners*

A floating line is the only type needed when fishing all three surface stages of mayflies. Though different fly patterns are used, it's generally a matter of casting the flies to rising fish and allowing the flies to sit stationary. An occasional slow pull on the flies, or a slight lift of the rod tip, may draw a fish's attention to them.

The fly selection should include imitations of the emerging adult, the dun, and the spinner for Tricos, *Callibaetis*, and the Hexes, but only the spinner for the Gray Drake. For the Tricos, consider a Trico Parachute, Trico, and Trico Poly Wing Spinner, sizes 18 to 22. Top choices for the Big Yellow May would be the Parachute Hex, Yellow Extended-Body Compara-dun and a Crippled Hex, sizes 6 and 8. A Parachute Adams, tan Sparkle Dun, Parachute Hare's Ear, Crippled Callibaetis, and

A fly pattern with a fan-like wing design sits low on the water and presents a very realistic silhouette to the fish.

MijCadMay Emerger in sizes 12 through 16 all have a place in my fly box. Flies for the Gray Dun would be a Gray Poly Wing Spinner and a Gray Compara-dun with the top of the wing cut flat, sizes 8 through 12.

## Damselflies and Dragonflies

Of all the aquatic insects of interest to the fly angler, damselflies and dragonflies may rank at the top of the "Most Intriguing" list. First, they are ferocious predators, both as nymphs and as adults. They are of the insect order Odonata, a word of Greek origin meaning "toothed one." This is a reference to the serrated teeth located on the insect's chewing mouthparts, the mandibles. How can you help being a little fascinated with an insect that has serrated teeth? As adults, they do us an excellent service with those teeth—among other tasty items, damsels and dragons eat mosquitoes.

As nymphs, damselflies and dragonflies are outfitted with a labial mask, a nifty structure that covers the mouth. The mask is actually a grasping tool that rests on the bug's face. If a snack disguised as a swimming insect or little fish swims near, the mask is extended on an arm attached under the damselfly or dragonfly's head. This movement is faster than you can blink, grabbing the prey and bringing it back to meet those chewing, serrated teeth.

Dragonflies are among the world's fastest flying insects. In short bursts, they can exceed 30 miles an hour. Combine this speed and the serrated teeth with the excellent vision provided by compound eyes that can almost see in every direction at once, and you have an airborne killing machine—not as benign as it looks.

Dragonflies are one of the world's fastest flying insects—bad news for those bugs chosen to be eaten by these predators. Mosquitoes are one of their favorite snacks.

Adult damselflies can be identified by their long, slender abdomens and four membranous wings of identical shape and length that are held back and parallel over the abdomen, unlike the dragonfly, which has two pairs of wings that are not identical and which are held out to the side of the insect, perpendicular to the body. In fact, the wing differences distinguishing damsel adults from dragonflies are noted in the taxonomical names for these insects. While both are members of the same order, Odonata, the damselflies are of the suborder Zygoptera, literally meaning "paired wings." Anisoptera, the suborder of Odonata to which the dragonflies belong, means "not equal wings" in Greek. The rear pair of the dragonfly's wings is broader than the forewings.

While dragonflies and damselflies are excellent fliers, the dragonflies are very clumsy when attempting to walk, and damselflies cannot or will not walk. The next time one of these lands on the picnic table, just watch. They land and take off from the same spot. In addition, with those see-everywhere-at-once eyes, these insects are difficult to catch. The eyes of the damsel are separated, while those on most dragonflies touch.

There are a couple of other distinguishing features that enable the observer to tell the difference between these two insect groups. The dragonfly abdomen is usually much stouter than the slender abdomen of the damselfly. Sky blue banded by black is a very popular color scheme for many of the damselflies, particularly here in the West. The abdomen of the damselflies may also be brown, green, olive, red, or yellow. Worldwide, dragonflies can be found in just about any color imaginable.

### Nymphs

Damselflies and dragonflies undergo incomplete metamorphosis: egg, nymph, and adult. Damsels have a life cycle that can range from one to three years, while a dragonfly's can extend to four years.

Damselfly nymphs have pronounced thoraxes, slender abdomens, and three caudal lamellae extending out the rear of the abdomen. The lamellae look like three brushy tails but are

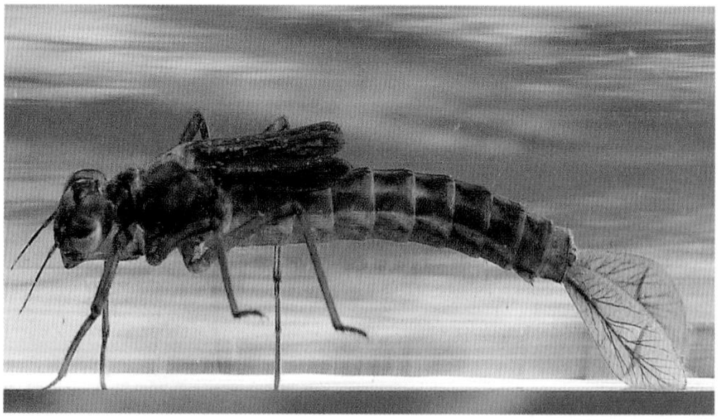

When damselfly nymphs slowly swim on their journey toward the shoreline, hungry fish go on the hunt. (See photo on page 104.)

actually gills. As the nymph swims, it is also breathing, as dissolved oxygen is extracted from the water by the gills.

It is among the stillwater vegetation that damselfly nymphs prefer to hunt and hide. With the extendable lower jaw, they will eat aquatic insect nymphs, larvae, pupae, small crustaceans, and tiny fish.

The dragonfly nymph body—depending on the taxonomic family—ranges from short and rounded to elongated and stout, not easily confused with the sleeker damselfly. Some dragonfly nymphs will exceed 2 inches in length.

Dragonfly nymphs can be classified by their hunting activities and hunting locations. There are crawlers, sprawlers, and burrowers. The crawlers patrol the vegetation and debris on the pond or lake bottom, hunting for prey. When needed, they can swim in short, fast bursts to apprehend their food. Whereas the crawlers can be 2½ inches long, the sprawlers may be half this length. Sprawlers are experts at ambushing their prey, as they hide on the mud and debris of the bottom, camouflaged by their environment. They are covered with tiny hairs that cause bits of their surroundings to cling to their bodies, making it difficult for unsuspecting wandering or swimming insects, crustaceans, and fish to escape before the labial mask extends to grab them. Lastly, burrowers dig themselves into the mud and silt to wait in ambush and to stay out of sight of predators that might eat them. They are the smallest of the dragonfly lot, barely an inch long at nymphal maturity.

Dragonfly nymphs have rectal gills situated within the rear portion of their abdomens. At the extreme rear of the abdomen is an opening where water can be taken in and the abdomen can swell. When the abdomen is squeezed, the water is expelled forcefully, propelling the nymph forward—think jet propulsion. As the insect swims it also breathes, as oxygenated water flows over the internal gills. At rest, the dragonfly nymph can respire by gently pumping its abdomen to force oxygen-laden water to the gills.

### *Fishing Dragonfly and Damselfly Nymphs*

With multi-year life cycles possible, dragonfly and damselfly nymphs of assorted sizes and stages of maturity can be available to stillwater fish year-round and are always important additions to any lake angler's fly box. However, optimal time for fishing the nymphs will be during their migrations, as they make their

The Carey Special, and variations of it, are good choices for imitating dragonfly nymphs.

Dragonflies predate the dinosaurs, with the oldest fossils calculated at more than 300 million years old. Today there are more than 5,000 living species identified. The nymphs, depending on the environment and species, may live up to 4 years before transitioning into the adult stage. As it grows, the nymph can molt more than a dozen times, shedding its old smaller skin for a more spacious one. Dragonfly nymphs are fierce predators and some of the larger species may actually eat small tadpoles and fish.

way to exposed structures to transition into the adult form. The timing will vary from location to location, depending on seasons and water temperature. Be on the lookout for the presence of adults during spring through early fall. If adults are present, there's an excellent chance the fish will be seeking out the migrating nymphs.

When the water is murky or the light is dim, a brighter mottled coloration scheme can make the fly a little easier for the fish to locate.

Damselfly nymph imitations should be elongated and thin and retrieved in a manner that imitates the swimming movement of the insect.

During their hatching migrations, damselflies will usually travel in the upper 3 feet of the water column. They have a very distinctive side-to-side undulation of the abdomen as they swim.

Swimming bursts are separated by pauses, short periods of rest before resuming the swim. If the angler can simulate this recognizable swimming movement with his retrieve methods and the materials incorporated into the fly tying design of the fly, he could be well on the way some epic fishing during this hatch.

Because the migrating nymphs tend to swim high in the water column, a floating line is often the best choice. If the wind comes up, use a slow-sinking or intermediate line. Though the lateral movement of the swimming nymph is difficult to emulate with a line length of more than 6 to 8 feet beyond the rod tip, the fish can often be fooled when the fly fisherman alternates three or four short strips of line with a pause of three or four counts. Sometimes it can be effective to cast the fly and wait for it to sink, and sink, and sink. Or, let a damselfly pattern sit motionless underneath an indicator.

Because nymphs that blend with their surroundings have a better chance of survival, the color choice of your damselfly and dragonfly nymph patterns can be extremely important. For my damsels, I carry flies in shades and blends of tan, brown, gold, and olive. Because the mature nymphs may be from 1 inch to almost 1½ inches long, I must carry multiple sizes, too. The Goat Damsel and Marabou Damsel are my mainstays, in sizes 8 through 12. If you tie your own flies, keep the abdomens thin. Color can be absolutely critical. Do whatever it takes to capture a natural.

Since dragonfly nymphs migrate along the bottom, sometimes out of water 20 to 30 feet deep, an array of sinking lines is necessary. Flying or resting adults are your clue that the migration is underway, especially if you discover the first adults of the season. This will usually be in early to midsummer for most locations. Use a countdown of the fly to calculate when you have reached the bottom in any given location. Strip the fly in short, quick bursts, interspersed with pauses, to imitate swimmers. Use a slow hand-twist retrieve with pauses to mimic crawling nymphs. Make note of when in the retrieve the strikes come.

Dragonfly nymphs can be black, dark brown, and shades of olive. Choose fly colors accordingly. The fly pattern should be fairly stout, with fly sizes ranging from 6 to 10. Flies like the Carey Special, Randall's Lake Dragon, Carey Bugger, and Marabou Carey Special are good.

This might seem like a little detail, but consider casting away from the shoreline to retrieve your fly toward the shoreline, the same direction most of the damsel and dragon nymphs are headed.

## Adults

Because they are strong fliers not prone to being blown into the water, and the egg-laying females deposit their eggs in the water and on surface plants in such ways that do not expose the adult to hungry fish, artificial imitations of the adult dragonfly should not take much, if any, room in your fly box. Adult damsels are a different matter.

Damselflies are equipped with two pairs of wings and can move their front and back wings separately while in flight. This enables them to stop quickly, hover, change direction, and fly backward. These high-speed insect hunters can form a "basket" with their forelegs, which are adorned with spiky *setae* used to sweep small flying bugs in for a meal.

Fishing adult damselfly patterns when the females return to the water to lay their eggs can be the most exciting dry-fly fishing of the entire stillwater season.

In the adult stage, damsels and dragons live from several weeks to several months. This is a good length of time—in the aquatic insect world—for accidents to happen, especially for the damselfly. Unlike their stronger cousins, damselflies can be blown off lakeside vegetation and into the water. Also, it is not unusual to see a low-flying damsel hit the water where it may burble and splash before regaining the air. If a fish is nearby, it may apprehend the luckless damsel before it flies off.

### *Fishing the Adult Damselfly*

There isn't much sophistication in fishing imitations of the damselfly adult. On a breezy day when the damselflies are in evidence in the air or on exposed vegetation, cast the fly near cruising or rising trout and let it sit. Do not hesitate to slap the fly onto the water, like the real thing doing a crash landing. Give the fly a quick twitch like it's trying to fly away. Hold on tight. This can be very exciting fishing.

There are some good damselfly patterns out there. The vast majority have bodies of blue and two pairs of wings perpendicular to the body of the fly. Though it makes little sense for the damsel imitation to have the wing configuration of a dragonfly, the fish don't seem to care. Such wings assist the fly in floating on the surface. The body of the fly should be about 2 inches long. Patterns include Foam Body Parachute Damsel, Pearl Wing Blue Damsel, and Poly Wing Damsel.

# Water Boatmen

In many of North America's nutrient-rich lakes, there's an interesting little bug that propels itself through the water by means of tiny "oars." The hind legs of the water boatman are elongated, stout, and densely covered with hairs that provide significant surface area and rowing power to move the insect through the water just like an oarsman in a boat. They are fun to watch and effective to imitate when fishing lakes and ponds at certain times of the year.

Water boatmen and backswimmers (their close cousins) are members of the Hemiptera order of insects. *Hemiptera* is literally translated from the Greek as "half wing." The forewings of these insects are hardened and leathery at the base, while the rest of the wing has a membranous appearance. Backswimmers can be distinguished from water boatmen by their larger size (½ inch or slightly larger, while water boatmen rarely exceed ½ inch) and by their orientation while swimming on their backs. Both insects have piercing mouth parts, with the backswimmers likely to inflict a painful bite on any human who handles them, while the boatmen are gentler little spirits, not inclined to bite your finger. Although backswimmers can be dining fare for stillwater fish, the boatmen are more important more of the time, in my experience.

The lifecycle of a water boatman is the incomplete type. After the final instar, or molting, during its growth, the nymph becomes a winged adult. The adult looks almost exactly like the nymph and continues to live underwater just as it always has. This transformation usually takes place in late summer or early fall.

Water boatmen have a very distinct swimming movement, propelled by their hind legs, which act as oars.

Flies that imitate water boatmen should have a pair of prominent legs and be fished in a manner to mimic the short-spurts swimming movement of the insect.

Unlike other aquatic insects that have gills to extract dissolved oxygen from the water, boatmen breathe air. They do this by coming to the surface to capture and hold an air bubble, or plastron, along their body or under the wings. When the air bubble is used up, boatmen must return to the surface to grasp another. Because of this, these insects stay in the shallow periphery of deeper lakes, and it is along the periphery or shallow shoals that fish will seek water boatmen.

Each pair of the boatman's legs performs specific functions. The short forelegs are designed for sifting and sorting bottom debris when searching for food. Also, they are rubbed on the insect's head and antennae to produce a stridulation, or chirping sound, either warning competitors to stay clear or attempting to attract a mate. The middle pair of legs grasps the substrate or vegetation to hold the boatman in place, preventing it from drifting to the surface because of the buoyancy of the air bubble attached to the body for breathing. The rear legs are the oars for swimming.

Mating and egg laying may occur in late spring, late summer, or fall, depending on the species. Late summer and fall timings seem to be most common. The female boatmen dive into the water to deposit the eggs on plant stems or on the lake bottom, or attach them to submerged wood. It is during these egg-depositing flights, when thousands of insects rain down on the water, that fish will key on the water boatmen as a food source. It's easy and abundant pickings for the fish as they intercept the diving, swimming females.

## Fishing Water Boatmen

Some key things to remember when fishing imitations of water boatmen include their distinctive short-spurt swimming movement, prominent legs, size, color, the presence of the air bubble clinging to the body, and the fact that they inhabit shallow water.

The back or dorsal surface of a water boatman's oval-shaped body is typically shades of brown and black, often mottled. The underbody can be shades of olive and yellow. The rear legs are long and prominent physical features that need to be part of the fly design. Because the air bubble clinging to the body is easily observed by fish, this too should be mimicked in effective fly patterns.

Because water boatmen are usually in 10 feet of water or less, a floating line or a slow sinker are the logical choices. If the wind is reasonably light, the easy casting and pick up of the floating line is preferred. Quick short strips of the line, mixed with pauses, imitate the swimming and resting of the insect. If you need a rest from casting, a slow troll along the shoreline, enhanced by short line strips and releases of the line, can be very productive. Experiment with the line length; a longer line is required when trolling during windless conditions. Because water boatmen must frequently return to the surface to replenish the air bubble, fish are accustomed to finding them at any part of the water column, surface to bottom.

My favorite patterns include the Rubber-Leg Boatman and Biot Boatman, sizes 12 through 16. If a bead is incorporated into the fly, I use silver or glass to best approximate the silvery gas bubble clinging to the insect. Beadhead patterns are particularly useful when the boatmen are "raining" down on the water during their dispersal flights or egg laying. Splat the fly onto the water to simulate a crash landing. The bead helps the fly sink and dive, just as the real bugs do. This is a fun technique, different from the mainstream presentations of most lake and pond flies.

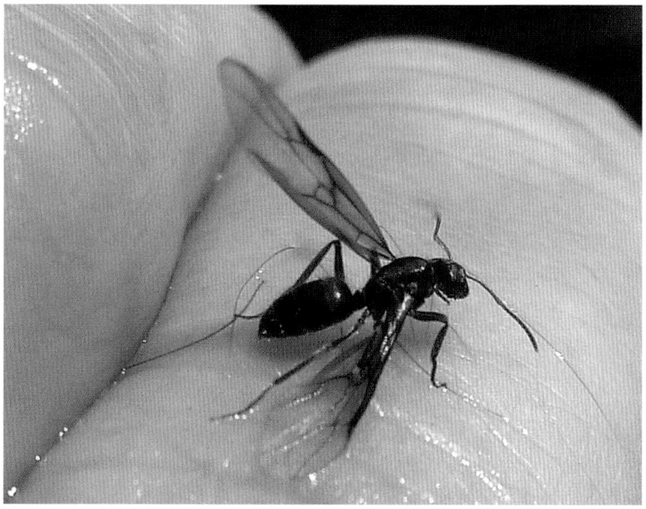

Flying ant swarms are a bit unpredictable and sometimes not very obvious. Apparently, they are particularly tasty to fish, so make sure you have a few winged patterns in your fly box.

# Terrestrial Insects

## Ants

Under the right conditions, land-based insects can be of occasional importance to stillwater fish. Beetles, crickets, and grasshoppers, among others, can be piscatorial snacks, especially for shoreline cruisers. However, one group of terrestrial insects that distributes itself over the broad reaches of a lake is ants. I find it difficult to predict when ants will quietly shower down on my fishing waters, but I am never unprepared when they show. Though they may be small and their numbers sparse, ants helplessly drifting on the surface will cause fish to actively seek them out.

### *Fishing Ants*

Ants are poor swimmers. Their skinny legs may move frantically for a bit, but they make very little headway. Fishing an ant imitation is a straightforward affair: heave it and leave it. For the impatient angler, this can be tortuous fishing. If you can locate an area with fish rising consistently, get ready for some fun action. Ants obviously taste good to the fish. In survival situations, ants are one of the more desirable food items for a starving human in the wild. My friend Joe Uffelman has eaten ants and says they aren't too bad. Pop them into a hot pan over a fire, and serve 'em up.

The fly patterns are simple concoctions of a fur or foam head/thorax and abdomen, separated by a hackle feather, in black and cinnamon, sizes 10 through 16.

# Important Non-Insect Stillwater Foods

## Scuds

Commonly referred to as freshwater shrimp, scuds are very important food items for lake fish. How important? In lakes where they live—and there are many—scuds can be second in importance only to chironomids as a food source. In the fall of the year, it can be a dead heat between these two groups as to which will top the list of preferred fare. Fly fishers must have scuds in their fly boxes. Though scuds may be relegated to a secondary food source when insects are active and hatching, they increase in importance to foraging fish during quiet times. On those days when fishing is tough and nothing seems to entice the fish, think scud.

With two pairs of antennae, many pairs of leg-like appendages on the underside, and a semitransparent, obviously segmented exoskeleton, scuds have a very distinctive appearance. Though they can live among the rocks and detritus of the lake or pond bottom, jungles of vegetation are common habitats for the freshwater shrimp. Thus, they tend to concentrate along the shallow margins of lakes where sunlight can penetrate, producing abundant plant growth. Experts at camouflage, they blend well with their surroundings, typically dressed in shades of olive, gray, and brown. As it outgrows its old exoskeleton, a newly molted scud will have a bluish pearl appearance for a short time. Two families are of particular importance: Gammaridae and Taletraide (or Hyalellidae, depending on the taxonomical source). Within these are the scuds of the genera *Gammarus* and *Hyalella*, which look and behave identically, except for their fully grown sizes; the *Gammarus* scud can be twice as large as its smaller cousins, exceeding 3/4 inches at full

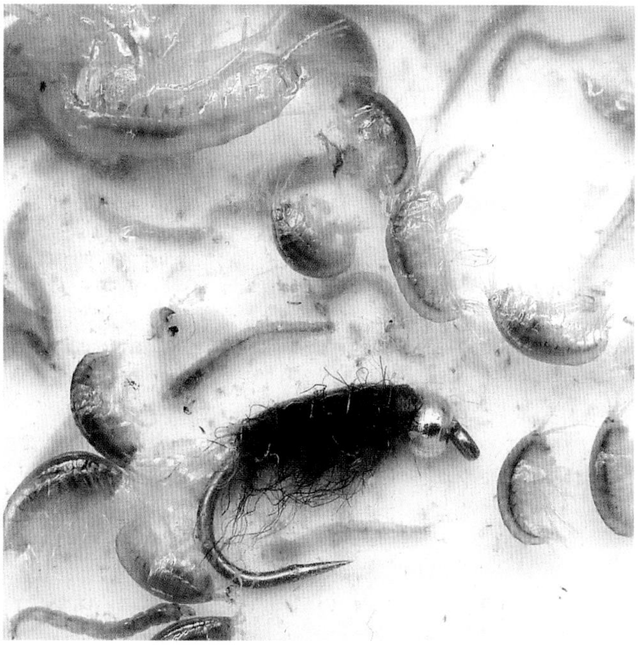

Where present, scuds can be one of the predominant food sources for lake and pond fish.

maturity. *Hyalellas* top out at about 5 mm, less than 1/4 inch. *Hyallelas* are more widespread than the *Gammarus*, having a broader tolerance of water chemistry.

Scuds will produce multiple broods of young in a year. The pregnant females can be identified by a bright orange egg mass situated under the thorax. The young scuds are carried in a pouch, or marsupium, under the thorax of the mother until they are eventually released to fend for themselves.

Being light sensitive, scuds tend to be most active during low light times of day, early morning and evening, or on overcast days. They swim slowly in short bursts, and then pause to rest. As they pause, they sink a bit before resuming their travels. The fly fisher must be cognizant of mimicking this alternating movement and rest rhythm as he retrieves his scud patterns.

### *Fishing Scud Flies*

Because scuds are commonly found along the shoreline and weedy shoals of lakes, floating, slow-sinking, and intermediate fly lines are best. After casting, allow the fly to settle near the bottom. Retrieve the scud with slow, short (1/2-inch) strips, alternating with pauses of three or four seconds. I have sometimes found it effective to speed up the strips, while still keeping them short. A scud fly tied with a shellback of buoyant deer or elk hair may help to keep the fly from impaling debris and vegetation on the bottom when fished on a sinking line.

There are times when suspending the scud just off the bottom under an indicator can be effective. After allowing the fly to rest motionless for twenty or thirty seconds, slowly strip 6 inches of line, then allow the fly to rest again. Periodically, check for vegetation on the hook as a sign that the fly is a bit too deep. Move the indicator a little closer to the fly.

The Tied-Down Caddis Shrimp, Plastic-Back Scud, and Beadhead Hare Scud (#10–18) tied in shades of olive, olive gray, and brown are all good flies. A dot of orange dubbing to imitate the egg mass carried by female scuds can add a bit of realism to the fly.

In my fly box I also carry a few scud patterns tied in pearly light blue color to imitate those shrimp that have just molted. In addition, I have a few scuds tied with a predominantly orange body. It is not only the pregnant females who exhibit some orange coloration; there are a few other factors that produce the orange shrimp. At certain times of the year, scuds may build up fat reserves, inducing an orangish tinge to their bodies. In other instances, an orange spot may form on a scud's back because of a parasite that also causes the scud to exhibit an unnatural behavior, exposing it to foraging fish. The fish become accustomed to seeing and eating "crazy" orange shrimp. Lastly, dead scuds turn orange, and fish will use these as food, too. So when it comes to blue and orange scuds, it never hurts to throw the fish a changeup.

Leeches are a food staple for stillwater fish. If there is one fly pattern found in every lake and pond fisherman's fly collection it is the Woolly Bugger and its variations.

This pretty little leech was foraging the shallows of Horseshoe Lake, BC. Leeches—like most aquatic organisms—rely on a body color scheme that blends with their environments. A camouflaged creature is harder for a hungry fish to discover.

## Leeches

Repulsive. Ugly. Creepy. Icky. Blood-sucking. These are a few of the commonly used adjectives used to preface the word "leech." They are every freshwater swimmer's secret nightmare. However, there is something very endearing about leeches: fish love to eat them. When there are no hatching or swimming insects, or scud activity, fish look to leeches for food.

Leeches are segmented and flatten when stretched out. Common colors include black, brown, maroon, and shades of green. Some are concolorous, while others are mottled. They swim in an undulating, wavelike movement, usually near the

When in doubt, reach for a leech. Pictured is a fly tied with a mix of claret, brown, and black. Tasty!

bottom where they scavenge on decaying or dead plant and animal remains. They will also feed on insects, scuds, and snails. They prefer dim light, usually hiding out during the bright part of the day.

### *Fishing Leeches*

Any angler, whether beginner or veteran, knows to have an abundance of leech patterns at hand when fishing lakes and ponds. Leeches are everywhere, or so it seems. I am sure that even in waters that contain few leeches, lively fly patterns meant to imitate leeches may be taken by fish that are opportunistically looking to consume anything that looks alive. Fly-tying materials like marabou, fur, soft feathers, and mohair contribute to add life to the flies in which these materials are used.

Leech flies can be fished on all types of fly lines, from floating to Type VI full-sinking types, and everything in between. All manner of retrieves will prove effective at one time or another, from short and slow strips of the line to long and fast. You can cast, troll, or use a combination. Experimentation is key to discovering what the fish want today.

One key part of every leech pattern design I want includes weight on or near the head of the fly. Because real leeches swim in an undulating fashion, this movement is emulated in an artificial fly when the weighted front of the fly drops forward and dives a bit in between line strips as I swim it through the water. I either secure a metal bead to the front of the fly as I tie it, or I wrap lead wire along the forward third of the hook shank before dressing it with fur, yarn, and feathers.

A bizarre but effective method for fishing leeches, especially Micro Leeches, is suspending them under an indicator. It is incredible to me that fish will intercept a leech pattern hanging just off the bottom with little or no movement. After a minute or so, I will strip the indicator a foot or two, then let the fly sit for another minute. Mysteriously, the fish catching with this method can be excellent.

My favorite leech patterns include New Age Woolly Buggers and Dubbed Buggers in size 8, and Micro Leeches in size 12, with black, brown, olive, maroon, and combinations of these colors predominate. Whereas most of my stillwater patterns are tied in a range of sizes, for my leeches I have settled on sizes 8 and 12 to keep it simple, with no discernible detriment to my fishing effectiveness. I can vary the length and silhouette of any leech pattern by adjusting the length and amount of materials I put on the hook, reducing the number of hook sizes I must stock. When I use metal beads on the front of the fly, I tend to use silver and copper on the vast majority of my leeches.

## CHAPTER 3

# Chironomids Rule!

A group of chironomid pupae sampled from a trout's throat, still alive and nearing emergence.

Chironomids are so important in the diet of stillwater trout that they deserve a chapter all to themselves. They are one of the few stillwater food organisms available to fish 365 days a year. What they may lack in size, they more than compensate for in numbers. When midges are hatching during the prime times of spring and summer, it is an underwater snowstorm of pupae slowly ascending to the surface. These are vulnerable, easy targets for gorging trout and other species. When it's not "snowing," which is most of the time, wandering midge larvae can be discovered by roaming trout. And, when conditions are right, it's the adult midges that interest the fish and provide fly anglers with exciting surface action.

With the ability to survive, even thrive, in a broad range of habitats, midges are widely distributed all over the planet. Chironomids of the genus *Belgica* are found in hostile climes of Antarctica. A diverse abundance of midges inhabits virtually all Arctic regions of the northern hemisphere. Midges exploit practically all damp freshwater environments, and some can live in saltwater marshes. They can be found thriving in sewage treatment ponds. When I lived in a rented house in Heppner, OR, for a year, some mornings I would discover adult midges on my bathroom sink mirror. They crawled and flitted around while I shaved in the morning, having hatched from the sink drain, unaffected by hot soapy water or residue from my washing and shaving efforts. Chironomids are quite hardy and adaptable, and available as food just about anywhere freshwater fish live.

Philip Rowley, a British Columbia fly angler, author, and TV show host, has an excellent knowledge of aquatic organisms,

Chironomids are a major source of food for stillwater fish year-round.

A throat or stomach sample from a feeding trout will often provide a major clue about fly selection.

especially as they relate to the stillwater trout diet. Concerning chironomid consumption, Rowley's data indicates that approximately 39 percent of the diet of the average trout in lakes he's sampled is comprised of chironomids. All other aquatic insects combined tally about 26 percent, only two-thirds of the chironomid component. The balance of the diet includes scuds (19 percent), leeches, forage fish, zooplankton, snails, and terrestrial insects. In some productive lakes, the consumption of chironomids in all stages, as a percentage of the total diet, can exceed 50 percent.

To further emphasize the importance of midges in the stillwater trout's daily consumption, biologist Brian Chan maintains that a trout of 3 pounds might ingest in excess of 1,500 chironomid pupae in a single morning or afternoon feeding session. Again, although the fare may sometimes be quite small as individuals, collectively 1,500 chironomids eaten in a few hours is a big meal—quite analogous, I think, to the human consumption of a large bowl of popcorn. One significant difference: chironomids are probably a healthier food choice.

A growing army of good lake and pond fly fishers are coming to understand the significance of midges in their trout fishing success. New fly patterns and angling methods are continuously being developed specifically for this very diverse group of insects. Because the number of identified species of Chironomidae exceeds 2,500 in North America alone, a new crop of chironomid fly patterns utilizing new fly-tying materials are created every year. If there is a growth industry in fly pattern development and new methods to fish them in stillwaters, it's about midges, and nowhere is there more overwhelming evidence of this than the Internet. Search YouTube. A fly tier could spend the rest of his waking life trying to reproduce the ever-running flood of new chironomid fly innovations there.

The days of merely trolling a Woolly Bugger behind a float tube are gone for serious students of catching worthy fish in quality public waters. Though dragging a leech in circles has its place and time, determined anglers who want to maximize their fish catch have to learn, adapt, and act. They will most certainly become students of the chironomid as they seek wisdom.

It's important to understand the chironomid's life stages because you can't know too much about an insect that can make up more than half of a trout's diet in certain lakes. And it's a safe bet that on certain days in certain lakes, chironomids make up 100 percent of a given trout's diet.

## The Larva

Pupal imitations may seem to get a disproportionate amount of glory when it comes to catching stillwater trout in spring and summer. However, if you consider the fact that midge larvae are available to be eaten 24 hours a day, 365 days a year, it should come as no surprise that their artificial counterparts are a go-to fly for the savvy angler. Let's give a little more love to the larvae. The fish do.

Chironomids in the larval stage are skinny little nine-segment worms, with stubby prolegs front and rear. Every single one of them appears anorexic, so think thin and tie thinner if you are creating an artificial fly. They are crummy swimmers, but excellent wigglers. To locomote, they have a spasmodic thrashing movement that appears to be a miniature seizure. The head end thrashes one direction, and the tail end in another. Somehow they make it from point A to point B, though not gracefully. A midge larva could never elude a trout, but if the fish watches too closely before attacking, it might grow confused or dizzy, missing the snacking opportunity.

There are free-roaming chironomid larvae and those who prefer to live in tubes burrowed into the lake bottom of stable mud or silt. Some free-living sorts inhabit the detritus that has settled to the bottom, while others seek out vegetation for their refuge and foraging. If they stray too far from cover, they can easily fall victim to fish on the prowl. The tube builders can hide out in their burrows, capturing food that drifts near or into their retreats, but staying in their tubular subterranean retreats is, apparently, no guarantee against being eaten. Brian Chan maintains that bottom-cruising trout may actually vacuum suck the larvae from their tubular cases. To support this theory, he has extracted live larvae and remnants of their tubes from throat samples. What makes the cruising and hoovering feeding activity of the fish worthwhile is the density of the larval populations in productive lakes. The population of larvae in a given square yard or meter in a target-rich area may number in the thousands.

There are several other scenarios where trout will find a bounty of midge larvae to prey upon. Each spring and fall, lakes with adequate depth located in climes where water surface temperatures reach 39 degrees F (4 degrees C) or lower undergo "turnover." Vertical convection-cell currents occur when sinking denser water displaces less dense water at the lake's bottom. Such convection currents can lift and carry hapless chironomid larvae from the safety of their homes or hiding places, exposing them to be eaten by fish.

The second situation occurs when larvae that will winter over in the lake migrate en masse from shallow water to deeper areas, which provide the best opportunity for their survival in the coldest part of the year. Herds of larvae begin their writhing journey to the depths—kind of a slower, smaller-scale version of the wildebeest migration on the Serengeti Plains of eastern Africa. It's one more opportunity for predatory trout to thin the herd before the wormy migrants find shelter.

The larvae are found in a myriad of colors. The free-living varieties, many of which inhabit vegetation, are usually various shades of green for camouflage. Other colors include cream, brown, olive, tan, maroon, and red. The maroon and red larvae have a hemoglobin-like component in their circulatory systems. Just as in vertebrates, the hemoglobin helps extract, carry, and dispense oxygen in the bloodstream. It is the hemoglobin component in the larvae that makes for a rich red appearance. Known as bloodworms, scarlet larvae get the most fly-tying press because red is a fun color. It trumps brown, drab olive, and tan any day. From a more practical standpoint, the bloodworms can exploit low-oxygen environments that would be lethal to other chironomid species not equipped with the hemoglobin that ensures they have sufficient oxygen to live. This means less competition for food and housing from other less adaptable midge larvae.

Some effective chironomid larva flies can be extremely simple designs. This fly is merely V-Rib wrapped on a hook.

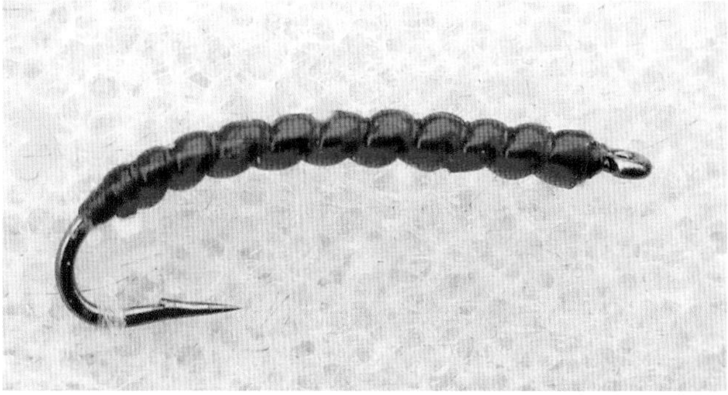

Flies imitating midge larvae are simple to tie. Effective colors include shades of red, brown, green, and olive.

As for size, some of the largest species produce larvae that are close to an inch long; 3⁄8-inch to 3⁄4-inch is a more typical range. As is common with many other insects, there is a downsizing as the chironomid progresses through its various life stages: the larva is larger than the pupa, which is larger than the adult. To do a little logical scaling when tying flies, if you observe numerous adults of a particular size on a lake's surface, fish a pupa that may be a hook size larger. If you capture pupae, or use a stomach pump on a fish for some pupae samples, know that the artificial larval imitation should probably be a hook size larger than the pupa. Considering typical lengths, segmentation, and color, a fly tier would do well to create larval patterns that are an inch long or less, skinny, and segmented, in a variety of colors. Flies can't get much simpler than chironomid larvae. I wrap small brown, olive, green, or red V-Rib along the hook shank. If more lifelike movement is needed, a few strands of marabou or pheasant tail fibers of the appropriate color wrapped sparsely on a hook with a wire ribbing are excellent patterns, too.

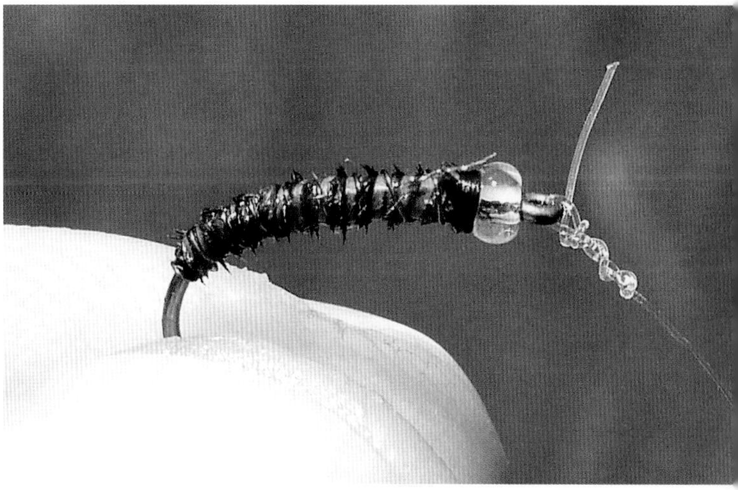

Chironomid pupal imitations with thin bodies of pheasant tail or turkey tail fibers are very effective.

At what depths in a lake are anglers most likely to be effective fishing chironomid larvae? The majority live in water ranging from 2 to 8 meters, or 6 to 25 feet. Early in the season it may be better to fish the shallow end of the range because the water will be warmer in the shallows. As the shallows warm, and the larvae have transformed into pupae, and then the pupae into adults, the angler should move out progressively deeper in late spring and summer. The larvae population in shallow reaches has been greatly reduced as the insects transform and eventually hatch. Logically, you want to cast your flies where the food is abundant; that's where the fish are. As for more details on angling techniques, appropriate gear, and strategies for fishing midge larvae, these will be addressed in depth in a subsequent chapter.

## The Pupa

Midge pupal body design exhibits many more interesting features than the slim, uniform larval worm. The abdomen is slim, tapered, and distinctly segmented. The thorax of the pupa is bulbous, with the developing wings, legs, and antennae tucked tight inside the comma-shaped profile of the pupa body. Prominent white gill filaments protrude at the top of the comma from the front dorsal region of the thorax. Productive artificial pupal fly patterns should incorporate and represent all these bodily features. An additional feature may be present in some large "bomber" pupae: caudal gills that protrude from the extreme tip of the abdomen. Though less prominent than the filaments protruding from the thoracic region, a hint of white at the end of these pupal patterns can add a touch more realism to an artificial.

Though the larval and adult stages are important to the fish's menu, it is the pupal form of the chironomid that takes center stage for pattern development and the creation of most refinements in angling techniques. When the majority of anglers make reference to "fishing chironomids," they are referring to fishing the imitation of the pupa. It is the pupal emergence that will concentrate the fish as they gather for easy pickings during the pre-staging hover of insects near the bottom and the *slow* ascent of the insects to the surface, where—if the bugs make it without being eaten—they will split their pupal skin and the adult will emerge. Savvy, or lucky, anglers who are parked in the zone fishing the correct pupal patterns where the underwater snowstorm is occurring can have crazy-good fishing.

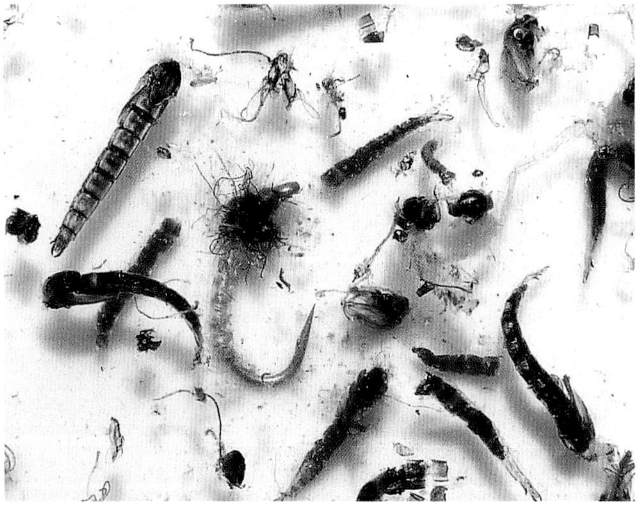

Sometimes chironomid patterns that may not closely match the size and color of the real insects being eaten can still catch trout, especially in popular, heavily fished waters. It can pay to show the fish something they have not seen before.

The stage is initially set when the larvae mature to the point that it is time to pupate. Tube-living larvae will seal off their mud tubes; free-living varieties may encapsulate themselves or undergo the transition to their pupal stage within their old larval skin. After a week or two in a dormant state, the transition is complete, and emergence from their tombs or capsules will occur when the water temperature is right. The pupae will cut, chew, or wriggle themselves free, to emerge from their confines. Gas is generated or trapped under the pupal skin for buoyancy to assist in the dangerously slow rise to the water's surface, where the lucky will finally change into adults. A split forms along the thorax of the pupa, the adult emerges, and it soon flies off to mate. Mating may very well occur within a day. Females laden with fertilized eggs soon return to deposit on the lake's surface; the dropped eggs will sink to the lake bottom. Some eggs will find fertile territory in which to grow and thrive, and the carrying on of the species will begin anew. In just a couple of weeks, the eggs will have hatched to produce the larvae of the next generation.

Most pupal emergences happen in relatively shallow water, 3 to 20 feet deep. However, some emergences may occur from depths that exceed 30 feet. Hatches are largely keyed to water temperatures; 50 to 60 degrees F (10 to 15 degrees C) at the surface is an optimal range, indicating that the water temperature at that depth is warm enough to prompt the insects to begin their move toward the surface.

The shallowest depths warm first in the spring, so the earliest major midge hatches are usually in 3 to 10 feet of water. As the spring and summer sun continues to warm lakes and ponds, the hatching activity gradually progresses to deeper and deeper water. Smaller numbers will continue to hatch throughout the entire fishing year until many stillwaters freeze up. In those that remain ice-free, a few rebels can be found emerging out of sync with the high seasons of spring, summer, and early fall. It is these pupae that provide the occasional trout snack on winter days, giving cold-weather fly fishermen hope that they can catch a stillwater trout on an artificial even when there is snow on the ground in January.

As for the daily timing of hatches, during the heart of the spring and early summer, midmorning to midafternoon is generally a good time to expect a hatch. On hot days, early and late are better. In the winter and very early spring, the hatching will most likely be at the part of the day when water temperatures peak, mid to late afternoon.

After stealing a trout's lunch with my stomach pump, I inject the stomach contents onto a white plastic lid of a small yogurt container I carry in my vest. When this is done during a chironomid hatch, it is not unusual to find wriggling, live pupae in the mix. As I watch, the transition from pupa to adult for many of the survivors continues. Before my eyes, the thorax of an insect will begin to split, and the adult midge will slowly emerge through the opening. Given an additional minute or two, adult insects will dry their wings and fly away from the yogurt lid. Having once been swallowed by a feeding fish, on the threshold of certain demise, a fortunate few have been freed by my stomach pump to possibly find a mate and actively participate in carrying on the species. Jonah the Midge has won the lottery.

Another fascinating change occurs in the coloration of some of the living midge pupae I have rescued: their colors undergo a transformation right in front of my eyes. From a shade of brown, olive, green, black, or red, they transition to a metallic-looking gray or silver. The gasses trapped underneath the thorax and abdomen, which assisted in their ascent to the surface, continue to cause separation of the adult inside from its old pupal skin. Once the adult has managed to separate itself from its skin, it is free to crawl out of it. Finally extricated, the adult will unfold and dry its wings, then fly off.

This body sheen and color change can happen underwater, too, as pupae drift up toward the surface. Selective trout may focus on individual insects with the distinctive shiny appearance. There is a fly pattern called the Static Bag Chironomid that attempts to specifically mimic this sheen. You may also encounter the term Anti-Static Bag (ASB) Chironomid: it's the same thing. This plastic bag is used in the electronics industry to protect components that may be damaged from electrostatic discharge during storage or shipping. Next time you buy a computer or related accessories, save the bags to tie some pupal patterns. Cut into strips about 2 mm wide, it is very effective at creating fly bodies with the magical sheen exhibited by chironomid pupae.

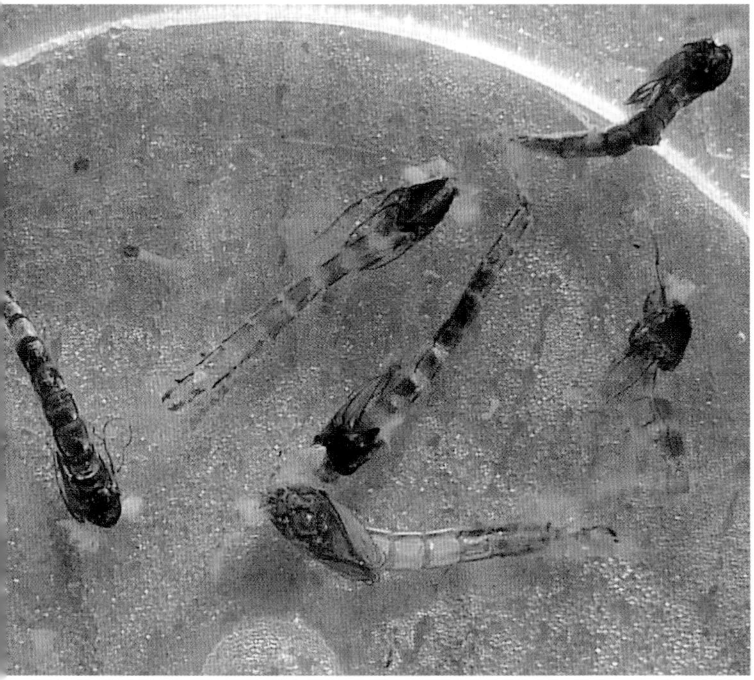

Gasses underneath the pupal skin make it easier for the adult insect to extricate itself during emergence and give the pupa a silvery sheen.

A chironomid pupa pattern with a shiny gunmetal gray body and copper rib is an excellent simulation of the gas-inflated pupa ascending to the surface.

While this metallic sheen sounds like a Magic Bullet that should be regularly applied to all chironomid pupal imitations, most of the living pupae I have examined, at least here in Oregon, do not exhibit a silvery or gunmetal sheen, appearing as straight-up, standard shades of black, olive, red, and brown. So my fly box has patterns both with and without the shiny body materials incorporated into them, excluding the wire ribbing.

It can take several days for chironomid pupae to collect enough gas underneath their skin to the point where they are adequately buoyant for their ascent to the lake's surface. Envision thousands of helpless midge pupae suspended just off the bottom of a lake, waiting for just the right moment. Can you imagine the available feast for cruising trout that happen upon this scene? Chironogeddon. For the astute fly angler who fishes the correct size and color pupal pattern at the correct depth, this event holds promise for a very memorable fish-catching day.

## The Adult

As you might recall from the previous chapter, adult midges are identified by slender, tapered, segmented bodies, with no tails. The two wings are held flat along the back in a "V" or delta shape and are distinctly shorter than the body length. The thorax is somewhat humped. The males have plume-like, hairy, "bottle brush" antennae, which assist in locating a female at mating time.

At mating time, male midges can gather in large clouds along the perimeter of a lake, pond, or stream. They entice females to join them with the release of attractive pheromones. Once the females join in the commotion, the male antennae are used to promote a heterosexual union at the Big Dance.

The body color of the adult chironomid initially may be little different from that of its pupal stage. As the body hardens and the wings unfold and dry for flight, the pupal sheen or brightness can fade. This change in color intensity can be important for fly selection if fish get choosy. Newly hatched, preflight adults are easier to apprehend. Capturing these newly emerged adults is an angler's best guide for color when choosing a fly.

It is always fun to catch fish with surface flies, be they emergers in the film or dry flies sitting on top. The visual thrill of watching the take never grows tiresome. When the easily intercepted pupae have diminished significantly at the conclusion of a hatch, what remains for fish on the prowl are the adults. Not all adults immediately take flight for safety and mating. Some may continue to struggle to free themselves completely from their old skins; others may linger just a second or two too long before liftoff, flitting or skating on the runway, unable to go airborne, drawing fatal attention to themselves with their telltale movements. The commotion may alert a cruising trout still not sated from its recent meal of pupae.

It is not certain that all insects in a population will successfully hatch. Some are unable to extract themselves completely from their pupal skin. They are referred to as stillborn. Stillborns provide for easy capture, as they cannot emerge and fly to safety. Fish recognize this predicament and may become selective for these. The experienced stillwater angler is aware of this, prepared with appropriate fly patterns and methods. Gentle, methodic rises while the trout feed offer a clue that the fish are feeding on fare they know will not escape before they intercept it, so why hurry? There's a lot to be said for eating slowly and enjoying the experience.

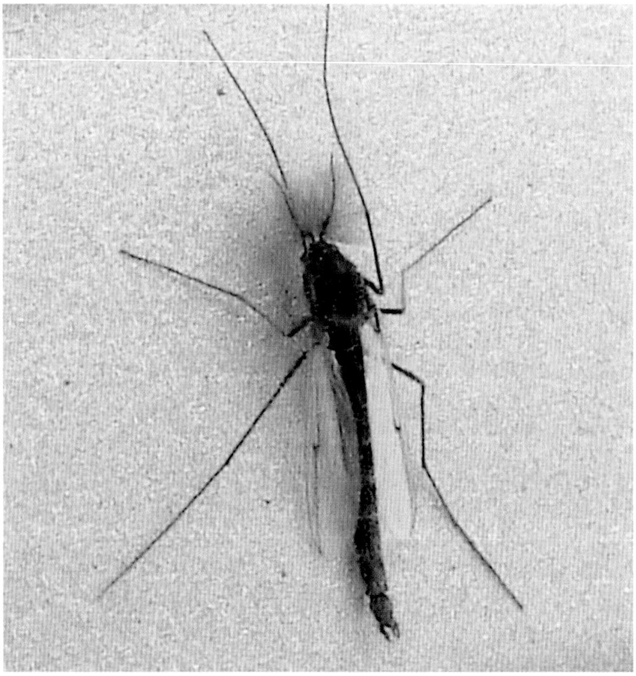
Adult male midges have sensitive brush-like antennae to locate females at mating time.

Trout may also look for adult midges when the females return to the water to lay their eggs. As the female midge dips to the surface to deposit her payload, an alert fish in the immediate vicinity may be able to grab the insect, especially if the bug is temporarily slowed or caught in the surface film. Or, after the culmination of her mission, the female may crash land on the lake, having fulfilled her destiny. She is available one final time to be consumed.

Even though the size of the midge decreases as it changes from larva to pupa to adult, some of the adults may still be relatively large, approaching an inch in length. Biologist Brian Chan says that a reasonable range for the adults, depending on species and growing conditions, is 2 to 20 mm. Translating to inches, this spans from less than 1⁄10 inch to about 4⁄5 inch. You might remember, 1 mm is about the thickness of a dime. So, to realistically simulate an adult midge the length of two dime thicknesses, you will be using a tiny, tiny fly.

Because some chironomid species are capable of producing more than one hatch cycle during a single season, smaller individuals are produced because of a shortened growing time. Smaller fly patterns are in order when fishing waters populated by multiple-generation midges.

## Now That You Know, What's Next?

I have tried to build a reasonable case to emphasize the importance of chironomids to trout and other species in stillwaters, in order to convey their importance to fly anglers in pursuit of fish-catching success. Let's assume you are convinced, maybe even excited, to fish chironomid patterns on your very next fishing outing. As you plan, anticipate, and circle a date on your calendar, know that preparation with the right fly-fishing gear and fly patterns will be only part of your success. A strategy with contingencies built into your approach is also crucial.

An excellent strategy does not cut any corners on its assembly. The following are some of the key elements of a well-planned lake fishing outing. Besides the obvious items for your angling comfort and safety as you fish, necessary equipment includes:

**A selection of appropriate fly lines and leaders** to fish effectively from the surface to the bottom of the lake you have chosen. This would include a minimum of three fly lines: floating, clear intermediate, and full-sinking Type III or Type IV.

**Effective fly patterns in a broad array of sizes, colors, and designs** to imitate all three life stages of chironomids that fish use as food. If you are a fly tier, take your tying gear to create patterns that you may have overlooked or did not anticipate.

**A floating craft that allows you maximum mobility.** A float tube is fine on a small body of water, but on a bigger lake it will take an angler too long to get from Point A to distant Point B in a tube. Fatigue or the physical work necessary to cover much distance can be very limiting. At a minimum, a pon-

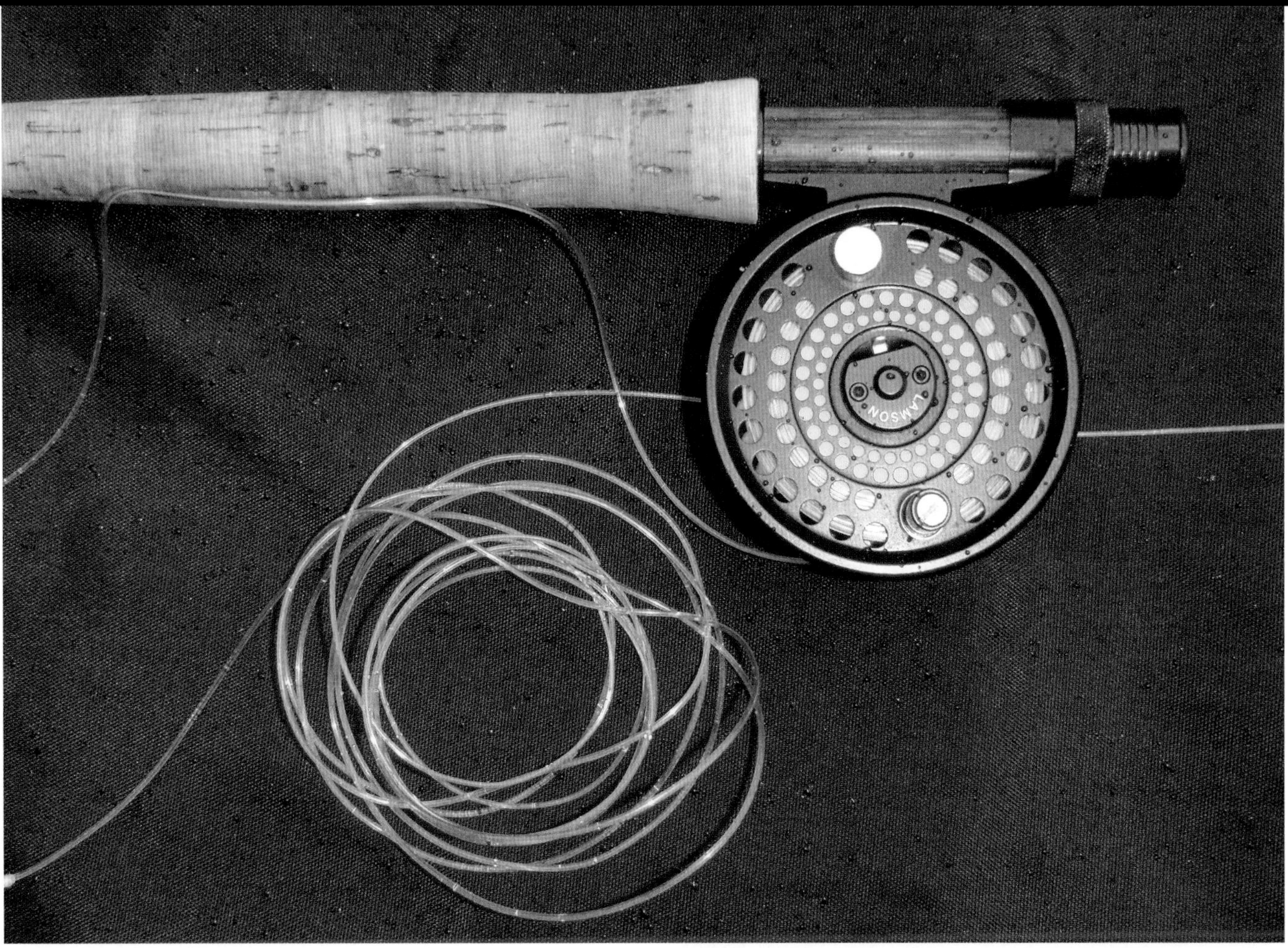


A very slow-sinking, intermediate fly line allows you to get under wind-driven surface currents to enable a slow retrieve of the fly in shallow water without the hook sinking immediately to the bottom to be fouled by vegetation or pulled through the silt, like a faster-sinking line would. A clear finish adds an element of stealth to the fly line.

toon boat equipped with oars is needed, or a boat with oars. A cartop boat with a small motor has some big advantages. The more fishing ground you can cover quickly, the better your chances of finding and catching the fish. One more consideration for whatever craft you select: an effective anchoring system is important, even when fishing in a float tube. Remaining stationary when you are in the kill zone is a necessity most of the time. Trying to remain in place even in a slight breeze can be a distraction to your concentration and your attention to the small, yet significant, details of your fishing.

**An electronic depth finder (fish locator)** is not a luxury; it is a necessity. If nothing else, you need to know the depth and contours of the lake bottom, since much of the time effective angling must be done on or very near the bottom when fishing larval and pupal flies. Misgauging depth can cost valuable time as an angler experiments with leader length to finally get it right. Since some feeding events can be short lived, devoting of too much time to discovering the exact depth can leave you with the bite over and gone. At this point, it may not matter that the fisherman has the right lines, leaders, flies, and angling method. If one crucial factor—the exact water depth—is left out of the success formula, it will undermine the effec-

Patrick Gorman brings to hand a rainbow trout that fell for a chironomid pupa fished under an indicator.

tiveness of everything else. In such a case, it is natural for an angler to doubt his equipment, his flies, and his methods, but the lack of success was entirely the result of ignoring a puzzle piece deemed unimportant.

A stomach (or throat) pump is a necessity. What the fish are eating specifically can quickly be determined. Because trout can be quite selective, the pump is indispensable. Though examining the stomach contents of every single fish is usually not necessary, it is important to remember that food preferences can change. A black-bodied chironomid pupa fly with a red wire rib, size 14, may be the answer for a while, but this preference may change as the fish change to the green pupa with a copper wire rib, size 16. It is not unusual to have multiple hatches of different chironomid species occurring simultaneously in the same location. Though it is not legal in British Columbia to fish more than one fly at a time, in much of the United States it is okay to do so. I often fish two diverse midge patterns at once. At times it becomes very clear that fish prefer one over the other. To confirm whether the position of the fly on the leader—upper or lower—is attracting the fish, I may switch the two flies' positions. If I have fair to good success with one of a pair of flies and not the other, I can replace the ineffective one with a totally different size, color, and/or design. Now and then, the newly introduced pattern can outfish the fly that had earlier proven the best. Fishing multiple flies can hasten the discovery process when fish are being selective. Not only can time be money, time can also be fish. Save as much fishing time as you can.

I also carry binoculars with me. Without being too obvious, and at a nonthreatening distance, I will search for anglers who are catching fish. They may be part of a group, or they may be all by themselves with no one nearby. Are they fishing the lake's edge? Are they in one specific spot or on the move? Are they trolling, casting, retrieving, or using a strike indicator? Or, if I can see no one catching fish, with binoculars I can scan for birds swarming an area of the lake where hatching insects are food for them. Hatching insects can mean fish are eating them before they get airborne for the birds to eat. There is also a chance I can scan an area where I spy rising, feeding fish. Magnified vision can offer many clues to move an angler toward fishing success.

## More Elements for a Successful Game Plan

### Choose your lake.

The angler needs to select a lake with proven fish reserves. Not all lakes are rich, food-abundant bodies of water. There may be very few fish present. Chances of fishing success may be limited or nonexistent. Conversely, some productive lakes can be so overfished and the remaining fish so educated or alarmed that success can be limited. Popular stillwaters in Oregon, such as Diamond Lake, can be so busy and pounded that fishing can be

Gently holding a landed fish in the belly-up position will often minimize its struggling as you take a throat or stomach sample.

challenging to fool those trout not killed and thrown into the cooler. Though Diamond can and does put out some large fish, the chance of catching a true trophy is greatly diminished by the fact that vast majority of larger fish are killed by anglers before they ever have a chance to reach huge proportions. There are very productive lakes that can prove disappointing because of the "unnatural selection" by anglers. The naïve and careless fish in the population are quickly extracted, leaving only the wary and difficult. Choose your lake wisely.

### Time your expedition.

Don't go lake fishing in December with unrealistic expectations. Plan your attempts when there is a reasonable chance of success. Timing is steered by local conditions; know what they are since they vary with latitude and elevation. I look at archived fishing reports on the Internet, paying particular attention to the dates of the postings. Some lakes can be prime in April, while others at high elevation may be best in August or September.

### Locate the fish.

Besides the benefit of my electronic devices, other clues can be available to the observant angler. Are anglers clustered in one or several specific areas on a lake? It's always worth investigating. Locating a concentration of anglers can also prove helpful if you draw close enough to watch and listen to them. As they talk among themselves, which is quite common, a listening angler can get some clues about fly patterns and depth. Observing the angling methods being used is extremely helpful. Are they fishing flies under an indicator? Are they casting and retrieving their flies? Floating line or sinking? What kind of retrieve is being used? When I observe a fly fisherman consistently catching fish, I often mirror their exact retrieve of the fly. If they impart two short pulls on the line followed by a pause, I do exactly the same. If they cast their line and wait ninety seconds before they move their fly, you can bet I will copy their every move.

### Sometimes the exact retrieve of the fly is the single most important element in coaxing the fish to bite.

Though my aim may be to specifically fish chironomids, I will troll different flies as I go from one fishing point to another. Since I must get from my launch point to my final destination where I will fish chironomids from anchor, I might as well put my flies in the water as I go. I have nothing to lose, and perhaps something to gain. Let me illustrate. While in British Columbia during the summer of 2011, I hooked some excellent rainbows while trolling, even though the chironomid anglers were doing quite well. I have specific memories on Roche, Heffley, and Leighton Lakes, where I got vicious strikes and landed some fine trout on small leech patterns while I was looking for likely areas to fish, or just thinking about what method or fly I should try next. I can still see in my mind's eye a steelhead-size jumping rainbow on Roche Lake that somehow managed to escape before I could hold it for a moment. What a fish! Trolling is a great no-brainer method that demands little mental focus as I ponder my next move. It serves the old adage that says something to the effect of "You can't catch a fish if your fly is not in the water."

I usually have a minimum of three fly rods set up and ready to fish at any given time. Even when I fish from my float tube, I have two rods stretched across my stripping apron, over my lap, as I troll the third one. Depending on the depth, I troll my intermediate or Type III. Unless I am convinced otherwise, there is a small leech as my dropper. About 30 inches beyond that, I trail a Beadhead Prince. If I catch a fish, I pump its stomach. Even though I may have caught it on a leech, it could be stuffed with chironomids. I make a mental note of the exact size and color, or I may place the stomach contents in a small glass vial I carry in a vest pocket to study later, especially if I must tie a fly of a size and color I do not already have in my fly box. The vial contains a 50/50 mixture of isopropyl alcohol and water. This potion will adequately preserve what I deposit in the vial.

Because I use barbless hooks, it is important to keep steady tension on the line, even when the fish jumps.

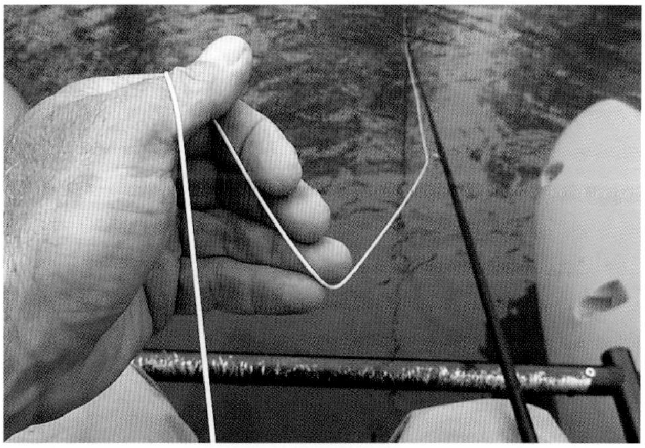

Too many anglers retrieve their flies much too quickly. A slow hand-twist retrieve—rather than slipping or pulling the line—can be very effective. Occasionally pause the retrieve, letting the fly actually stop.

Such samples are also useful when I discuss aquatic entomology with my OSU classes.

## Work within your time limitations.

If you have only a few hours for fishing a lake, pare back your expectations for success. Even if you have every hour of daylight for an entire day, the time may be too brief to discover and put together all the essential puzzle pieces for a successful fishing day. If you understand that your available time can limit your fish-catching results, it can ease the intensity of your disappointment. You must be protective of your determination and optimism. If they are damaged by your own unrealistic expectations, it can discourage your future efforts. If you are new to lake fishing, you will find that as your experience grows and you continue to learn, the time it takes for you on any given day to assess the fishing conditions and implement a smart and successful game plan will grow significantly shorter on successive fishing trips.

Experience doesn't always guarantee you will always catch as many fish as you had hoped, but you can still catch enough to encourage you to persevere. Some days I have caught only a few fish but still ended up as the high rod for the day. It eases my anxiety to realize that other anglers I have watched all day, fishing within easy view, caught not a single fish for their efforts. My first day ever on Edith Lake, BC, I landed six trout, which I thought was mediocre at best. But after talking with most other anglers on the water that day, all of whom lived in the area of the lake, the next highest fish total by any one angler was three, and some recorded zero. Perspective.

## Review and evaluate your overall game plan, especially when fishing was poor.

What were your strengths, and where were the flaws? Returning to my first day on Roche Lake in 2010, it was easy to see that one major flaw in my planning was starting at high noon. I should have been on the lake at least four hours earlier, but I had stayed up so late the night before completing my journal entries that I'd slept too late. It was an easily correctable glitch in my overall plan, one which negated—at least in part—other elements of my plan. Equipment, flies, techniques, and trick strategies were for naught because of my tardy start to the day. An angler with whom I spoke as I was preparing to launch had had a very successful morning, and even generously handed me a fly with which he'd caught many fish. His day was rewarding and complete before mine had even begun. If the bite had continued, the angler would have stayed on the lake, but he was headed home. There are times that plans have obvious flaws. Recognize the problem, put the blame on the man in the mirror, and do better next time.

The author on Edith Lake, BC. This day did not produce many fish, but such days can teach valuable lessons.

All of the elements I have suggested here for a successful approach to chironomid fishing, of course, apply to any lake fishing expedition, even those where you may never even tie on a midge imitation during the trip. It just seems most appropriate to address planning and strategies in this chapter because chironomid fishing can be so precise, so challenging, that a good plan and attention to details seem especially critical when these insects are the specific interest of the fish on the day you fish. Chironomid fishing has such important potential to take you to both the depths of discouragement and the tops of the mountains of achievement that I want continue to convey with clarity the nuances and fine points of this game. In chironomid fishing, as with many other worthy challenges worth meeting in life, the devil is in the details.

## Following the Leaders

In my experience, it is the British Columbia lake anglers who have led the way in chironomid fishing and pattern development, and who will probably continue to do so. I do not know if their love of hockey could ever be replaced in the Canadian psyche by any other sporting activity, but among lake fly anglers in British Columbia, chironomid fishing has to be in at least a close second place.

One of the fascinating aspects of chironomid fishing is that it is never static (despite the Static Bag chirono pupa pattern): fly pattern preferences by the trout can constantly change, hour to hour, day to day, and location to location. An angler must be willing to change flies often, change locations, change depth, alter equipment, and resort to different methods in a full fishing day. Those anglers who refuse to be aggressive or dedicated to the flux and flow of the fishing day can be left wondering if there are any fish in the lake or just assuming they are off the bite. Successful chironomid anglers anticipate and look for the fish and fishing to change at any time. Their goal is to, as quickly as possible, discern the change and adapt. In the search for clues, an electronic depth finder is indispensable. Get one. Every serious chironomid angler has one—and probably a spare for security.

One of the best ways to stay on top of the constant change in food preferences, methods, and productive locations in a lake is to fish with a group of comrades. This prompts me to reference a group of anglers I will call the Group of Four on Roche Lake. These guys plan on spending the first day or two of their annual buddies' trip on this lake finding specific locations where the fish seem to be concentrated and tying up specific fly patterns that will imitate the chironomids that they have extracted pumping the stomachs of the fish caught and released during the scouting days. Or they examine the stomach contents of the trout kept and dressed for the frying pan. After a couple of nights at the fly-tying benches at their campsites, these guys have a broad assortment—with much mixing and matching of sizes, colors, materials, and design styles—of chironomid pupae flies to be shared with everyone in the group.

Once on the water, the members of the group are in constant communication. They talk endlessly to each other about fly size and color combo, the length of their leaders and the depth at which they are fishing, and share specific details about anything other than a heave-it-and-leave-it. The leader of the conversation is the angler who has landed the last fish. His buddies want to know if he has used a different fly, altered his leader, or changed his method to catch the most recent fish. With this type of information sharing and the possibility for experimentation, a knowledgeable committee can account for many, many fish hooked while outsiders watch with envy.

Now as the Group of Four speak to each other, nearby anglers (like me) can hear what they say. However, there are a couple of complications. They speak in a code, especially about the fly patterns. If they have named them, there may not be any clue about the color or design of the fly. When a fly is referenced as "that skinny dark one I gave you yesterday afternoon,"

On popular waters like Roche Lake, BC, other anglers can help you locate the fish, and observing them can provide clues as to how to fish your chosen fly.

This Diamond Lake rainbow ate a fake chironomid pupa fished under an indicator. The lake's shallow south end can provide sight-fishing opportunities.

this does not tell an eavesdropper much. Even when color combination is given, it usually offers nothing about the materials or the design features of the fly.

Another important puzzle piece for success is the exact location being fished. Fish can be concentrated in a very small area near a spring, a channel, a drop off, or a weed bed where insects are active. Four guys—and a few other anglers who have knowledge of the fishing at that moment—can position themselves strategically, anchoring their craft so that there is no room for a late arrival to approach the area where the fish are ganged. Besides witnessing this on Roche Lake, I saw the same a few days later at Leighton Lake. A group of angler boats quickly gathered in a particular location near the southeast corner of the lake in early afternoon. Five boats anchored in a line, evenly spaced over a distance of about 200 feet. Trying to join the fun without encroaching on anyone's personal space, I was the sixth boat, anchored on the north end of the line. The fishermen in the other five boats were in constant communication. All five of them regularly hooked fish. I even hooked and landed a few rainbows myself. We were all using the same technique: chironomids under an indicator in about 15 feet of water. That meant I had about 14 feet between my indicator and fly. This set up was significantly easier to cast than the longer leader for fishing at 20 feet at Roche Lake.

A few weeks later, I was fishing Oregon's Diamond Lake with my good friend Chuck Wagner. It was not hard to locate the best concentration of fish at midmorning; find the boats clustered and you will find the trout. As we maneuvered Chuck's powerboat through the maze of assorted fishing craft, it was difficult to not trespass into someone's casting or trolling territory. The spacing was not static, since there were many anglers in float tubes and small pontoon boats always on the move. A reasonable open space to anchor without intruding could suddenly shrink and become crowded. This is messy and uncomfortable boat maneuvering when none of the other anglers are your acquaintances.

Most fly anglers at Diamond were fishing—surprise!—chrironomid pupae under indicators. Through a bit of trial and error we discovered the depth and patterns that were attractive to some passing fish and caught our share of nice trout. As on Roche and Leighton, other anglers had led me to the fish, but it is usually left to me, or my angling companion, to figure the right fly, depth, and method.

Of course, like all parts of your chironomid fishing game plan, there must be contingencies when circumstances call for adjustments. There are not always bloodhounds to lead you to the fish on the lake you have chosen. No rising fish. No swarming birds. You forgot your best box of flies. Accidently kicked off a fin, and it sunk to the lake bottom. Oops! Just broke a rod. Smile if you can and embrace the challenge. There may be a multitasking opportunity: you can work on building your character as you pursue fish.

# CHAPTER 4

# Equipment Essentials

Compared to wade-fishing streams and rivers, most stillwater fishing endeavors are gear-intensive. They require a boat, waders, fins, multiple rods, and a million flies . . . just for starters.

I remember clipping a thought-provoking photo from the sports section of my local newspaper some years ago. At the finish line of a major horse race were two horses, with the nose of the winner merely a couple of inches ahead of the beaten horse. It was literally a photo finish. The winner—the one who got all the horse-racing glory and most of the money that day—had a slight edge, all that was needed to win. Like the winning horse, the most successful stillwater angler is one who develops all the "edges" he can: an edge over the weather, over the conditions, over other anglers, and over the fish. Good and appropriate fishing gear can provide a significant edge for a lake fisherman because of the unique "musts" for meeting the challenges of the lake angling environment, compared to stream and river fishing.

## Fly Rods for Lakes

Rod selection starts when you think about what you need to accomplish when casting to quality lake fish. I have used the term quality to distinguish these from naïve hatchery trout that often take little skill, strategy, or good equipment to catch. I am addressing fishing for bigger, educated fish that are wary and easily alarmed, like those conditioned by heavy fishing pressure on public lakes. An essential ingredient in the mix is the ability to make long, smooth casts when dictated by the circumstances.

Multiple rods strung with a variety of floating and sinking fly lines can save valuable fishing time.

Additionally, thought must be given to the challenges and obstacles to making reasonably long—50- to 70-foot—casts. For instance, the fact that a caster sitting low in the water in a float tube must be conscious of slapping the water behind him with the fly line on a backcast pleads the case for a longer rod. More length, let's say 9½ or 10 feet, elevates the line slightly, decreasing the chance that an adequate caster will kill the cast as the line touches the water to his rear.

Dealing with the wind is another consideration in rod and line weight selection. A fast-action rod that throws a tight line loop may be the best choice when casting into a stiff breeze. However, a fast-action rod can break a light leader when the hook set is too powerful. A compromise rod action may actually be a better choice. It's one more reason to think things through before you buy.

When looking for the right lake fly rod for you, the number of choices may seem overwhelming. Be patient. Search and cast before you buy.

Fly rods come in a variety of lengths and line weight designations. Let's consider each with our end goal to find the ideal lake rod for you.

Six to 16 feet is a range of rod lengths that you may encounter in a well-stocked fly shop. This range provides the typical lake fly angler—man or woman—the optimum combination of casting ease, casting distance, comfort/minimum fatigue, and line control. For lake fishermen, the most popular lengths are between 9 and 10 feet.

It is the suggested fly line weight inscribed on the fly rod blank that indicates the appropriate quarry for a particular rod. When the rod is matched with its recommended fly line, the rod's performance can be maximized, and the fly most easily presented to a fish at a reasonable distance.

Fly line weights range from 0-weight through 14-weight. These whole numbers correspond to an actual physical weight of the tapered portion of a fly line, the first 30 to 40 feet. The unit of weight measure is a grain. 1 ounce = about 454 grains.

The following is a general summary of line weights/fly rods matched to the typical target species:

0–3-weight fly lines/fly rods: panfish and small to average trout
4–6-weight: typical trout
7–9-weight: typical steelhead, salmon, bass, and light saltwater
10–14-weight: big species saltwater or mountain rescue

Now, let me remind you that the above classifications are accepted generalizations. I have landed 7-pound rainbows on a 3-weight fly rod, and I have captured 6-inch saltwater snappers on a 10-weight. However, it is usually best to select the appropriate rod for the particular species sought. There is no such thing as a "one-size-fits-all" fly rod. Let me demonstrate with a couple of sporting analogies.

I usually golf once a year with my nephews as part of our annual 4th of July party weekend, and I've noticed the equipment used in golf serves as an excellent analogy for fly rod selection. A variety of clubs is used to play a round of golf. A golf bag might have ten different clubs to select from in a given situation. A good golfer will not use the same club to hit from the tee, lift a shot out of the woods, escape from a sand trap, and putt on the green. Yes, I could hit off the tee with my putter. Yes, I could catch a 6-inch trout with a flagpole. Get the appropriate tool for the job.

The typical lake fly rod casts a 4-, 5-, or 6-weight fly line for pursuing trout and smaller warmwater gamefish, such as crappie and bluegill. For all-around general use, consider a 6-weight for longer casts and dealing with the wind. While a 6-weight can beat a 10-pound lake trout, you can still feel and enjoy the scrappy fight of an 8-inch fish.

As for largemouth bass, a 7- or 8-weight rod may be a better choice. This has little to do with the size of the bass; it has to do with casting large, heavy, or air resistant flies, and being able to extract a fish that has burrowed into the underwater vegetation. Many bass anglers will immediately apply tremendous fighting pressure on a hooked bass to prevent it from entangling itself in the cover-rich environment quality bass prefer. A heavier rod is required to do this successfully.

I own many rods, including lightweight models that cast a 2- through 6-weight fly line, which I dedicate to lake fishing. I have the luxury of matching a specific rod to a specific situation. If the wind is down, short casts will suffice, and if the fish are not bigger than pan size, a 2- or 3-weight is a lot of fun. My 3-weight gets a lot of use when I am trolling flies for BIG fish on a light leader. The soft, light tip of the rod bends like a rubber band when a hard strike comes, a strike that would normally snap my spiderweb line on a 5- or 6-weight rod. Additionally, when a strong, fast fish sprints away from me at high speed, my light rod tips absorb the sudden shock, keeping my light leader intact.

## A Big Fish Story

I was fishing with my friend Matt Sentena on a warm June day at Crane Prairie Reservoir in Central Oregon's Cascade Mountains. In this man-made lake it is possible to find rainbows ("Cranebows" is a common colloquialism) that will easily exceed 10 pounds. That blue-sky afternoon, the rainbows preferred a trolled damselfly nymph on transparent, slow-sinking line. We patrolled a particular stretch of water not too far from Osprey Point. The strikes were hard, sometimes vicious. If there was a heavy-handed response on the hook set, it was time to tie on a fresh fly. Because I was fishing a lightweight leader, I used my 3-weight rod with a soft tip to protect the line from a break-off. When the hard strike came, the tip absorbed the impact. Though we never landed a 10-pound trout, we brought to hand an abundance of fish in the 4- to 6-pound range.

How hard were the strikes? For whatever reason, I momentarily lost my focus as I looked at other fishing activity on the lake. When a tremendous pull came on my line, my rod was pulled from my hand and started to swim away from me.

A lightweight flexible fly rod aids in landing large fish on fragile tippets with small flies.

A slow-action rod tip will cushion a hard strike or an overly enthusiastic hook set and make a small fish seem just a little bit bigger.

Simultaneously, it began to sink slowly. Instinctively, I pivoted my float tube 180 degrees with a few quick kicks of my fins and went in desperate pursuit. In a couple more kicks, I was near the sinking rod. I thrust my left arm straight down as far as I could reach. With any less effort, my fingertips would not have reached the descending rod. In retrospect, I was fortunate not to have capsized my tube with such a forceful lean.

As I gathered my errant rod and my wits, I soon realized the culprit trout was still attached! Holding my rod securely, I eventually landed another spectacular Cranebow.

## Bend with No Fear

I am often asked if a light rod is at risk of being broken by a big fish. Maybe, but participating as a guide or angler in the capture of hundreds of large and extra-large lake fish, I have never witnessed the breaking of a rod while fighting these fish. Modern graphite rods can easily withstand tremendous bend. But if you perceive jeopardy when a strong fish puts a dangerous bend in your rod, merely drop the rod tip to a lower position toward the fish. You can minimize the bend to any degree you want, even to the extent where you position the rod horizontally, pointing it directly at the bruiser. However, with no shock-absorbing bend in the rod, there is an excellent chance you will break off a worthy fish.

## Rod Action Choices

Rod action—the extent to which a rod bends over its entire length with a big fish on the line—is usually chosen to suit the angler's casting comfort. A fast-action fly rod generally bends readily in the upper quarter to one third. A medium-action rod bends to its midpoint, while a slow, or full-flex, rod bends all the way to the grip. Each has its pros and cons.

Each type of rod action has its advocates and detractors. Most inexperienced fly fishers think that a fast-action fly rod is the best choice. I am sure they think of such a tool as a high-speed sports car. Because the rod tip is powerful and recovers quickly to its unbent resting position quickly, the fast-action rod is capable of propelling a fly line at higher velocities, resulting in greater casting distance. However, just as in driving a sports car at high speeds through the curves, timing and control can become overwhelming issues. Some casters can master the timing stroke and cast a long beautiful line. Others bully or mistime the casting stroke rhythm of a fast rod, losing the distance potential. The fast rod will seem unmanageable and unpleasant.

There are occasions—low, clear water, for instance—where a light tippet is required to fool large lake fish. With a fast-action rod, there can be a high impact force imparted to the leader that can easily break off the fly. There may be too little "give" in the rod tip if the hook set is too forceful, and little, if any, shock absorption. An overly powerful response to a big strike will part the leader. An escaped fish with a fly still in its jaws may jump, responding to the sting still in its mouth. That way, at least, you may see the fish you might have landed.

In contrast to the tip-action rod, there is the slow or full-flex action. The bending and recovery of the tip takes longer than the other actions, and the casting stroke is much slower. An impatient caster may move the rod back and forth too quickly, not allowing the bending rod to reach the natural terminus of its flex in either direction. Calmed relaxation is a good mental posture with this action type. This is not the rod action for the hyperactive.

The longer, extended flextime of the slow-action rod allows a focused caster to better feel the bend of the rod. Also, the slow action accentuates the feel of the unfurling fly line as it straightens out on the backcast. This signals just the right moment to move the rod tip in the opposite direction during the cast. An attentive angler has time to process and prepare for the next stroke to begin. This I call a "forgiving" action. The slower flex makes more allowances for imperfect timing—within reasonable limits—of the casting stroke. And, for those who may have fished quality bamboo or fiberglass fly rods in their careers, the slow action feels quite normal.

The possibility of breaking off a fish on the strike is reduced with a full-flex rod. The rod acts like a springy shock absorber, so the impact of a reasonably hard hook set against resistance (the fish) is cushioned. A heavy-handed angler who tries to turn a big, stubborn fish will have a lesser chance of a break-off than an angler performing the same maneuver with a stiff, fast-action stick. It is the same effect as playing a good trout on a lighter, more limber 3- or 4-weight fly rod.

The majority of fly rods will fall into the broad medium-action category, flexing most commonly down to the midsection. Take a fast-action and a slow-action model, and then split the difference. It is here that most fly anglers will settle when it comes to selecting a fly rod.

I highly recommend that you cast any rod you consider buying. Even an expensive rod can feel clunky, uncomfortable, or too heavy in the tip. The grip might look pretty on the display but be too big or too small for your hand. Even if your casting skill is minimal, cast before you buy. You would not, I think, buy a mail-order bride without a photo, nor buy a car sight unseen. Always take a rod for a test drive in the alley or on the lawn before plunking down your cash. Its appearance on the rack may have little bearing on the rod's feel and performance.

## Instruction for Inspection Perfection

Examine the components on the rod: the cork grip, reel seat, the guides, the thread wraps on the guides, and the epoxy or urethane finish work on the wraps. The majority of the guides—usually twisted "S" snake guides—need to be made of chrome-plated stainless steel or some space-age alloy. Do not settle for mere stainless steel guides. They will wear with time and corrode more easily if ever used in saltwater. They may have to be replaced in a few years—not an inexpensive proposition. If you do not know their composition, ask the guy or gal behind the counter. Read the manufacturer's literature.

Count the number of guides tied on the rod, not including the tip-top. On a quality fly rod, there should be at least one more guide than the whole number of feet in the fly rod's length. Example: a 9- or 9½-foot rod should have at least 10 guides. As the rod is flexed forward and backward during a normal cast, the line in the guides should mirror the flex. If the guides are too far apart because the manufacturer or rod builder cut corners on work time and materials, the line will slap the rod blank during the cast, creating friction that slows the line as it slides through the rod guides and decreasing casting distance. Additionally, when you hold the rod horizontal on the forward stroke as the cast is completed, the line sags between guides that are spaced too widely, again causing distance-killing friction.

More guides than I have recommended are not necessarily better. One rod manufacturer attaches two more guides than the whole number of feet in the rod length. No problem, but any more are certainly not needed and will only add excess weight and stiffness to the rod.

Just as an inexperienced driver can get a feel for the vehicle that suits him and his budget, an inexperienced fly caster can feel an affinity for a certain rod. It will seem comfortable

High-quality, high-performance fly rods will also have top-notch aesthetics. Most of these rods also come with a warranty in case of breakage. If possible, cast a rod before you buy it to make sure it suits your casting style.

and pleasant to cast, even though the casting stroke is far from perfection. No matter your experience level, to make a wise choice put your pride aside and do some comparison casting. You will not know what suits you unless you compare. It may preclude you saving a few bucks by buying that deal on the Internet or from the bargain bin, but look long-term. The right rod may be fished for a lifetime. If you amortize a few extra dollars over a lifetime, it can mean only a few pennies a year. How much money did you waste on that pair of shoes that never fit right, or that CD you listened to once in six years? Compare, and don't skimp on the cost. By investing the time to find the right rod for you, you may only have to buy once.

## Fly Lines

Here are some of the possible variables you will deal with when selecting the fly line, or lines, for your lake fishing needs: taper, color, length, full-floating, full-sinking, floating/sinking combination, length of sinking portion, sink rate, quality level, price, and manufacturer. Combining all these factors presents the angler with more than two hundred choices. Yikes! Unless you have a good reason backed by personal knowledge or experienced advice, I suggest that you consider using the lines I personally have found useful and effective.

For most lake anglers getting started, I recommend two fly lines: the first is a high-quality, high-visibility, weight-forward, tapered, floating fly line. A high-quality line lasts longer, casts better, floats higher and longer than a cheap fly line. As for color, you want to be able to see—approximately—where your fly is drifting as you fish it. Yes, fish can see color; however, it is not the fly line color that startles a fish, but the shadow and splash as the line lands.

The second must-have fly line for stillwaters is a clear, or "camo," slow-sinking (intermediate or Type I) model. Sink rates are usually designated with a Roman numeral from I to VI, Type I or "intermediate density" being the slowest, sinking at a rate of between 3/4 inch and 1 1/2 inches per second, and Type VI being the fastest, dropping at 8 to 10 inches per second. If you add a third line to your arsenal, make it a Type III density-compensated one, in a dark color.

To cast effortlessly and have the fly line and leader fully extend on the cast, a standard fly line must be tapered. In my opinion, a double-taper fly line—which most beginners have heard of—is a specialty fly line with a couple of serious limitations for the majority of average fly rodders, including casting long distances and overcoming the wind. A weight-forward taper, when properly cast, maximizes distance, performs better than a double taper in the wind, and does a better job of presenting heavy and air-resistant large flies at distance.

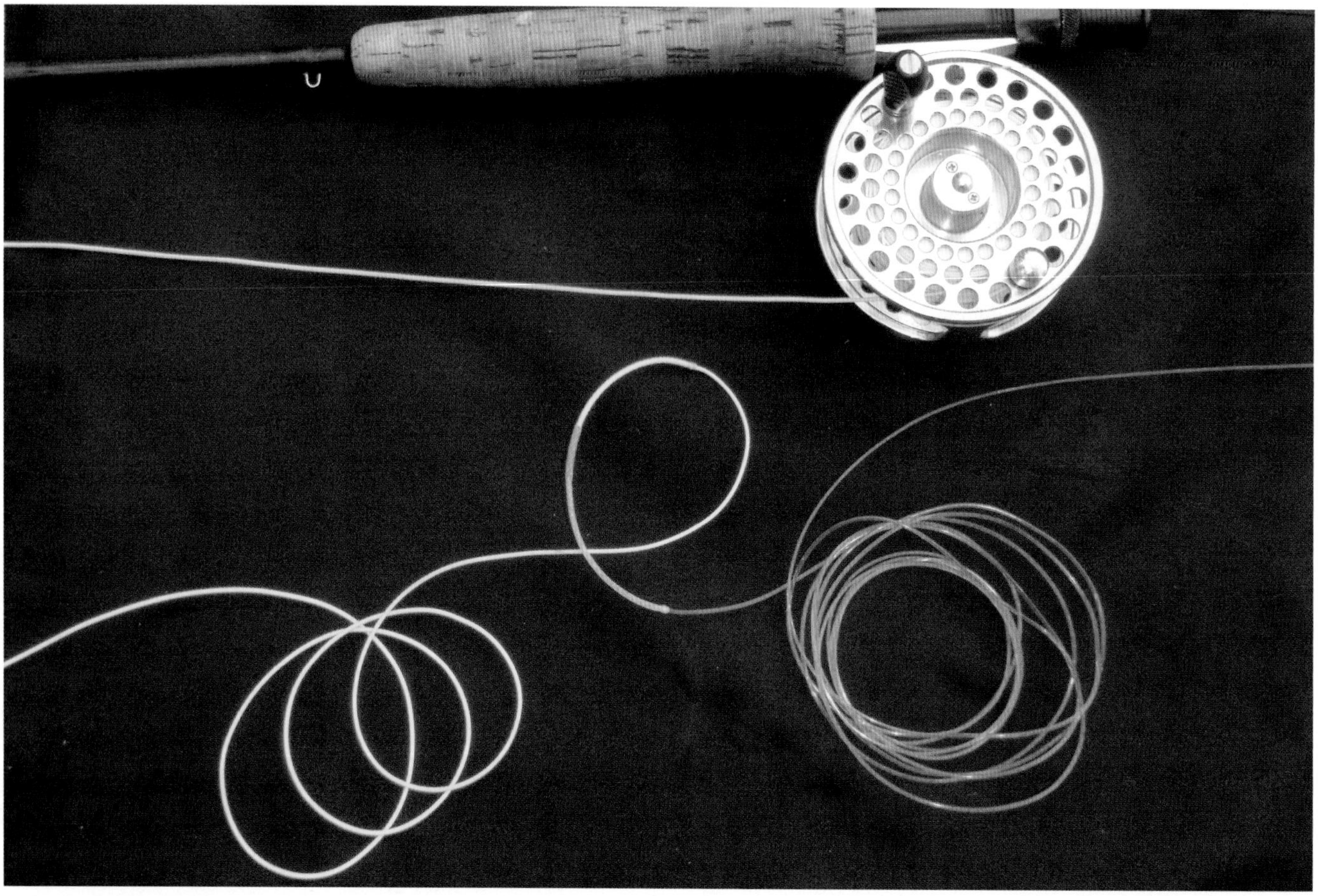

A clear-tip, slow-sinking fly line is one of my top four choices to be carried during a typical fishing day. The floating portion serves as a very visible strike indicator and also makes the line easy to pick up off the water for the next cast.

To be fully effective, an angler must have a variety of fly lines for stillwater fishing.

Use a floating fly line to present dry flies, shallow-running wet flies, and nymphs in shallow water. The floating line is also used when suspending nymphs and midge larvae and pupae in water of any depth. The floater is also the easiest line to cast, mend, visually track, and pick off the water to recast.

When circumstances require a sinking fly line, I most often use my clear (transparent) slow-sinking line in shallow water, usually not more than 10 feet deep. I use this line in shallow water where I might normally prefer my floating line, but because the wind is blowing, my slow-sinking, clear line descends below the surface currents. When the wind blows a big curve into my floating line, I miss or may not even detect subtle strikes; I do not have a straight-line contact with my fly. Because the clear intermediate line sinks below the surface, I have the straight-line contact I need. If the water where the fish are cruising and feeding is shallow, it is the slow-sinking line that keeps my flies from dropping immediately to the bottom where they would then be caught in the vegetation or pick up debris on the hook point. The Type III full-sinking line is most useful for me where the water exceeds 10 feet.

## Your Insurance Policy: Fly Line Backing

Peeling all the fly line from your reel during a panicked run is not a difficult task for a huge lake fish. As insurance, have 50 yards of braided Dacron backing knotted to the rear of the fly line. This material—I use and recommend 20-pound breaking strength in most situations—has virtually no stretch, is very strong for its diameter, and does not deteriorate significantly over time, as monofilament will. Do not even consider using monofilament. Exposure to sunlight over a couple of fishing seasons will greatly weaken it. Then you set yourself up for a

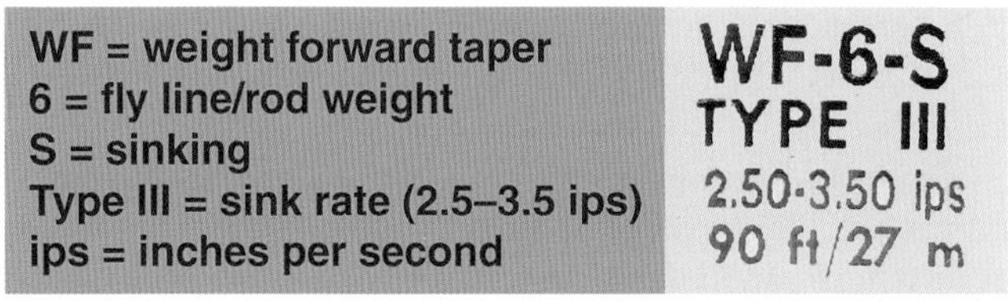

A Type III density-compensated sinking fly line is very useful in water depths of ten feet or more.

two-for-one: if a big lake fish pulls out your entire fly line during an epic fight, and then your mono backing breaks, you not only lost your fish, you lost your expensive fly line, too!

## Smooth under Pressure: The Fly Reel

Once a nasty, strong trout or bass is on the end of the line, the final scene in the drama—capture or escape—is largely determined by your fly reel. The rod presents the fly to the fish, but the reel resists and tires it. A reel that does not release line very smoothly at high speed is worthless to me. If I consistently hooked fifty huge fish in a day, the disappointment of lost fish due to reel malfunction would not be as intense. However, a biffed chance by most of us mere mortals who feel lucky to hook one or two monsters in a fishing day is serious heartache. I would rather use a mediocre fly rod and an excellent fly reel than vice versa. Like I tell my students, "Put a star by this statement: Get a GOOD fly reel!" Even if you are a natural-born skimper, do not try to be frugal with this piece of fly-fishing gear. I guarantee you will be sorry.

The drag mechanism in a fly reel adjusts the amount of resistance against the force of a steelhead pulling line off the

An excellent fly reel is well worth the price in large fish landed and can serve you well for a lifetime.

reel. This pulling force varies throughout the battle in duration and intensity. The drag must smoothly and instantly adjust to these changes.

Examples of common drag designs include spring and pawl, caliper, and disc types. Disc drags are the most widely used in quality steelhead fly reels. Simply, a smooth, flat surface on or geared to the turning spool of the reel works against a stationary, flat, smooth surface on the inside of the reel frame. Drag (resistance against the pull of the fish) is increased or decreased as the angler tightens or lightens the drag by means of a lever or knob on the reel. Too little drag and the fish feels no tiring resistance. Too much drag causes the leader to break when the fish pulls hard or suddenly against the resistance. Experience gained through a little trial and error will enable the angler to discover what is too little and what is too much.

Frankly, I do not like spring and pawl reels for fishing, though I know some very good fly fishers who love them and would use no other. They love to palm the spinning spool and cherish the whirring scream of the instrument when a fish peels line from it. In the first case, I can set my disc drag exactly where I want it, taking the guesswork out of palming the drag and not risking a miscalculation that could result in too much tension on the spool rim, breaking the tippet. Secondly, it is rare that I want to draw attention to the fact that my clients or I have a fish on the end of the line. Spring and pawl reels loudly proclaim, "Look at me! I got one! Come over here, and bring your friends." I have disengaged the clicking pawl in all of my disc drag reels, converting them to silent running.

## Choosing a Reel

I am beating a dead camel, but if there is one comment about fly reels I hear above all others from would-be and beginner fly fishermen, it is some variation on this: "I have heard that the reel is merely a device for holding the fly line, and it is not really necessary to buy a really good one. It is smarter to put the saved money into buying a better fly rod." And, I will agree with them—if the biggest fish they ever hook does not exceed 10 inches.

Once I hook an exceptional fish, my success in playing and landing it relies heavily on the performance of my reel. The reel must release line smoothly at high speed. If the spinning reel spool catches momentarily or binds up, the game is over; the fish has won. Smooth performance under high-speed stress is the ultimate test for a good fly reel, especially when its internal workings get wet from a dunking or fishing in the rain.

If water penetrates the minute space between the two drag surfaces in a disc drag reel, hydroplaning may result. Just as steering and braking control in a car may be lost as it travels through standing water at high speed, wet drag surfaces in a faulty reel will lose the friction necessary to retain the resistance needed for battling a steelhead. The reel spool will spin madly as drag is lost, creating a hideous backlash tangle of line that guarantees a break-off of the fish. Before you shell out \$100–\$300 for a fly reel, extract a guarantee from the seller that the reel's drag will perform when wet.

Even when a quality reel's drag system gets soaked, it must still release line smoothly at high speed for an angler to land a large fish prone to hard, fast runs.

Some drags are lousy when put to the test by a big fish even when they are dry and properly lubricated (if lubrication is required). Immediately return the reel to the seller. As best you can, resist being cajoled into sending it back to the reel manufacturer yourself. Let the seller of the item be responsible for packaging, handling, and delivery charges if the item must go back to the manufacturer for repairs or replacement. Oops! Bought it through the mail or on the Internet? It's rarely worth the time or hassle of attempting to get customer service. Consider dealing face-to-face with a local merchant. The service provided by a local fly-fishing specialty retailer is a good investment. You might also receive some quality fishing advice as part of the deal.

To ensure continued good performance, get a lube kit for your fly reel. Just as your car must be maintained occasionally, so must your fly reel. Pop off the spool now and then to clean the inner workings with a soft cloth. Then lube the spindle. If it has a cork drag, apply a light coating of neatsfoot oil. Now listen to your reel purr.

Size matters. Virtually all modern fly reel models come in a variety of sizes. For instance, the Acme Wizbang series has four different sizes to best accommodate a broad spectrum of fly line size (line weight) and desired amount of backing. Your clue to the reel size appropriate for your particular fly line is the stated "reel capacity" in the owner's manual. If you have a WF-6-F fly line and want to back it on the reel spool with about 100 yards of 20-pound braided Dacron, select the Wizbang model that has the closest approximation to the capacity you need. It is rare that any given reel will have exactly the stated capacity you desire. Since most manufacturers tend to overstate the amount of backing that can actually be held on the spool, I suggest you choose a reel with a stated capacity that is slightly too big over a reel whose capacity is slightly too small. Think in terms of buying shoes. With no size fitting perfectly, are you going to buy slightly larger or slightly too small? If you have ever worn shoes that were too small, you know the right answer.

## Leaders and Tippets

Starting with the obvious, the leader is the transparent segment of the total fly line system. The fly is tied to its end. Lengths range from 3 feet to 16 feet or more. Typically, I start with a 9-foot tapered leader, often lengthening it by adding tippet material; the final length may be 10 to 15 feet. I tend to use the longer length when fishing chironomid pupae under an indicator in deep water. The standard is 9 feet for wet flies and dry flies, though I may resort to 10- to 15-foot leaders when then there is no breeze on the water to riffle the surface.

The profile of the typical out-of-package 9-foot tapered leader is 0.024–0.021 inch at its heavy butt section, narrowing to 0.004–0.011 inch over the next 7 feet. The final 2 to 3 feet of the leader, where the fly is tied on its end, has a uniform diameter. This taperless portion of the leader is the tippet.

Nine-foot leaders are often adequate, but in deep water, leaders of 25 feet (!) might be necessary for some fly-fishing methods.

A tapered leader's length is naturally reduced by changing flies, breaking the leader on a lost fish, or casting into trees. To replenish the length, pull tippet from a spare spool and tie it to the shortened leader with a double surgeon's knot.

Leaders and tippets are available in an assortment of line technology chemistries: monofilament, copolymer, first-generation fluorocarbon, and second-generation fluorocarbon. Without getting too technical, know that monofilament leaders and tippets are cheapest and have the lowest breaking strength for their diameter; copolymer types are more expensive but up to 50 percent stronger; second-generation fluorocarbon lines are as strong as the copolymer varieties, have significant invisibility, and are three to four times as expensive as the copolymer.

Distributors and wholesalers of leaders and tippet materials can choose from a list of variables to create unique leaders and tippets. Besides the general chemistry of the line, these variables include color, taper design (leaders), suppleness/stiffness, knotting strength, and abrasion resistance.

## My Personal Choices for Leaders and Tippets

For fishing trout and smaller warmwater gamefish in lakes, I gravitate toward supple, soft leaders for minimal influence on the natural action of the fly on or in the water. Even with a soft butt section, my casts lay out generally straight at all distances, even in a significant breeze. Even when I am skating a dry fly on a tight line across the surface, I like the subtle bobbing and weaving of the fly allowed by a soft tippet.

Because fluorocarbon tends to be stiffer, I prefer a copolymer leader. I cut off the tippet portion of the leader and replace it with fluorocarbon tippet. In the tippet, I am sacrificing a little suppleness for invisibility, kind of like sacrificing my queen to win the chess match. I always prefer a second-generation fluorocarbon tippet, no matter the leader. Second-generation is stronger than first-generation tippet for the same money. It seems like a no-brainer.

Losing a worthy fish to an unexplainable break-off is disheartening. When you witness these too often with a particular tippet brand name, it leaves a lingering bad impression. Not all second-generation tippet materials are the same quality. For knot strength and minimal mysterious breaks in the middle of a fish fight, I prefer one brand name above all others (so far). Readers are invited to contact me personally through one of my websites to discover my choice. Because new and better items come to market all the time, I may discover something even more to my liking in the future.

I admit to being addicted to fluorocarbon. It is the invisibility factor that has me hooked. This, I think, is imperative in clear water where wary fish are on high alert. Plenty of stillwater fish succumbed to my flies before the advent of fluorocarbon tippets and leaders. However, at the end of a lean or—yikes!—a

There are many materials and brand names of leaders and tippets. Some are definitely superior to others. In clear, heavily fished waters, opt for high-quality fluorocarbon tippets, well worth the extra cost.

fishless day, I do not want to wonder if a willing biter would have struck a hook if only I had used fluorocarbon. Removing this doubt is important. The type of tippet is under my control, a variable in the fishing success equation I do not want to have to reflect on. There are too many other factors I cannot control. Even though fluorocarbon is expensive, it is a small cost in comparison to the much larger costs of my other equipment, including, rods, reels, waders, boat, and travel. I might use $2 to $3 of tippet in a day. Keep perspective.

Tippets come in a variety of diameters and should be matched to the size of the fly you use, balancing both the natural "swimability" of the fly and a diameter adequate to fully extend the leader and fly on a good cast. The table at the right shows the diameters of commonly used tippet sizes, measured in terms of "X" number commonly found labeled on leader and tippet packaging and an equivalent diameter measured in inches. Note that when the "X" number and final digit in the inches measurement are added, the sum is 11.

Example: 3X = 0.008"
3 + 8 = 11

**TIPPET DIAMETER**

| "X" number | diameter in inches |
|---|---|
| X | 0.011" |
| 1X | 0.010" |
| 2X | 0.009" |
| 3X | 0.008" |
| 4X | 0.007" |
| 5X | 0.006" |
| 6X | 0.005" |
| 7X | 0.004" |
| 8X | 0.003" |

Note that there is an inverse relationship: the larger the "X" number, the smaller the diameter, so the diameter of a 6X tippet is smaller than the diameter of a 1X tippet.

As I said, it's key to get the right combination of line extension during the cast coupled with an effective drift of the fly once it hits the water lies in the diameter of the tippet. For generally matching the tippet diameter to the fly size, use the following equation:

Fly (hook) size / 3 = "X" number

____________ = appropriate "X" number

3

The "X" number found on a tippet spool and leader packaging is a reference to diameter. If you look closer at the labeling, you will usually discover the translation into inches. Example: 2X = 0.009". Using the equation above for common stillwater flies, you will probably find 3X, 4X, 5X, and 6X tippets to be the most useful diameters.

In case you are new to this information, know that there is an inverse relationship between the hook size number and the actual physical size of the hook. That is, the larger the hook number, the smaller the hook's measurable size, specifically the measurement between the main body of the hook (the shank) and the point of the hook. This is a measurement of the hook's gap or gape. For example, a #6 hook is larger than a #12 hook.

In tough clear water conditions, I will often give up castability for a better drift and tippet invisibility. Instead of using the 2X tippet suggested by my mathematical formula for a #6 fly, I may instead use a smaller 3X or 4X diameter so there's a diminished chance that an eagle-eye steelhead won't be able to detect a line attached to my hook.

In my everyday fishing, I only use two knots: the double surgeon and the clinch. I use the double surgeon to add tippet to my leader and the clinch to secure my flies. These are very commonly used, and schematics and tying instructions can be found in any fishing knots book or online. Both are quick, easy, and strong. I make sure to lubricate the knots with my moistened lips before I pull them tight. Use a nail or tube knot to tie the backing and leader to the fly line. A small tube the diameter of a cocktail straw is necessary to tie this knot. It is somewhat tedious, so practice and patience are necessary.

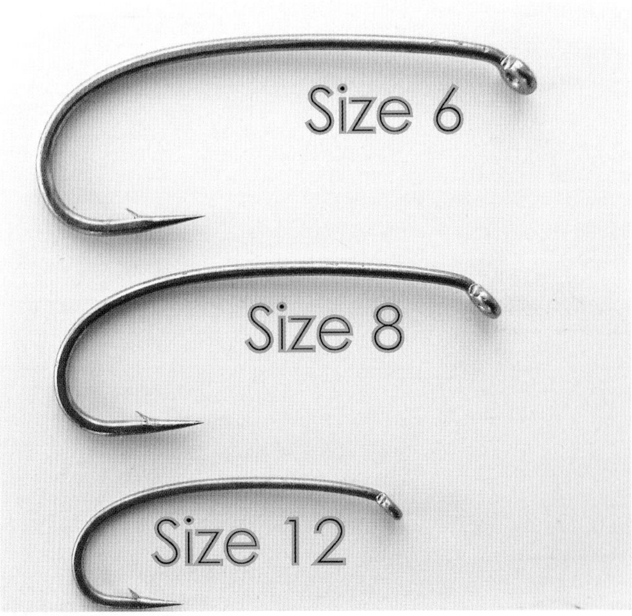

Just as there is an inverse relationship between the "X" number and its measurement in inches, so, too, is there an inverse relationship between hook number designation and its actual size.

CHAPTER 5

# Finding the Fish

Once on the lake, the angler's first job is locating the fish. If there are no rising fish and no other clues as to where fish may be concentrated, trolling is an excellent searching method. Carrying multiple rods with fly lines of varying sink rates aids in this process.

Often, fish in a lake tend to concentrate in very specific locations. They may be drawn to the cooler or warmer waters of a spring or creek mouth. In the dead of summer, they may seek out the cooler, more oxygen-rich depths of submerged old river channels and springs. When aquatic insects are hatching, or scuds and leeches are active, lake fish gather where the buffet is available. On a large lake whose surface area is best measured in square miles, it might be necessary to locate a block of water that measures a mere 100 feet by 100 feet. If this "hot spot" location is not specifically a spring, submerged river channel, or tributary mouth, the fish may relocate tomorrow, and the search will begin again. Locating a specific "red zone" can be the difference between a few fish for your day's efforts and a stellar day where you expect a strike on every cast.

On a large expanse of water, with no clues about where the fish are concentrated, an angler could spend weeks locating them by trial and error. If you only have a day or two on a large lake, you had better find a way to greatly shorten the time required to locate the fish because there are still the matters of the right fly fished with the right technique at the right depth. So let's find those fish in a hurry.

A watercraft is essential on most stillwaters to get to the fish and move in pursuit as they relocate throughout the fishing day. Pictured are my drift boat, float tube, and pontoon boat. On smaller waters, I much prefer the smaller craft for stealth and very precise trolling. When fishing with guests, the drift boat is the obvious choice.

## You Need a Pursuit Vehicle

There's no getting around it: you need a boat to chase stillwater fish. To start, you can begin the chase on the thrift, for less than $100. For less than a C-note, a budgeter can buy a float tube and fins. This is where most fly anglers start, and it is the most intimate way to fish lakes and ponds. You are sitting in the water, surrounded and held by it. For some of us, it feels quite natural and cozy, even comforting.

Float tubes come in a variety of designs: the round donut, the "V" or "U" boat, and the pontoon style. The round or donut tube is mostly a remnant of the past. It had some serious safety issues as the angler attempted to enter and exit the craft. The simplest and least expensive of those that remain are the "V" or "U" boats. Most are lightweight and easily transported, inflated, and deflated. For bigger payloads (stocky or husky guys), the pontoon float tubes are a smart choice.

All float tubes are propelled by fins on the angler's feet. When in motion, the tubist is moving backward as the fins are kicked. It is necessary to occasionally turn around to stay on course and avoid collisions with other watercraft that may also be moving backward. I think there could be a market for float tube rearview mirrors.

While float tubes are inexpensive and very portable and packable, they are slow when you have to cover a serious distance. Anyone who can kick a float tube at a speed of 2 miles per hour for more than ten minutes is a beast. For those in poor physical shape, going very far in a float tube can be tedious. Also, if a tuber gets blown by a strong wind far from home base or has to battle against the wind to return to his starting point, he may be inspired to get a boat with oars or a motor—assuming he gets out of the ordeal alive. I remember an afternoon on Montana's Clark Canyon Reservoir when a hurricane-force wind came out of nowhere. The lake was calm one moment, and the next, my friends and I were kicking like men with their hair on fire. Swells on the lake were crashing over our tubes and washing onto us. Fortunately, we were within a few hundred feet of the shore. If we had been a half mile out . . . I can't even guess.

I love fishing from a float tube on small lakes and ponds. It's very quiet, and I can control my every little movement as I fish. I can turn on a proverbial dime to cast in the opposite direction in three heartbeats. And, a float tube is the absolute best vehicle for trolling flies. As I troll flies, their speed and direction can be changed subtly and quickly. Trolling—for those who truly know it and appreciate it—is a fine art, with many nuances. A float tube allows for intimate control of every movement of the fly, and it's these little adjustments that can be the difference when reluctant fish must be gently coaxed and enticed to bite the fly.

The next craft on the continuum of boats is the pontoon boat. Though there are variations on the theme, pontoon boats are basically a chair secured between two floatation chambers. Pontoon boats typically range in length from about 6 feet to 20 feet. Eight to 12 feet is probably the most common range of lengths for one-person craft. Some larger fishing pontoon boats can accommodate two anglers and an oarsman. The largest can hold even more passengers and are commonly used on large whitewater rivers.

Almost all pontoon boats are of the inflatable type. The pontoons are filled with air for floatation and can be deflated for transport or storage. For my personal use, I have boats with hard-shell pontoons, with no inflation or deflation required. It is the ultimate Lazy Man watercraft. My boats are 75 inches long, about 3 feet wide, and weigh no more than 40 pounds. I can quickly bungee two stacked, nested little pontoon boats on the standard roof rack of my 4Runner, and I'm down the road. I can travel at the speed limit on the freeway and my boats are secure. There is little lost fishing time when I get to the water. The boats are quickly unstrapped and launched. When I need speed, I fit the oars into the locks and hit it.

With an inflatable pontoon boat, just like a rubber raft, the need to repair a puncture or serious abrasion may arise. Carry a repair kit, or at least a full roll of duct tape, the handyman's best friend.

Cartop boats are those boats made of wood, aluminum, or fiberglass, commonly 10 to 12 feet long, which can be secured on the roof rack of a car, carried in the bed of a pickup, or towed on a small trailer. They can be fitted with oars, an electric motor, or a small outboard motor. They are light enough to be handled by two people; one person will suffice if the boat is trailered. Such boats easily accommodate two fly casters, though I occasionally see three people onboard. These boats generally have a flat bottom, are very stable, make excellent casting platforms, and are very popular for serious lake fly fishermen. All the fly-fishing experts using these will equip them with anchors fore and aft to maintain a fixed orientation even when the wind blows. Virtually all will be fitted with an electronic depth finder.

Wood, aluminum, or fiberglass drift boats, popularly used on Pacific Northwest rivers, are sometimes called to do double

A flat-bottom cartop boat is a very popular stillwater watercraft, providing a stable casting platform with lots of storage, with the ability to cover a large expanse of water when equipped with an electric trolling motor or small outboard motor.

Many anglers who fish whitewater rivers will use their drift boats for double duty on lakes and ponds. These provide a high casting platform for long casts.

duty as lake boats. Traditionally outfitted with oars to negotiate moving waters, a little modification will enable the mounting of a motor on the stern. Adding a bow anchor and the necessary electronics makes a totally adequate stillwater craft.

Bottom line: you must get to the fish. Some type of boat is mandatory to get into the game. Properly outfitted, a stillwater fly fisherman has an effective tool necessary for getting to the fish, which is the obvious starting point in the fish-catching success formula.

## The Baying of the Hounds

It is possible sometimes to let others do the work of locating the fish for you. This can save an immense amount of fishing time, especially on a new lake. The added bonus to this approach is that there will inevitably be talk among the herd that offers more clues about the fishing, such as the flies being used and how they are being fished by the successful anglers within the group. Even if an angler catching fish says nothing, an observer can get an excellent look at the type of fly line being used (sinking or floating) and how the fly is being presented to the fish.

### Roche Lake, British Columbia

My good friend Jeff Hilden and I were based in Kamloops, BC, in mid-June to sample the fishing in a variety of lakes, including my nemesis, Roche Lake. I had fished it one day the previous June, and the fish had humbled me. My only consolation was that I had lots of company, most of whom were Canadians who fished the lake often.

When I refer to a lake as "big," this is a relative term. If you are an angler in a float tube kicking against the wind, Roche's 300+ surface acres can seem big. However, compared to Lake Superior, it's a tiny, tiny pond. Nonetheless, if you only have a day or two to locate the willing concentration of fish an area of 300 acres, it can be a daunting task.

To further complicate the mission, the bite may only last for a few hours before the fish take a break to digest their meal and frolic with their friends. This seems particularly true in productive lakes like Roche where the trout can gorge themselves for several hours on the fare du jour, then—apparently—become sated. The angler who finally arrives at the red zone after the feeding frenzy has ended may not even know he has found the magic spot, since very few or no fish will be caught. Or, upon arriving at the right spot, the angler is not able to discover the right fly fished with the correct technique and depth in time to catch fish before the bite has ended.

I knew exactly how I was going to find the trout on Roche Lake 2011: I would follow the bloodhounds who would lead me there. How would I be able to identify the bloodhounds from the mutts and mongrels roaming the lake? Easy. The bloodhounds would have bent rods playing fish.

As Jeff and I rowed our pontoon boats out into the lake, my preliminary sorting began with spying the largest concentration of floating craft. Didn't take long. There was a major cluster at the east end of the lake. Within the cluster was a row of five anchored boats in a straight line, all casting in the same direction, that of the prevailing breeze. And, as we circled and watched, it seemed that some member of the Line of Five always had a fish on. These were our bloodhounds.

Four of the five anglers, the Gang of Four, were friends on their annual Roche Lake fishing week. They knew the lake well and were experienced resourceful anglers, as we discovered later talking to one of the group members. Arriving a few days before us, our source related that he and his comrades had spent a day and a half looking for the fish, even with their previous weeks on Roche in years past. It was, again, impressed upon me the importance of discovering exactly where in the lake fish are concentrated before dropping the anchor.

Every angler in the Line of Five was fishing a chironomid pupa under an indicator. Because it is legal in British Columbia, each fisherman was fishing two rods. The only legal stipulation is that you must be the only angler in the boat. Each of the five was fishing solo. Realistically, only one rod can be held while waiting for a fish to bite. The second is put in a rod holder, or propped on or in the boat. I was amazed repeatedly when a fish would grab the chironomid on the unattended rod and actually hook itself with no help from the angler. The Kamloops trout took so hard that the resistance of the line and indicator being pulled through the water often secured the hook point in the fish. One guy in the group actually had two fish on at once. He did not have enough arms and hands for this frantic, comical situation.

## The Moving Red Zone

A few days later I went back to Roche Lake. The Gang of Four plus one were in the same location as a few days earlier . . . almost. Interestingly, they'd formed their anchored line of boats about 80 feet farther east than four days earlier. Still fishing chironomids and indicators, they caught more fish than others in the area. They correctly perceived through experimentation and communication with each other that the red zone had moved a short distance, and their bent rods served as testimony to their perceptions.

### Diamond Lake, OR

It was late June when fraternity brother Chuck Wagner and I met up at southern Oregon's Diamond Lake, one of the state's most productive and popular waters. Diamond is a food factory for the rainbow trout that live there. It is truly terrifying to think of the fish sizes this gem could produce if the trout could not be killed. As it stands, tens of thousands of trout are harvested here each season. And it's a guarantee that the vast majority of the largest trout caught are thrown into the cooler, with no chance that some might reach epic, monstrous size. Oh well.

Mt. Thielsen is a very recognizable landmark seen from Oregon's Diamond Lake, one of the most productive stillwaters in the state.

The hounds had gotten onto the scent early our first day on the lake, long before we launched. Because most of the fishermen at Diamond Lake use conventional spinning gear, we were specifically seeking out the congregation of craft where the anglers were casting flies. Human nature as it is, fly fishermen tend to seek out other fly fishermen. We soon found what we were looking for in a corner of the lake not too distant from the shoreline. The area of focus, spanning a few acres, was only 6 to 7 feet deep. What a refreshing change from fishing chironomids 20 feet under an indicator as had been necessary a few days earlier at Roche Lake.

As we carefully picked our way through and around the clustered pontoon boats, cartoppers, drift boats and expensive boats with powerful, high-performance motors, we watched several anglers at any time with rods bent hard against fighting rainbows. Watching my depth finder readings, there were no indications of channels or holes. The bottom was fairly uniform and flat. Initially, there were no apparent intriguing features that might cause the fish to concentrate in this one particular area. Most, but not all, of the successful fishermen were fishing chironomids under indicators. Because the small inflatables had no anchors, their positions were constantly changing, pushed by the wind. I attempted to read a pattern where the fish were being caught. It appeared random.

The first two places we anchored produced no strikes. Was it our location? Maybe. Was it our flies? Maybe. Was it our

Anglers ply the shallow portion of Diamond Lake's south end. When the breeze is light, cruising fish can be easily seen here.

leader length, tippet size, fly size, or technique? Knowing the exact depth and seeing the adult chironomids landing all over our boat, we were fairly certain of these last four variables. Over the course of the next few hours, we changed, moved, and anchored until we finally discovered some patches of underwater vegetation. Casting into and around the vegetation, we started getting some strikes and landed a few fish. Over this same two-hour span, many of the craft in our immediate area had headed for the shore or launch sites to take a break, leaving us to roam with little fear of interfering with someone's personal fishing space.

One of the few boats remaining held a man and woman team. They were casting and retrieving flies, instead of the more popular heave-it-and-leave-it technique with chironomids. As they settled into my field of vision for the first time, they both quickly combined for three or four hookups, landing a couple of fish.

After only a few minutes of no strikes, I watched the man pull the anchor, start the little motor, and peer over the side into the water in search of something. Weed beds? Within a minute he found another spot, dropped the anchor, and they resumed casting. Almost immediately, she had a fish, then he had a fish. They obviously had all the puzzle pieces: location, fly, depth, and effective retrieve of the fly. Fish on! After a short duration of no strikes, their anchor was pulled, a new location selected, and more fish caught.

In the meantime, Chuck and I were getting only the occasional strike; a few more landed fish on chironomids. When I landed my second fish, I pulled out my stomach pump to extract the stomach contents of a 13-inch rainbow. After sending the fish home, I emptied the stolen lunch mixed with water onto my white yogurt lid: dozens of chironomid pupae with a single leech of almost 3 inches. Our chironomids were a close enough match to those artificial on the ends of our leaders. Was the couple fishing leech flies? The frantic casting and retrieve were definitely not remotely reasonable for mimicking the actual movement (or non-movement) of a living chironomid pupa. One fact, for sure, was that they moved around a lot. They did not wait for the fish come to them; they quickly and aggressively went after the trout. It prompted a question in my head: Do specific trout in stillwaters tend to patrol a specific beat, a specific area? This seemed a logical question because the man and woman anglers would apparently sting and put down all the willing biters in a specific area surrounding their anchored boat. If more "new" fish from nearby had been swimming into their casting range to replace those fish that had been hooked, released, and put down, then the couple would not have needed to move position; a constant supply of new, untouched trout would swim by and some would bite their flies.

I drifted back years in my memory to a day on Lenice Lake, WA. Having parked my pontoon boat in the cattails nearby on that sunny spring afternoon, I was standing at the edge of a channel watching fish cruise parallel to the channel's edge. It seemed that most of the rainbow trout were cruising in one direction for a time, and then the fish reversed course and swam the channel edge in the opposite direction. One of the fish was distinctively marked. I saw this individual several times, cruising right, then left, then right again. Perhaps its companions were doing the same thing, but I could not recognize them easily as the same fish I had seen before. It's more support for the possibility that specific fish patrol—at least for a while—a specific area. If an angler would hook or alarm most or all of these fish, there might not be other unsuspecting fish to replace them immediately. It would make sense, then, that a lake angler should move on once the "bite" stops to seek out new fish in a new area.

This leads me to pose another question. When the fish seem to go off the bite, could it just mean that the specific fish in a specific area can no longer be coaxed to bite our artificial flies, but are more discriminating and careful to more closely inspect what they are considering eating, no longer being quite as gullible as they were the hour before? That is, the fish are still eating but are less gullible, especially if they have been hooked and lost, or hooked and released. Where fish are frequently caught and killed, those fish that remain in the lake are those with the natural ability to discriminate between real food and fake food, and are not easily caught.

Following this line of thought, there may be a "large" area—let's say a square acre—that is being fished by a couple dozen boats. Everyone will eventually disperse when the bite, apparently, ends. Everyone agrees with everyone else—consensus agreement—that the bite has ended for now. However, the bite for real food may actually continue, while the bite for artificial food has stopped by those fish that are naturally wary

This stomach sample taken from a trout reveals the extremes of sizes of trout food items on any given day.

or those that have learned through immediate experience to be careful of fake foods.

In the course of my observations, I hooked and landed a third trout. Were its dining preferences any different from those of the previously checked fish? Using the stomach pump again revealed a digestive tract jammed with food items. From this single trout, I extracted perhaps seventy chironomid pupae, some of which were still alive and squirming, and two leeches. Though *Callibaetis* mayflies were drifting by us on the wind-driven surface currents, neither fish checked had a single mayfly nymph or adult in it.

Our second morning at Diamond Lake, Chuck and I eventually anchored in a location where we observed trout swimming near us constantly. The silty bottom was light-colored, so the fish were easy to observe, especially since it was only 6 feet deep and the light was excellent. Dangling my chironomids under an indicator within two rod lengths of the boat produced five of the seven fish I landed that day. The constant presence of fish left no doubt we were in an excellent location. Chuck and I hooked more fish than any other single boat or pontoon we observed. When the wind chased us from the lake, we had a firm game plan for our third day, which included anchoring in exactly the same location.

Even though there was a traffic jam at the boat launch at 8 o'clock the next morning, we managed to get to our predetermined anchoring spot with very few other boats in our immediate area. Through some simple triangulation, I was able to determine our desired anchoring position. Initially, not many chironomids were hatching. We could not discover any fish swimming near our boat, whereas we had been constantly surrounded by trout at this position the day before. Maybe we were a bit early.

Within forty-five minutes of our arrival, a motor-powered drift boat with two anglers parked about 150 feet directly north of us. Within his first few casts, the angler at the stern of the boat loudly announced he had a fish. Some guys like an audience. He was casting 40 to 50 feet of fly line, hesitating very briefly once the line was on the water, then stripping the fly in short, quick pulls. Soon there was a second fish, and another, and another. Most annoying!

Since neither of us had gotten one strike on a chironomid, and with no observable fish swimming in our vicinity, I switched rods, casting an assortment of nymphs on my slow-sinking clear fly line. To get my retrieve right, I watched the successful angler's hands to mirror his movements exactly. I must have tried ten different nymphs and wet fly patterns in the next half hour, casting around the compass with each. Not a strike. Back to the chironomids. Chuck had gotten a strike during my stripping flies experimentation.

When I could not stand the show-off (whom we unaffectionately called "Whoopi") any longer, and still saw no fish cruising in our immediate area, I suggested to Chuck that we move. When we settled in again on anchor at our new location, we were directly west of Whoopi by more than 100 feet.

Immediately, we saw fish cruising around us. Now it was just a matter of finding the right fly pattern and fishing it in the right way. Because of the previous day's success, I initially opted for making a very short cast off the stern to dangle a chironomid. Fifteen minutes passed. Nothing, and more nothing.

Needing to change something, I cast in Whoopi's direction. In less than thirty seconds it was "Fish on!" There was definitely something special about the expanse of water between us and the drift boat. My first five casts produced four hooked fish on my chironomid. The action remained fairly constant for most of an hour, as long as I cast in the direction of the drift boat. Casting in all the compass directions, which I did for the sake of experimentation, produced very few strikes. The vast majority of our action that morning came from casting east. Interestingly, fishing chironomids under an indicator was somewhat steady for us, while Whoopi and his buddy pulled anchor and left when the action dried up on the active retrieve of their secret fly that they had used since their arrival.

These events seemed to further solidify my theory that feeding fish can be extremely localized. It does not matter, at times, how good your flies and effective your techniques. What really matters is being in the right spot, and this area can be quite small compared to the vast expanse of a lake. Hot spots can move from day to day, sometimes not far, but far enough that it will behoove you to hunt around until you find one.

## With a Little Help from My Friends

As illustrated by the team at Roche Lake, it can pay big dividends to bring your own "pack of hounds" on a fishing expedition. If your friends are experienced anglers, so much the better. They are best for sniffing the trail to the fish, but rookies can get the job done sometimes, too. If a rookie makes a lucky find—even if it's merely locating other hounds who are sitting on the fish—that is good work.

As your team spreads out to locate the fish and do some reconnaissance, radio contact can save a lot of valuable fishing time with instant communication.

Unless the matter of locating fish is obvious upon arrival, or someone in the posse is very familiar with the lake and where the fish will be, it is my preference to split up the group. Ideally, the pack members will not range so far that we can't see each other. If a discovery is made, we can see the discoverer screaming, waving, or holding a bent rod, and move toward his location.

Two-way radios are an excellent means of reliable, instant communication on a lake when cell phone coverage is not available If something of significance is learned, the finder agrees to let everyone else know promptly. It is human nature once a fish is finally caught, the mystery apparently solved, to keep fishing and disregard all else, such as telling your friends. I admit that I have been guilty on this count more than once. So the gentlemen's agreement is: "Catch a couple, then call your buddies." Sometimes the bite may not last very long, so time may be of the essence.

Another advantage of two-way radios is that you don't have to yell or wave your hat; communication can be done quietly. There may be an obvious advantage to doing so unless, of course, you want to meet and make a lot of new fishing friends. If you are catching fish when others are not, it is amazing how you can immediately become Mr. Popular. Understandably, some anglers yearn to bask in the spotlight. Suit yourself.

## When the Lights Go Out

I know how important a depth finder is to my fishing, especially in unfamiliar waters. This tool can often take the guesswork out of tracking down fish. On a small lake or a pond, a lone angler with an electronic fish locator has a very reasonable chance of success. On lakes of fifty acres or more, it is wise to have done some homework—studying maps, reading fishing reports, querying friends or sources who might be familiar with the lake, or looking for pertinent magazine articles—to narrow the scope of where fish might be found. The electronic depth finder is not the final answer. It is one tool of many, yet an absolute must, especially on new lakes.

Recently, my finder/locator went down in the middle of a weeklong fishing trip at Jimmy Lake. Fishing alone, I was floating on a new lake without success. There were very few other anglers, and they were trolling anywhere and everywhere. I was getting very few readings indicating fish. Knowing there was a good population of trout in the lake, I just needed to explore until I found them. I trolled a small leech pattern that had proven itself reliable a thousand times. No strike, and the search continued.

My finder/locator is secured to my float tube or pontoon boat by means of a nylon strap with a click-to-lock-or-open buckle on it. Somehow I hit the buckle inadvertently and popped it open. In a blink, my electronic finder/locator was heading to the lake bottom. I lunged deep and fast with my left arm and rescued the unit, but apparently the twist-on handle that housed the batteries was not as tightly secured as it should have been, so a little water seeped inside the finder to mess with the electronics. For a short while it worked sporadically, then finally died. I was blind. I did not know the depth of the water I was fishing, could

The electronic depth finder is an indispensable stillwater fishing tool—especially if you can keep it onboard and operating.

not read the contours of the lake bottom, and had no idea if there were fish in my vicinity. I had no bloodhounds and no underwater eyes on a new lake. It was time to leave. As I was 600 miles from home, it suddenly seemed a good idea to have a second electronic depth finder with me. If I needed a slap-in-the-face reminder of how critical this piece of equipment is on an unfamiliar large expanse of water, I got it at Jimmy Lake.

## Contour Maps and a GPS Unit

It is possible to find many contour lake maps online. Such a map can get you in the ball park of where you might want to fish. Look for indications of shoals, springs, drop-offs, creek mouths, submerged old river channels, and depths of less than 30 feet where sunlight can penetrate to produce habitat for food organisms.

If you locate an online map of your chosen lake, you can track the GPS coordinates of the cursor as you move it around on the map. Locate the cursor over a river channel, spring, shoal, or other feature of interest. Then program the coordinates into the GPS. Once at the lake, your GPS will lead you to where you want to go. It's hard to know the accuracy of the map readings and the accuracy of your particular GPS, so you might need to fine-tune your position on the lake with the aid of an elec-

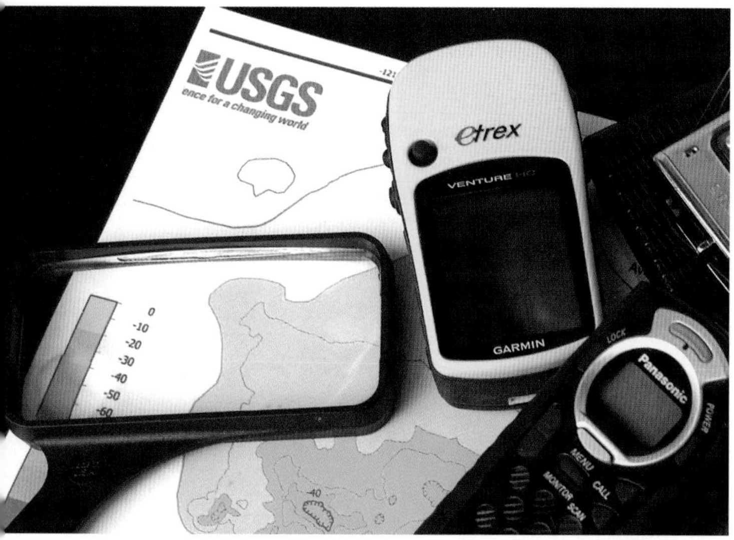


A map of a lake's underwater topography and depth profile, in addition to a GPS device, can enable an angler to mark and return to productive fishing areas on a large lake.

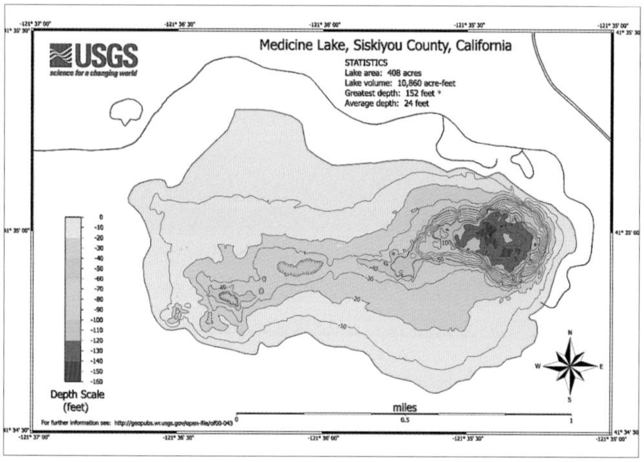


A depth/contour map of a lake bottom is helpful in formulating a fishing game plan by locating specific areas of interest in a lake. Map courtesy of U. S. Geological Survey at pubs.usgs.gov.

tronic depth finder. As you crisscross the zone of interest on the lake, noting the depth changes and bottom contours displayed on the screen of the depth finder, you have an excellent chance of pinpointing the bottom feature you seek. Once you have discovered the exact location, the new coordinates can be entered into the GPS.

## The Observant Online Detective

Sometimes good general lake locations for finding the fish can be gleaned from fishing reports. Some anglers will reveal a general location on the lake where they had good fishing success. If you have no clues at all, this can be a starting point. "In front of the resort," "just west of the boat launch," and "in the SE corner of the lake" are worth paying attention to. I often cut and paste the reports into a printable computer document, highlight key info with a yellow marker, and tuck these hard copies into a folder I carry with me on my fishing trips to new lakes.

It is not unusual for Internet postings to include a photo of the hero and his fish. If you examine the surroundings or backdrop in the pic, you might see a clue about the location. Something distinctive about the landscape, a boat launch, a building, a sign, a campground, or a recognizable landmark may present you with a valuable lead. Think and observe like a detective.

## Trolling down the Boulevard

Trolling flies—pulling them through the water as you propel or wind-drift your boat—has many advantages for an angler. One plus is that you have your flies fishing without having to watch or pay much attention as you do so. When I troll, I am looking around and listening for clues about where the fish are. I can watch for rising or working fish, or I may hear porpoising, splashing fish as they feed before I see them. If I spy insect-eating birds, such as swallows, gathered and feeding in one particular area of the lake, I'm going to move toward the activity. Should aquatic insects be hatching, the fish may be feeding on them. I want to be there. Of course, if there are other anglers on the lake, I want to watch them, especially those who are catching fish. There is no need to crowd them, and I do not want to do so, but I do want to note how they are fishing and the particular area of their success. During all this watching and listening, I am actively fishing.

When I hook a fish while trolling, part of my multi-tasking approach to discovering at least one area where fish might be caught, I make note of specifically where I am when the fish struck. I make a quick triangulation, if necessary, if I am a long distance from the shoreline. If I am near the shore, let's say within casting distance, I merely need to note features along the shore that will orient me to the position where I got a bite. After losing or landing the fish, I may continue along the same path for a few minutes to see if I can fool another fish. If a second and third are hooked, I will note my position again when the strike occurs. If no strikes come within a few minutes, I turn 180 degrees to retrace my same path, trolling at least as far back as where my fly was located when I got my very first strike.

Should I get a strike as I retrace my original course, I may be on to something. There is a chance I am trolling over an area where the fish could be concentrated, or at least a zone they are regularly patrolling in their search for food. The important thing is I have found an area with more than one willing fish.

As for what follows my discovery, my usual plan is to troll back and forth at least one more time to see if more strikes can be had. If yes, then I may choose to cast and retrieve my flies from a stationary position for a while, which is my preference. Depending on what happens, I can experiment with the retrieve to see if I can enhance my success, change one of the flies (remember I fish two), switch to a floating line and indicator, or resume trolling. Should the fishing action stop, I resume exploratory trolling until I discover another potentially productive area.

Trolling with a thoughtful game plan is an effective way to prospect for fish while freeing the eyes to look for rising fish and floating or flying insects, and to observe anglers on the lake who are catching fish. When it comes to trolling speed, slower is better.

As I troll, I make sure to vary my speed, even stopping to pause briefly. Such activity alters not only the velocity of the flies, but the depth as they rise and fall in response to my movements. It is certainly possible to run my flies through a pack of fish but get no response, no strikes, because my flies are swimming too quickly or are too high in the water column. I could have found the fish, but I did not troll at the proper speed or depth to interest them. This part of the success equation must be taken into account as you scout for trout—or bass, crappie, perch, bluegill, and so on. When in doubt, troll s-l-o-w-l-y.

An additional aid that is always in play as I troll, of course, is my electronic depth finder. I look for readings on the screen indicating that fish are in the area, or not. Many times, the readings indicate few fish in my immediate zone. But because I do not always troll in a straight line, my flies may locate willing fish that did not show up on my screen because I did not get close enough with the device to get a reliable reading. However, if I locate a hot spot where I consistently get strikes as I troll back and forth through it, I will eventually go through the area to see if I can get situated in a location where I also get a healthy number of fish blips on my screen.

## Elevate Your Game

On Memorial Day weekend many years ago, a contingent of mis amigos and I were in eastern Washington State to fish Dry Falls Lake for the first time. Dry Falls is not too far from Lake Lenore, home to Lahontan cutthroat. We knew about Lenore but had no specific plans to fish it. However, when Dry Falls proved ungrateful to our efforts, we stopped at the north end of Lake Lenore to at least look at it.

The north end of the lake terminates in a rather narrow bay. The water there is not very deep, and an angler can wade out a short distance on a solid lake bottom to cast. No one was there. No angler to watch or query. As we stood high above the lake on the highway side of the bay, we immediately saw cruising trout. And not just a few. There were dozens of cruisers in 4 to

After a quick photograph, a cutthroat trout is gently released to fight another day on Henry's Lake, Idaho.

5 feet of water. Because there was no one fishing, and fish seemed to be everywhere, we surmised maybe the lake was closed to fishing. But after checking the angling regulations, it was, indeed, legal to fish. Pinch us! Are we dreaming?

Forming a line, we all took up casting positions in thigh-deep water. Casting a broad assortment of flies, we cast out into the lake with great expectations. It took very few casts before someone hooked a fish, and backed to the shore to beach it. The fishing action was constant. Sometimes we had two or three fish hooked at once. Crazy! And no one else around. Lenore's north end was our private playground.

Circumstances had aligned themselves for our good fortune. The sun was high, the water shallow, and we had a high vantage point to easily see the fish. Any time I have access to a high bank, an easily climbed tree at the water's edge, or a big rock to stand on, I'm looking for cruising fish. When I use my drift boat or powerboat to fish lakes, I will stand on the bow or the deck to get as high as I can. Besides the excitement of watching the fish, it gives the angler great confidence in his chances for success. It all starts with knowing you have found the fish. Seeing them confirms it. If you can continue to watch the fish from your elevated perch as you cast and retrieve your flies among them, you can note their reaction to your attempts. It doesn't get much more exciting than this!

Many of the British Columbia interior lakes have light-colored shoals, expanses of shallow water that transition along their edges into deeper reaches. Many anglers will cruise from shoal to shoal in a lake until they visually locate the fish. No fish, no stop. This goes a long way to assure the angler that he will be fishing to the trout. Seeing is truly believing. And as I mentioned, the shallow portions of Diamond Lake where I fish are usually not much more than 6 feet deep. When the sun is high enough by midmorning in the summer, I can locate the trout visually. I can anchor and watch for cruising trout. If no fish appear, and I am catching nothing, I move to a new spot.

So an important factor in deciding which lake you might fish could be situations or conditions that allow for locating the fish visually. It's no guarantee that you will have a record-breaking day, but you have put the cornerstone of a successful day in place: finding the fish.

## Searching for Likely Ambush Points

There are times I have little advanced information about a lake I plan to fish, and I may be fishing alone. When approaching a new body of water in this situation, I begin with a visual inspection, scanning the shoreline for features which may lead me to

A shoreline of cattails is an excellent area to search for cruising fish as they forage for food. Here, Steve Severson battles a good rainbow he found traveling the bank.

the fish. Studying the lay of the land of a lake or pond can offer clues about where my quarry might be found. Specifically, I am looking for little coves and bays, inlets, outlets, rock slides, points of land or rocks, and shorelines of cattails. I look for islands, shoals, and surface vegetation, like lily pads. All such locales have proven productive for locating fish at one time or another on the scores of lakes, ponds, and reservoirs I have fished. Each has its own attraction for the fish.

When I launch with minimal specifics about where the fish in a lake might be, I will troll likely areas to begin. Inevitably, this means trolling not too far from a shoreline I perceive has some depth, let's say 8 to 15 feet, if I can find it. Fish like to cruise the shoreline. The depths along the periphery of most lakes are usually shallow enough to allow the penetration of sunlight all the way to the bottom. This translates into the growth of vegetation, which in turn supports populations of living food items trout and warmwater game fish are seeking. A shoreline of cattails provides an excellent hunting area for the fish in search of a meal. Some insects, small fish, and crustaceans use the cattail habitat to find food and stay out of harm's way when predators are on the prowl. Additionally, adult aquatic and terrestrial insects resting in the vegetation

Bluegill and other warmwater game fish are very cover-conscious. Shorelines and shallows laden with vegetation offer excellent locations to find and catch these fish. Bluegill populations can be large, providing fast action for beginners new to the sport of stillwater fly fishing.

Water lily pads make for superb fish cover, so casting to the edges is a good strategy.

may lose their purchase, especially with the help of a strong breeze, and fall into the shoreline waters. A forest of underwater cattail stalks offers an alert fish the chance to dodge and hide from a larger predator. So some shorelines can offer much attraction to a fish in search of both food and protection. I seek out such places.

If a lake supports the growth of plants like water lilies, it's definitely worth trolling or casting to the edges of these areas. The plants' leaves (or pads) collectively form a large floating mat on the water's surface. The large leaves, and roots that extend from the surface into the lake bottom, provide habitat and cover for aquatic organisms fish may want to eat. As with other prime feeding locations, fish may also escape danger in the underwater jungle. When the sun is high, the huge leaves of the water lily create a shading canopy where fish can remain hidden and comfortable out of the bright light. Bass, bluegill, and crappies are definitely cover-conscious. Lily pads are sure areas of focus when these species are present.

Little bays and coves can concentrate hungry fish. If the area is small enough, I can anchor at the mouth of the bay to methodically cast in a 180-degree arc, probing the shore of the cove from one stationary position. For the angler, bays and coves can offer a sheltered zone out of the wind on those days when maneuvering and casting become chores in open water. If the lake is busy with many boaters, fish can find a quiet haven here to feed and be undisturbed in the coves where traffic is minimal.

The perimeter around an island is always worth exploring, especially if part of the island's shore tapers quickly into deep water. This quick transition from shallow to deep offers the fish an area of interest as it can cruise the shallows in search of food, but quickly drop into the safety of deep water if trouble should arrive. The vegetation associated with the island can also hold

Small bays or recesses in the shoreline can provide shelter from strong winds and are always worth exploring for feeding fish.

Largemouth bass are particularly inclined to frequent areas with an abundance of submerged logs and fallen trees.

fare that drops or gets blown from it into the water. Typically, I will troll my way around an island, surveying for likely areas where I can eventually cast toward it from a stationary position. Casting toward the island shore, then retrieving into deeper water can be a good tact.

Think of shoals as underwater islands. The edges of shoals slope into deep water. Fish cruise onto and off of shoals, having a good possibility of finding food coupled with deep water safety close at hand. Troll the perimeter to survey various areas or to maybe spy cruising fish, then return to likely positions to anchor and cast onto the shoal, to retrieve the fly from the shallows back into deeper water.

Trolling and casting along the lava flow at the northeast end of Oregon's Davis Lake is a dependable area to search for lunker rainbow trout. Davis also has an excellent population of largemouth bass.

As for other submerged cover that can be easily seen, submerged fallen trees and logs can provide food-hunting areas and shelter for fish on the prowl. Warmwater game fish in particular have an affinity for submerged wood, but trout can be attracted to such locations, too. In Oregon's Cascade Mountains, famous Crane Prairie Reservoir is a well-known fishery with lots of wood in it. In addition to many submerged logs of trees that have fallen over the years, there are still many standing remnants of trees flooded when the lake was created in the late 1920s. In addition to other insects, this woody habitat has created an immense population of dragonfly nymphs, a staple food for the lake's renowned Cranebows, some of which may tip the scales beyond 10 pounds.

Points of land or rocks jutting out into a lake can direct cruising fish to a narrow line of passage around the point. Trolling and casting near these protrusions into the lake can be productive. The same holds true where rockslide areas or lava flows slope into the depths. Not too far from Crane Prairie is Davis Lake. One of the best areas to hunt the lake's rainbows is at its northeastern portion, along a huge, ancient lava flow. The shoreline drops off quickly into an area where rainbows can always be found, patrolling the area for its abundant insect life. The depth here is adequate to stay cool enough year-round, ensuring that the lava flow is a consistently dependable location to find fish at Davis Lake.

Certain times of year, trout may collect at the mouth of an inlet stream. In addition to the possibility that the stream may sweep food into the lake, early spring finds rainbow trout seeking moving water to spawn. Brown trout will do the same in the fall. If the lake water warms to uncomfortable temperatures in the dead of summer, an inlet's flows may be comfortably

A rod in one hand and a camera in the other sometimes makes for a lucky photo. Rainbow trout, in particular, like to dance.

cooler, and, thus, attractive to fish. At such times as these, an astute angler may seek out the creek or river mouth as an ambush station.

Lake outlets are locations where drifting food items may collect. The outlet acts as a funnel into which insects with poor mobility are swept, especially when they are in a helpless hatching mode. For the wise fish, the current created by the lake outflow acts as a conveyer belt delivering food as the fish holds its position, minimizing its energy expenditure at mealtime.

The best way to break the quiet is with a screaming fly reel as it resists a large fish.

During all these searching activities, I am watching my electronic depth finder. I will deviate from my searching routine to concentrate my fishing efforts on a discovered concentration of fish. Rarely will I leave fish to find fish. It isn't often I will leave an area of willing biters unless I have caught so many that I decide to see some different scenery and challenge myself to catch fish elsewhere on the lake.

In summary, the starting point for all successful fish-catching days is putting your fly in front of the fish. A systematic plan, replete with adjustments along the way, can minimize the search time. Of course, locating the fish is not the whole solution to catching them, but it is the cornerstone upon which all the other puzzle pieces rest. Locate the fish. Figure out what they want. Then hold on tight—and have the camera ready.

CHAPTER 6

# The Art of Effective Trolling

Trolling is an excellent searching method when there are few clues as to where fish are located. My eyes are free to wander for fish and fishing clues while I effectively present my flies. If I troll through a zone and get a strike, I will eventually reverse course to troll through the same area again.

The simplest of all lake-fishing methods is trolling. For the novice, unskilled beginner to get started in fly-fishing lakes, trolling is great, both easy and effective. The fly fisherman merely strips a length of line from his fly reel, letting it drift behind his moving watercraft. If the craft is a float tube or pontoon boat, the angler is propelled by fins he wears over his shoes. Propulsion, especially for larger boats, is with oars, paddles, or a motor. The flies are pulled through the water at the same velocity as the boat or float tube. Adjustments for depth can be controlled by adjusting the length of the line, the type of line used, and the velocity of the boat. It is always important for the astute angler to make note of the exact length of line and velocity of the successful troll. Once the right combination of line length and speed are noted when fish are being caught, these can be duplicated in order to continue the success until the bite fades.

Before we go a little further into trolling, a word of cautious advice is necessary. Though trolling for fish in lakes and ponds can be both simple and easy, these are not to be equated with effective. Consistently effective trolling is an art, with many details and nuances. It's attention to details that move a troller toward fish-catching efficacy.

Even though I am familiar with a broad variety of stillwater methods, it is a rare fishing day that I launch my float tube or pontoon boat and don't troll flies at least part of the day. Trolling allows me to fish and observe my surroundings at the same time. Because my fly line is tight as I move along, I will feel the strike, not needing to watch the rod or the line to know a fish has struck the fly. My eyes are free to wander, looking to discover where fish might be cruising or rising, what insects or other fish food organisms might be active, scouting for other locations of interest to fish on the lake, and perhaps determine what success other anglers on the water are experiencing.

## Effective Equipment for Trolling

I want at least four different fly lines for trolling. The first is a floater. There are times the fish are feeding near the surface, or patrolling shallow water of 6 feet or less. If the wind is slight, a floating line with a leader length of 12 to 16 feet can be the best choice. A floating line is easiest to pick up off the water and cast. Being the easiest and quickest to recast, a floating line will buy you more fishing time with the fly in the water. Sinking lines must be stripped back and lifted out of the water with more time and effort required than those needed with a floater.

The fly line I use most for trolling is a slow-sinking, or intermediate type, with a clear finish. With a sink rate of usually no more than 2 inches per second, this line allows me to get beneath the wind-generated surface currents that would put a large bow in my floating fly line, putting me out of touch with my fly. The intermediate allows me straight-line contact with my flies to detect even a soft strike. In shallow water, where a faster-sinking line would put my flies in the mud or vegetation in shallow water zones, the very slow-sinking intermediate line keeps me in the fishing zone longer before it finally touches bottom. I can troll slower in shallow water, which can be very important as I try to entice the fish. Because this line is as close to transparent as fly lines get and is not creating a telltale wake on the surface, I can usually fish a leader of 9 to 10 feet with little problem.

For deeper waters, say 15 feet or more, I usually resort to a density-compensated Type III sinking fly line with a sink rate of 3½ or more inches per second, with a 9- to 10-foot leader. A density-compensated line sinks in a relatively straight diagonal line to maximize straight-line contact with my fly. Those fly lines that are not compensated tend to sink in a shallow "J" shape, with the leader and tip of the line descending slower than the rest of the fly line. As a result, the strike is not easily detected, nor is the transfer of power through the line as effective when the angler sets the hook. The Type III is useful for me in depths to 25 feet, which covers the vast majority of lake depths I normally fish. I can always fish a weighted fly or flies if I need to get down at a faster rate. Faster sink rate fly lines are available if you perceive a need. Additionally, when I set the hook, the power of my lifting rod tip is immediately transferred through the line to the hook, burying the point securely in the fish.

As a fourth line, I carry a clear intermediate 10-foot sink-tip. This line gives me easier pickup and casting because all but 10 feet of it sinks. I have added sinkability and stealth with the clear tip. My leader is typically 10 to 12 feet. Easier casting makes this a top choice when I take a break from trolling the line to cast and retrieve my flies in certain locations.

## Trolling Fly Patterns, Tips, and Techniques

Every fly angler comes to have his favorite go-to flies. Over time, these favorites can change. This is only natural, particularly for those always searching to increase their success rate. Instead of being locked into the same known universe of fly possibilities, the adventuresome will experiment. As they do, new favorites are bound to be discovered.

If I don't have a few clues about what fly patterns I should try on the lake or pond du jour, I will start with a pair of flies separated by about 30 inches on my leader, with one significantly larger than the second.

Typically, I will tie a leech pattern on a short 2- to 3-inch dropper, and a smaller size 12 or 14 nymph on the point. For those who might need a specific suggestion, I have a couple of patterns that I currently prefer as my first choice exploratory trolling flies: a #8 Beadhead Midnight Woolly Bugger and a #12 Prince. Unless I have good reason to use something else, I fish these flies on a slow-sinking, transparent fly line.

Woolly Buggers and leech patterns are staples in every stillwater angler's fly collection. When the question is open, I prefer smaller to larger.

## Trolling Line Length: Be Precise to Be Effective

A key decision I must make as I finally begin my trolling is how much fly line to trail behind me as I move through the water. The length of line I strip from my reel depends on the water depth, water clarity, and the wind conditions. If the water is clear and there is no wind, I must let out a long length of fly line to have the fly far away from me as I fish. I assume my presence and activity will disturb the fish, so I may initially pull twenty strips of fly line from my reel. For me, and the sake of precision, a "strip" of line is the distance from my reel to the first guide on my rod. Though this exact distance will vary slightly from rod to rod, the variation is not significant. What is important is that this length is a fixed constant. It takes the guesswork out of estimating how much line is in the water when you find a particular line length that works to entice the fish into biting. If 16 strips of line—reel to the first rod guide—works, continue to use 16 strips until the action drops off. Then, try 20 strips, or 23, or whatever. Just remember the number of strips you have out when you start to get strikes. Then, do the same any time you have reeled in your fish and, then, resume fishing. This is a significant detail.

## A Precision Aid

If you are willing to "tattoo" your pretty fly line, length measurements can be put on the line with an indelible felt tip marker. The fish won't care. Marks can be made at 5- or 10-foot intervals, or whatever suits you. Color-coding possibilities are there, too, if you want. Do whatever is helpful to always know the length of fly line trailing behind you as you troll. Attention to little details such as this is what separates the good stillwater anglers from the mediocre.

## How S-l-o-w Can You Go?

If I am not getting strikes as I troll, before I change line length or flies, I experiment with my speed. Most anglers troll too fast. Even Olympian Michael Phelps cannot swim 10 body lengths in a second, nor can many aquatic insects. If you swim your ½-inch-long Prince Nymph 1 foot in a second as you troll, that's rippin'! Imagine what a wary fish is thinking. A fish attuned to its environment commonly sees its food swim much slower. Big fish with lots of time and experience behind them are particularly suspicious. So, in my trolling routine, I often slow to a crawl, sometimes stopping completely. Many days, it is then that I have the best chance to get a strike.

As I slow or stop my troll, the fly sinks. Following fish can find that very enticing. The same holds true when I have been stopped, and then resume my troll. As movement starts from a stop, the fly rises as the line tightens. Again, this rising of the fly may be a biting trigger for a nearby fish. And don't be surprised if a fish picks up your fly even after you have been stopped for a while. The effectiveness of stationary trolling is often discovered when I stop my craft to watch something of interest. I get focused on someone or something, and as I do so, a fish picks up my fly. Experience has told me that this may be exactly what the fish want—troll a short distance, stop, and let the fly sink. For impatient anglers, this is tough. Consider counting to 30 before you move the fly again—100, if you can stand it. You will be amazed how your patience will grow if you hook a few fish!

## Location, Location

Where to troll? If the water depth allows it, I often troll parallel to and not too far from the shoreline, especially in deep lakes. It is along the shore where vegetation grows in the shallower water where sunlight can penetrate. Plants need sunlight for photosynthesis to grow and thrive. Submerged vegetation provides habitat, food, and protection for many aquatic organisms. Since a smart fish goes where the food is, fishing in and around submerged vegetation makes smart fishing sense. Terrestrial insects such as ants, beetles, crickets, and grasshoppers may go for unplanned swims near the bank, too. Discover a reasonable distance from it where your flies are not grabbing the weeds, and trace the shoreline. If you discover expanses of elodea, lily pads, cattails, or other water plants far from shore, troll near them, too.

## How Low Can You Go?

Keep your rod tip low, almost touching the water, as you troll. Because many strikes, especially at low trolling speeds, are very soft, you need to keep your line straight and tight to sense the interception of your fly. When a fish bites something to eat, it doesn't usually grab its prey and quickly swim away to finish it elsewhere. Like we do, it devours it on the spot. Likewise, a fish usually takes a slow-moving artificial fly into its mouth and does not give you much indication that it has done so. An inexperienced fisherman may not even know he has an interested fish. If you fish with your rod tip elevated more than a few inches off the water as you troll, there is slack line between the rod tip and water. A subtle strike may not impart sufficient resistance to pull this slack tight. The angler may never know. There are enough other challenges fishing lakes. Keep that tip down!

Especially when fishing light tippets with the possibility of extra-large fish, consider not pinning your line against the rod grip with a finger or two as you troll. If the line is prevented from immediately being pulled from the reel with a correctly set drag tension, a hard strike from a weighty fish will instantly break the fragile tippet. Instead, adjust the reel's drag tension so that there is enough resistance to set the hook solidly on a hard strike, but not so much tension that the tippet will break. As line is pulled directly from the reel in response to the fish's strike, the shock of the sudden impact is absorbed by the release of the line, and the bend of the rod tip.

## Evasive Maneuvers

One of the problems with trolling in a straight path is that you may disturb the fish you kick or row over, moving them out of the line over which your flies will swim. This is especially true in shallow, very clear water. One solution is to lengthen your fly line so that, maybe, the fish will have time to settle back into the eventual line of travel of the oncoming flies. This also makes a case for slowing the troll speed to buy this time. However, there is an additional and more significant adjustment you can make: move in a nonlinear route.

Zig left. Zig right. Then, carve out a large circle. If you are feeling particularly sassy, track a figure eight as you troll. I do all of these, and it pays fish-biting dividends. Even as I startle the fish I travel over, my line and flies do not follow my exact path.

Because they do not trail me exactly, the flies have a chance of traveling over and through undisturbed fish. Additionally, depending on how I turn and zig, my flies will speed up and rise or slow down and sink. When strikes occur, try to detect a pattern in exactly where in the turn they happen. Seek clues constantly. There are always clues and lessons to be found if you are alert enough to look for them.

## Spice It Up

Rather than just a uniform swimming of the trolled flies, it can be effective to add some additional movement to them. This is accomplished by twitching or stripping the line with the fingers of the hand not holding the rod. Twitching or popping the line does not shorten the amount of line being fished; it is not retrieving any line without giving it back. While holding the line with my thumb and forefinger, I pop the line 3 or 4 inches with my bottom three fingers to make the flies dart the same 3 or 4 inches. When the fly line is stripped, the amount stripped is retained, not released back into the water; the line gets shorter with each strip. Again, I dart the flies only a few quick inches with each strip, gathering the retrieved line on the apron of my float tube or the side compartment of my pontoon boat. Twitching or stripping the trolled flies adds a quick darting movement on top of the horizontal velocity imparted to the flies by the watercraft pulling them. While the darting movement is short and quick, the component of the movement created by my float tube or pontoon is usually slow. There are times when popping the line or using a short-strip retrieve while trolling is exactly what the fish want.

Trolling with a Type III density-compensated sinking fly line, John Gorman brings another worthy fish to hand.

To prevent a break-off from a hard strike or an overly enthusiastic hook set, keep your fingers off the fly line while trolling. The reel's drag should be set correctly to offer adequate resistance to bury the hook point while at the same time allowing a little line to be pulled from the reel in order to safely absorb the impact.

There are times I will stop my troll and strip my flies back to me, experimenting with the length and speed of the strip. There are many combinations. Additionally, I may intersperse pauses here and there, allowing the fly to sink. For instance, I might make three short strips, and then pause for a count of three. If this produces strikes, I look for a consistent pattern as to when in my stripping routine the strikes come. Do they occur when I stop stripping and the flies sink? Do they occur when I start stripping and the flies ascend? Do the strikes come in the middle of my stripping routine?

Stripping or popping the fly are the only times that I actually hold the fly line when trolling. This can be dangerous. When holding the line, I risk a break-off by a big fish administering a hard strike. The response by the angler may be to hold the line tight against the strike on a light leader, with little or no give to the fish's hard pull. Even if my rod tip is soft enough to cushion most strikes, I want the fly line to be simultaneously pulled from the reel by the fish. This added absorption of the strike shock by not holding the line can be crucial to saving your fly and the fish. Unless you are stripping or popping the line, keep your hands off the fly line. Set the drag on your reel so that there is enough resistance to the strike that it buries the hook point in the fish's jaw, but not so much tension that line is not also pulled from the reel simultaneously to cushion the impact. No stripping, no popping, so no hands on the line!

If I stop my troll temporarily to strip-retrieve my fly line, instead of recasting the line to extend it them a considerable distance from my watercraft, I may instead wiggle my rod tip back and forth as I kick my tube or pontoon away from the line. So once my retrieved fly line gets, perhaps, three rod lengths from me, I hold the grip of my rod high and the tip low and "shake out" the line through the rod tip, releasing the line coils I had stripped in back into the water. I have re-established my long length of line trolled behind me without having cast the line. For beginners who are not yet comfortable with fly casting—especially the necessary gyrations and repeated false casts necessary to cast a sinking fly line—extending the trolled line again without casting can be convenient and effective. However, it will be important to all fly anglers who aspire to be consistently effective at stillwater fishing to learn how to cast, and cast reasonably far. Rising lake fish, especially in clear, shallow water, may dictate that long casts are necessary to catch them.

Henry's Lake, eastern Idaho. When trolling this lake, do not get caught with your hand on the reel or line, or you will pay the price in fish lost. Also, beware of the possibility of sudden strong winds that may arise to catch you in the middle of large western lakes.

## The Creative Stripper

Just as you can never have too many friends or too much money, a successful lake angler can never have too many effective fly-fishing methods. Trolling is just one of many stillwater fly-fishing techniques. Even with a large complement of methods, there are days when it seems that I am one short of having all the answers, keeping a fair lake-fishing day from turning into a stellar day. For determined fly fishermen, the silver lining of average fishing days, of course, is continuing to seek out or create another inventive way to present a fly in such a way that fish will be overcome by temptation to eat the artificial. If you subscribe to the idea that, more times than not, fish can be induced to eat even when we think the bite is off, you will eventually add to your fish-catching skills. Personally, I am a subscriber to this thinking. I am always in search of one more method, or a variation of a standard technique. Maybe I will create one. If I do, I suspect it will be a lucky accident, which leads me to a story to illustrate this point.

My friends and I were spending a long May weekend in eastern Washington state. It was an annual pilgrimage to lakes that enter their prime time earlier in the season than many of the lakes in Oregon, where we all lived. We had all come to associate the long drive into the scablands, cheap motels, and greasy diner food with great stillwater fishing memories. For three days, we would launch our float tubes and pontoon boats into three or four different lakes. The story that follows is set on Lenice Lake on the final day of one such trip.

As we had done in many previous years, we dragged or carried our watercraft over the sandy desert soil and through the sagebrush to reach the water by midmorning. We always wanted to arrive long before the afternoon wind kicked up to thwart our casting and blow us off our fishing targets. If you wore a broad brimmed hat, you had better crank down the chinstrap, or you would kick hard to catch it before it sank out of sight.

Using past successful ventures at Lenice as our guides, we anticipated trolling leech patterns paired with a Prince or a Hare's Ear variation as we got our day started. Such a method is a good opportunity to fish and observe simultaneously. It was always a good strategy to watch other anglers who had launched before us, to see where they were fishing, and discover if anyone had a bent rod. There were usually enough anglers for us to surmise that some had probably been fishing here for several days and therefore had figured out where to be and what to use. So we slowly trolled across the lake toward a familiar island of reeds and did our reconnaissance. There was not much going on, no whooping or hollering from the anglers settled into their fishing routines. Maybe the scene would be different once we reached the back side of the island.

The rainbow trout of Lenice Lake were being no one's fools that day. Even the dependable channel we patrolled on the back side of island gave up only an occasional timid strike. It was time to tie on a tan Compara-dun dry fly and chironomid pupa, one of our go-to Washington lakes setups. Everyone spread out to explore different parts of the lake, all looking for locations along the shoreline reeds where we might discover rising trout.

Sometimes a very unusual retrieve of the fly can pay surprising dividends. I wish I had a dollar for every time I vigorously strip my flies back to the boat in order to change them when a crazy fish chases it down to eat it.

The fish we sought were the bank cruisers who were looking for hatching midges and *Callibaetis* mayflies who showed up, typically, in late morning. A choice was made available to the prowling fish: an adult mayfly sitting enticingly on the surface or a suspended midge pupa hanging helplessly directly below the dry fly. The Compara-dun doubled as an effective fly and a float/indicator to keep the chironomid from sinking into the muddy bottom. If the dry fly suddenly disappeared, you had a split second to respond to a fish that had just intercepted the pupa. Great fun. And, now and then, a head would appear to suck in the indicator.

Invariably, members of our group would cross fishing paths with each other. Information was exchanged about fish landed and flies to try. Overall, this day's fishing was slow for us. Everyone had caught a few fish, but no one in our circle had cracked the code to consistent action, nor had anyone else on the lake.

Into late afternoon, the reports exchanged were always the same: the action was occasional and sporadic. So to mix up my routine, I parked my pontoon boat in the reeds of the island, extracted myself, and waded to the edge of the adjacent channel to cast from a standing station. My spot was well chosen. The angle of the afternoon sun allowed me to watch cruising rainbows patrolling the channel not two rod lengths in front of me. When the trout are being difficult, such a sight can be both exciting and frustrating as the fishing begins.

Since I had been trolling a Bugger and a Prince Nymph on my favorite clear, slow-sinking fly line, I continued to use the same as I stood and cast. Using this system, I could experiment with a variety of depths and retrieves as the fish passed in front of me. As I watched their reactions, or lack thereof, to my presentations, I would know what was interesting to them, or not. Anticipating their cruising paths, I could time the retrieve of my flies to swim them right in front of the passing rainbows. Above them, below them, fast, slow, and in between—but nothing interested the fish.

I was getting frustrated, so it was time to change my flies. Having already made a cast as my decision was made; I stripped my line as fast as any mortal can. I was in a hurry to make the needed change, to get on with it. As I yanked my flies through the water faster than any leech or little insect could possibly move in the real world, I got a hard grab from one of those naughty rainbows as it attacked my Prince Nymph!

My first reaction to this fluky event was that it couldn't possibly happen again. Nevertheless, it did; I landed several more good trout that fell for the Prince with SLH (strip like hell) retrieve. I had never retrieved a fly this fast in my career with the results I was now getting. I was baffled as to what these fish viewed and ate in the real world that I was mimicking. Frankly, at the moment, I did not care.

Once the action died at my position, I hopped into my pontoon boat to seek greener pastures. I kicked out of the end of the channel into the main lake. It was soon obvious that I could not troll the flies as fast as I could strip them. My solution to make the flies swim *really* fast through the water was to kick my fins and strip like a banshee simultaneously. It worked!

The fish always ignored the big leech, so the #12 Prince Nymph accounted for more landed trout. By the time I caught up with several of my companions, I had brought to hand no less than eleven rainbows on my new strip-like-hell-while-trolling retrieve. Though I was never accused of lying by my friends that afternoon, I will always wonder whether they believed me. As soon as I shared my angling insights, the fishing died. As my friends joined me in this laughable, frantic

This rainbow could not resist dining on a Beadhead Prince, an All-Star fly. Remember: The fish make the rules and it is our job to discover and obey them. A humble approach is always best.

retrieve of their flies, no one was able to duplicate the results I had just experienced. Nor could I give them a demonstration. I did not get another strike on this technique the rest of our stay.

In fact, I have never caught another fish anywhere in my travels using a frantic stripping retrieve with the troll as I did that afternoon on Lenice Lake. However, I did have it once. I hold on to the hope that one day when the fish refuse to bite for me, I will resort in desperation to my SLHWT method and crack the code again.

## I'll Be Baahhck!

When you locate a particularly productive area, take bearings as best you can with markers—trees, large rocks, identifiable landmarks—to make reference points about your exact location on the lake. The fish may be concentrated in this zone. Once you leave the special spot, the action stops. Strip in your flies, do a 180-degree turn, start kicking or rowing, let line out, and return to run your flies through the area again. Keep trolling through the magic spot in all directions until the party is over. Return to this area later in the day; the magic may happen again.

## One-Trick Pony

From my fly-fishing shop retail days, I remember a man new to fly fishing who was introduced to lake fishing by a mentor who had specialized in stillwaters for years. To protect the innocent, let's call the newbie Biff. Biff would occasionally bring me a photo of himself holding a large fish. He had obviously become skilled at seeking out big fish in lakes and getting them to bite. One photo I recall displayed a trophy that exceeded 12 pounds. Biff definitely had some clues about effective lake fishing.

A friend of mine invited Biff to join him for a day of fishing on a quality river, a guided fishing trip. When the guide set up the pair at their initial fishing spot of the day, Biff was immediately in distress. Try as he might, he could not get the fly anywhere near the fish. Because all he had ever done in his years of fishing was troll, Biff had never learned how to fly-cast. The only skill he possessed in getting his flies to the fish was to pull line off the reel, extending it behind his pontoon boat as he moved through the water. If lake fish demanded casting to be caught, Biff was out of luck. It was trolling or nothing.

Yes, trolling can be filthy-effective, and I employ this technique often, but sometime during the typical fishing day, casting the fly will be the only way to catch fish. Don't limit your options by being a one-trick pony.

## Look, Mom: No Hands!

So that my hands are free to tend my rod and reel, I much prefer trolling from a float tube or small pontoon boat. If I use a rowboat or a boat powered by a motor, I have to pay attention to steering anything but a straight path, plus manage the foot pedals that control the speed and direction of the boat. In my tube or pontoon, I have very precise control over the movement of my flies. I am able to stop, start, and turn in a heartbeat.

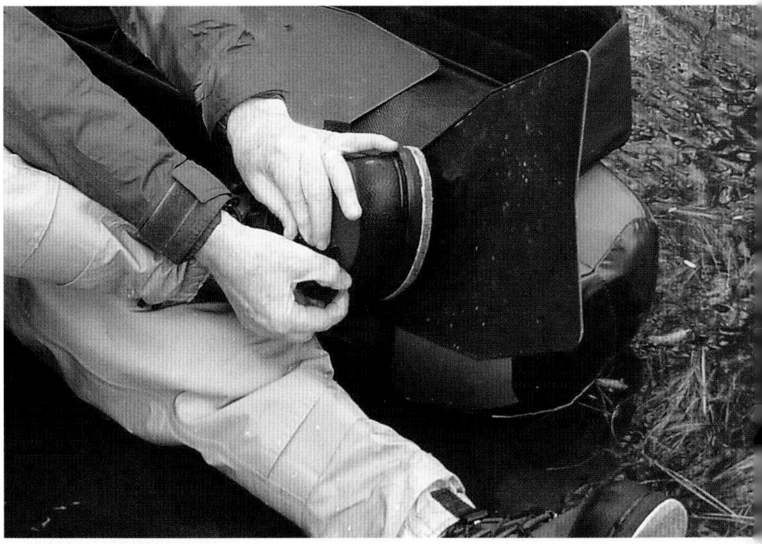

Being propelled by fins allows the angler maximum control over the speed, and the nuances of stopping and starting, of the troll. Such fine-tuned control is often the difference between catching and not catching fish.

Such control translates into more effective fishing, and more fish caught. From a traveling and hassle standpoint, I can easily transport several partially deflated float tubes in the back of my 4Runner. As for my 75-inch-long, hard-shell pontoon boats, I can strap two of them on my roof rack. Since no inflation of the pontoons is necessary, I can pull them off and throw them into the lake with minimal preparation, and spend my time fishing.

## Trolling Made Easy with Friends

Occasionally I invite friends who have no equipment and no skills to fish with me. To keep matters simple, I fish with them in my drift boat. Though designed to negotiate whitewater rivers, my roomy drift boat easily accommodates a pair of anglers with me on the oars. No need for waders, fins, small individual floating craft, or casting skills. Additionally, I can easily choreograph and instruct the guests who are seated in front of me, offering them tips about the little nuances of trolling effectively. I control the trolling speed and direction. When a fish is hooked, I can coach each passenger about what to do to finally put their fish in my net. Besides mentor and coach, I am also the photographer who captures their good time and fish-catching successes with my camera.

Because the drift boat sits high on the water, it is also an excellent, stable platform from which to teach the basics of fly casting. Sitting low in a float tube or small pontoon boat, the beginning caster will often slap the fly line into the water behind him. This can kill the cast and frustrate the beginning caster. In the big boat, the line flies higher without touching the water behind, and I am always within a few feet of the student, ready to offer suggestions.

With less experienced anglers in the boat, it is easy for a skilled oarsman to troll the flies with the proper speed, stops, and starts to entice the fish. The anglers merely hold onto the rods and reel in the fish.

For quick, simple, minimal hassle, effective coaching, and controlling the action, my drift boat is a great tool.

Another use for a bigger craft, such as my drift boat or my 16-foot power boat, is to transport pontoon and float tubes to a distant fishing site on a big lake. If there is no nearby shoreline access to a portion of a large lake where I want to more precisely troll from a smaller craft, I can throw the little boat into the bigger one and get to my spot with much less effort in much less time. I also have the ability to station a lot of fishing gear, supplies, and a large cooler with food and drink to my distant fishing spot onboard the Mother Craft.

## More Adjustments and Tweaking

Besides varying the speed, direction, and stripping movements of my flies, and my location, if the fish refuse to bite, other adjustments are in order.

Often, one of the last changes in my trolling efforts will be my flies. I may change my leech imitation from black to olive, and the size from 8 to 10. As for the smaller fly I have paired with the leech, I may replace the Prince with a Hare's Ear or a Pheasant Tail Nymph. If I have seen insects in or on the water, this could steer my fly decisions. In addition, I often use my stomach pump on the first few fish I catch, to discover what the fish have found to eat today. If there is a broad variety of organisms in the fish's stomach, they are not likely focused on just one food item. On the other hand, if one organism in the sample predominates over all others, I will choose to imitate this and find the closest match I have from my fly box.

A larger boat—the Mother Craft—can transport smaller craft to a distant location on a lake. The smaller boats are used when precision trolling is necessary.

Even when the fishing is good, the fish may overwhelmingly bite only one of the two flies I present to them. In this case, I replace the nonproductive fly with a different color or pattern. If I have some new experimental patterns to try out, this is an excellent time to tie one on. Because the fish are obviously on the bite, let's discover if they will eat my new creation. Every now and then, my experimental fly will catch as many fish, or more, than the pattern that has been today's early winner. Fun.

Be focused like a laser beam on the fishing details, but remember to check out the scenery now and then. Memorable photos are waiting to happen. Trolling can be an effective method for catching stillwater fish. To be *consistently* successful, a sharp angler pays attention to all the little things that contribute to his successful trolling formula. Remember where the devil is—in the details.

## Change Fly Lines

If the fishing zone today is deep—let's say greater than 15 feet—I will change to my Type III sinking line. It sinks at least twice as fast as my clear, slow-sinking one. I can now get deeper faster.

I can vary the depth at which I am fishing in a couple of ways as I troll. First, I can lengthen or shorten the amount of line I am trailing, making sure I always count the number of line strips I take from the reel. Second, the speed at which I troll can vary the depth of my flies. The slower I troll, the deeper the flies. Third, I can fish heavier or more lightly weighted flies. Just as before, when the strikes come, note the line length, the trolling speed, and how the flies were moving and/or being retrieved. Then the exact formula can be duplicated, and more fish caught.

CHAPTER 7

# Effectively Fishing Wet Flies and Nymphs

The ability to make a reasonable cast is necessary for maximum fish-catching effectiveness. Embrace the fact that the wind will affect your casting on larger lakes on most fishing days.

Though I enjoy trolling, and this method can be extremely effective, once the fish are located, I prefer to cast the flies to my quarry. For me, this is being more actively involved as I fish, which is my personal preference. An additional benefit of casting while riding low to the water in a float tube or small pontoon boat is that my casting technique improves. Sitting low forces me to keep my backcast elevated as the line travels behind me. Slapping the water to my rear can slow or kill the momentum in the line. If the mechanics of the backcast crumble, the forward cast that follows can be not only pathetic, but embarrassing, too. To execute a reasonable cast, I must be conscious of good mechanics. From a sitting position low to the water, little mistakes in good form can be magnified, which is good for learning to accentuate the significant details of casting a fly. This is particularly important since I teach fly casting to my students. Don't want my class members ending up like poor Biff, the one-trick pony.

Besides fine-tuning my casting stroke, I create less disturbance in the zone to which I am casting. I am not kicking my craft over and through my fishing water when I am casting from a fixed station. One more plus: I can fan my casts out in all compass directions quickly, enabling me to probe more water in a specific area much, much faster than I can troll through it thoroughly.

When do I fish wet flies and nymphs? Most of the time. If I don't see rising trout that are obviously plucking floating flies off the surface, I am fishing wet flies. Even when trout are observed rising, they may be actually taking hatching insects sitting in or barely under the surface. I have caught thousands of rising trout on emergers, pupae, and wet flies that were not floating on the surface. Often, when I pump some stomachs of these fish, it reveals that none of the insects eaten are winged adults, even though a surface disturbance was created by the fish as it intercepted the food. Fish quickly learn that insects with wings can fly away a split second before the fish snatches it. It's much easier to grab a morsel that helplessly struggles in or just under the surface, struggling to free itself from its pupal or nymphal skin. A little clue about whether fish are feeding on insect adults or the nymph or pupa: a fish's rise to a winged adult on the surface often leaves a bubble behind in the ring of the rise, whereas plucking an emerging insect subsurface usually does not.

## Fly Pattern Thoughts

Though I address more about specific wet fly and nymph patterns in other chapters, I want to emphasize that a good knowledge of the most common aquatic organisms in stillwaters is key to fly selection. If need be, circle back to Chapter 2, Stillwater Entomology. Depending on the time of year, staple wet flies and nymphs must include imitations of leeches, chironomids, *Callibaetis* mayflies, damselflies, dragonflies, caddisflies, and scuds. Specific lakes and ponds may demand particular flies outside the mainstream. Do your research. Also, though we all eventually have our favorite flies, slight variations in size, color, and design can make significant differences. You can never have too many stillwater flies. Those fish in clear ponds and lakes, especially when the light is good, can very closely inspect anything they might consider eating.

Searching the shallows along the lakeshore can give the angler some clues as to what the fish might be looking for during their dining travels, like this larva of the predaceous diving beetle.

## Armed and Dangerous

Typically, I will have three fly rods with me on the lake, each with a different type of fly line. Sometimes it's four rods. If the fish are sitting in shallow water, or begin to rise, I will choose to use a floating line for casting wet flies and nymphs. Because the floating line sits on the water's surface, it is easy to pick up and cast, and I may be able to do so without retrieving any line first. Another big benefit of using a brightly colored floater is that it may indicate a soft strike, one so subtle that I would not feel it. Experience has taught me to closely watch the end of my hi-vis fly line as I retrieve it. In between the pulls on the fly line as the fly is retrieved, the line forms little horizontal "S" waves as it hesitates. A strike may very well happen when the fly is at rest, and line is not tight. If I see the slightest straightening of the distant "S" in the line, the rod tip is lifted immediately to set the hook. Unless an angler knows this and looks for it, he will never have an inkling that a fish had momentarily intercepted his fly. Interception to release of the fly can span less than a second.

## Watch Closely

It was another bluebird June day on central Oregon's Crane Prairie Reservoir. Damselfly nymphs were everywhere; many swam to my float tube where they crawled from the water to seek a likely place to dry themselves just prior to the adult form slowly emerging from its nymphal skin. It was not hard to guess what fly to use. I usually fish two flies in tandem, but I didn't that afternoon. There is always a chance a big rainbow will find a submerged log, of which there were plenty, on which to entangle a second fly dangling free behind the frantic fish. A second fly in 6 feet of water filled with old wood is an invitation to heartbreak.

Because the water was shallow, I used my bright yellow floating line with a 9-foot 4X leader. I was casting my favorite Goat Damsel Nymph. It is a skinny little creation that looks like nothing special to me, but the Cranebows think differently.

Experience told me I was in a good location, near a submerged old stream channel. Crane Prairie was formed in 1922 when a timbered meadow was flooded by the damming of the Deschutes River. With an average depth of only about 6 feet over its five-square-mile expanse in an average year, sunlight penetrates every portion of the lake to produce vegetation that enables the production of an extreme abundance of trout food organisms. As the water warms in the shallow impoundment, the fish tend to congregate in the deeper reaches of old stream channels for comfort. Find the channels, find the fish.

Having landed a few fish soon after I had begun, life was good, the day already a success. Before making a particular

Watching the distant "S" curves in a brightly colored floating fly line can reveal a subtle take of the fly that the angler would never feel in the line. If the tip of the fly line straightens, set the hook.

Oregon's Crane Prairie Reservoir is a highly productive shallow lake known for its large "Cranebows." In the heat of summer, savvy anglers seek fish in the cooler depths of the old submerged river channels. This lake has put out rainbows as large as 19 pounds.

cast, I was chatting up one of my fishing companions. In spite of the pleasant interchange, I stayed focused enough to watch my line and fly settle on the water. My strategy, once the fly landed, was to wait fifteen or twenty seconds for the damselfly to sink, and then begin my retrieve. As I waited and bantered, I thought I saw the little curve at the end of my yellow fly line straighten out ever so slightly. At 40 feet away, it could definitely be my imagination, but . . . As I tell my guided clients and angling friends, there are no penalty points for setting the hook. If nothing is there when you set the hook, so what?

As I lifted the rod tip to tighten my line, I felt the familiar throbbing resistance of a strong fish! It had intercepted the Goat as it slowly sank, with no retrieving movement on my part. After a valiant battle, I gently pinned the big trout against my float tube for an admiring look, and removed the barbless hook from its jaw. As it turned out, this 7-pound beauty was the biggest fish of the day, a fish whose strike was so gentle it could have easily been ignored.

## Remember What You Are Trying to Simulate

I will digress for a bit to prompt readers to remember what they are trying to imitate with artificial flies. Understanding this will have great influence on whether the retrieve of the wet flies and nymphs may fool the fish.

Wet flies and nymphs are imitations of either immature aquatic insects that are swimming, crawling, or hatching, or other non-insect swimming or resting aquatic organisms such as leeches, small fish, crayfish, or scuds. Knowledge of aquatic organisms, specifically how they swim or propel themselves through the water, can add to the development of the retrieves in which you attempt to mimic the real life movements of living trout foods. The nymphs of the dragonfly, damselfly, and *Callibaetis* mayfly, for instance, have distinctive swimming strokes. When you become familiar with these movements, you can become more effective when specifically fishing imitations of these insects if you can duplicate how the fish see them propel themselves as you manipulate your fly line and rod tip. The same holds true for the wet flies imitating the distinctive movements of non-insect creatures such as leeches and scuds.

This two-tone marabou damselfly nymph is particularly effective because of the lifelike action and appearance of the marabou feathers and because of its very slender profile. With many proven wet flies and nymphs, thinner is better.

Keep in mind that most of these food items are rather small. As mentioned before, beginners tend to fish their flies with too much speed relative to the size of the organisms fish normally eat. Little fish would be the one exception. They have to move fairly quickly to survive, and they usually don't have the species survival advantage of huge numbers in a population, compared to the bazillions of chironomids in a lake. But beyond an exception like this, little critters can't traverse many feet in a few seconds. So, if you begin to wonder if you are retrieving your flies too fast, you probably are.

## The Cradle Will Rock

If there is a stiff breeze across the lake, it can definitely interfere with the retrieve and strike detection when you are using a floating line. The surface currents generated by the wind can blow the floating line into a large curve, adding additional speed to the fly, which you might not want. Additionally, the curve in the line puts you out of straight-line contact with the fly; there's a chance you will not detect the strike, or if you do, it may be too late to set the hook. And when you raise the rod tip to set the hook, the curving lay of your line may prevent you from getting an adequately forceful set of the hook as you try to pull the line tight before the fish releases the fly.

When the wind thwarts my ability to effectively use a floating line as I cast to fish in shallow water (10 feet or less), my slow-sinking, transparent stealth line is called into the game. It immediately settles below the wind and surface currents as it slowly descends. Because it sinks slowly, the line does not immediately take my flies to the bottom, where they might pick up debris or become entangled in the vegetation. Instead, there is a significant amount of time to retrieve the flies before they finally tap bottom. Once they do, it is time to strip them in to recast.

## Don't Forget to Stretch

One thing to deal with as you prepare to fish a slow-sinking, or intermediate, transparent, or camouflage fly line is that they tend to kink and coil as they rest between fishing trips on your fly reel. No matter who manufactures the fly line, they all tend to retain their springy coils. This requires that you stretch the line before it casts and shoots through the rod guides as it should. Even more importantly, if the line is kinked and coiled as you fish it, you may not detect strikes as you should. The coils can absorb the strike without fully tightening the line to relay the bite to the angler. Stretch that line.

If the lake I have selected for the day is deeper than 6 to 7 feet where I want to fish it, and there are no rising fish feeding

For overcoming the some of the inherent problems of fishing in the wind, and for added stealth, a clear, slow-sinking intermediate fly line is a must, especially in shallow water. This fish was caught in 5 feet of water where a faster-sinking fly line would have put the fly in the mud and vegetation on the lake bottom.

near the surface, I will usually start with my clear, slow-sinking line. If it's breezy, this makes my line choice easy. I take up a stationary casting position in an area that has produced for me previously, or one that has "the look." This could be a little cove or bay, the mouth of an inlet stream, a rocky point, or the edge of submerged or exposed vegetation. If I can locate a portion of the lake protected from the wind, so much the better.

A little breeze is always desirable on stillwaters. The fish are less wary with a riffled surface that obscures their vision and the vision of a would-be predator. My kicking and casting activities are not as noticeable. Neither is the splashy landing of my fly line. When the day is windless, the surface unruffled, and the sky bright, fishing can be tough. A little breeze is your friend.

## This Is the Setup

Most of the time in stillwaters I am fishing two flies on my leader. (Make sure multiple fly setups are legal on the waters you fish.) Typically, I separate the flies by about 30 inches. If I am fishing two flies of different sizes, the bigger fly is tied as my

A second fly—the dropper fly—is secured to the leader by leaving one of the tag ends of a double surgeon knot long enough to tie on the fly. Keep the drop short to prevent wrapping or fowling on the leader.

dropper, with the smaller pattern as my terminal, or point fly. The dropper fly dangles 2 to 4 inches off my leader on a short spur of tippet.

The spur of the dropper to which the dropper fly is tied is created by cutting off the lowest 30 inches of the fine end of a tapered leader. I then rejoin the two sections I have just clipped with a double surgeon's knot. As a result, two short tag ends of line are created, which would normally be trimmed close at the knot. Instead of trimming both tags, leave the one that is an extension of the upper, thicker portion of the leader. If you do a little planning as the knot is created, this untrimmed tag end should be about 4 inches long, plenty of length to tie on the dropper fly. The final dropper length from the main leader to the fly should be 2 to 3 inches. Longer than this and the dropper fly will tend to wrap around the leader and not fish properly.

There are good choices of knots to secure the dropper fly to the line. However, I use only one: the clinch knot. Many are familiar with the improved clinch knot, but I choose the unimproved, simpler version because I can untie this knot by gripping it with the fingernails of my thumb and middle finger, and pulling the knot away from the hook eye. After pulling this little section of now-curled line straighter by grasping the end with a forceps and the knot with my fingers, and pulling firmly, I can now tie on a different fly while preserving the length of my dropper line. Should you choose not to unravel the knot when changing dropper flies, then you must cut the line again to rejoin the tippet and leader with a new surgeon's knot, creating a new dropper spur.

I much prefer this tying my last 30 inches of tippet to the bend of the hook of the dropper. This latter setup is easy and fast to assemble, but it is my firm belief that significantly fewer fish will be hooked and landed on the upper fly using this scheme. Because there is no separation between the dropper fly and the leader, a fish that attempts to follow or intercept the fly from the rear will run its nose against the line. Two things may happen, both bad. First, the fish will be startled and retreat when its nose touches the leader as it nears the fly. Secondly, as the nose of the fish touches the line it will, in turn, push the fly away even as it attempts to grab it. The trap in using this method of securing the dropper fly to the leader is that an angler may land a few fish on the upper fly and think that the setup is effective. However, with the setup I prefer, with the dropper fly separated and dangling below the leader, maybe the same angler would have landed a dozen fish instead of a couple!

As for the overall length of the leader, this should be determined by several factors, including water clarity, breeze, and the wariness factor. Clear water, no breeze, and fish having survived heavy fishing pressure may demand a leader of 15 feet, and a small tippet diameter. If the water is murky, there's a bit of breeze to ruffle the water's surface and dapple the light underwater, and the fish are a bit naïve, a 9-foot leader can be totally adequate. For additional stealth consider using second-generation fluorocarbon leaders and tippets. Fluorocarbon is the closest material we have available to invisibility. It can be a significant edge when the fishing conditions are demanding. It's rare that you won't find me using a fluorocarbon tippet.

## Good Things Come to Those Who Wait

After your cast hits the water, what you do next can be critical to your success. Whereas the natural tendency is to start moving the fly through water to tempt a fish, be patient. Let the fly sink a bit. Your chances of getting a fish's attention are enhanced if you allow the fly to descend into the zone where the fish is cruising or feeding. It does not matter how enticing your flies or effective your retrieve if the fish are not seeing them.

I count during the descent of my flies before I impart any pulling movement to them. After my cast, I count to five then start my retrieve. I do this several times, varying the direction of the casts, fanning them around the specific area I hope the fish might be. If nothing happens, I will make another series of casts, counting to ten before I retrieve. I increase the count and waiting time until I get a strike or my flies start hooking the vegetation or debris on the bottom.

As for the specific retrieve of the flies, there is a vast combination of choices. At the extremes, I can pull the line an inch at time, or several feet on a single pull. As for speed, I can creep the fly, barely moving it, or I can rip it through the water as fast as humanly possible. Between these extremes of travel distance and speed of the fly, there is a very broad middle ground. The possible combinations are virtually endless, especially if pauses of varying durations are added to the mix. If these are not enough, on any one cast, I can change to multiple retrieves as the fly is brought back to me. So where should you start?

My initial choice in a retrieve of wet flies or nymphs as my stillwater fishing day begins is usually composed of short, medium-quick strips of the line interspersed with a couple of slower, medium length strips and pauses. So, here's how it might go: short strip – short strip – short strip, pause – two – three – four, slower medium strip – slower medium strip, pause- two – three – four, (repeat from the beginning) short strip – short strip . . . Before I change this retrieve, I will fan out a dozen

The hand-twist retrieve of the fly is an excellent choice for moving the fly slowly through the water in small, lifelike increments. Slower is often preferable to faster. Begin with the fly line between the first finger and thumb, fingers above the line.

Pull in a short section of line by rotating the fingers down and the thumb upward.

A finger of the rod hand pins the fly line against the cork grip while the fingers of the stripping hand move back to the beginning horizontal position, preparing to pull in another short length of line.

The fingers and thumb repeat Step 2. Continue until a fish grabs the fly or until the line is fully retrieved and it is time to re-cast.

casts, varying only the countdown of the flies as they sink before I start the retrieve.

If I find no success during my initial attempts, I may go next to a slow hand-twist retrieve, mixed with a couple of slow, medium-length strips of the line. The hand-twist is accomplished by grasping the fly line with the thumb and first finger. Next, the other three fingers pull the line toward the angler, rolling underneath the hand. The thumb and first finger release their hold to grasp the line again to start retrieving more line, as the three fingers roll underneath the hand to pull in another few inches of line. So I begin with four slow hand-twist retrieves of the line, followed by pause – two – three – four, followed by two or three slow, medium-long pulls of the line. I repeat this routine until the line is fully retrieved. If no strike, I cast in a slightly different direction, count, and then use the same retrieve. I do this for a dozen casts. If a strike should come, I note exactly what I was doing, or not doing, during that particular part of the retrieve. This will be my high alert moment when I repeat it on the following casts.

Remembering my Lenice Lake uberhigh-speed retrieve that was oddly successful, somewhere in my fishing day I strip the line fast, with short strips, long strips, and in between. If the strike count is low, the number of experimental retrieves of the flies should be high.

## Mirroring Success

There are times that an angler in my immediate vicinity has found the fish *and* the right retrieve to entice them. If necessary, I will move my boat to get into position to clearly see the fisherman's hands. From a non-invasive distance, I seek to observe the exact retrieve Mr. Success is using and mirror my retrieve to his. As he casts, I cast. If he pauses before retrieving, I pause. As he manipulates the line, I mimic his exact movements. By actually mirroring the exact movements and pauses, I can better remember exactly what he is doing than I would by merely watching.

The exact retrieve is only part of the success formula. I attempt to determine the type of fly line—floating or sinking—that is being used, and the leader length. What fly pattern, or patterns, and the exact location of where the successful fish-hooking casts are made are other key components of the whole success package here. But the fact that I know the exact retrieve of the fly allows me to eliminate the search for this puzzle piece as I can now devote my total focus to the others.

## More to Ponder on the Pond

Fishing alone with no one to observe, I know there's a chance I may actually have used the particular retrieve that the fish desire but gotten no strikes. It could be that the flies were wrong or the area being fished had few or no fish. With this possibility in mind, a sharp fisherman will repeat his favored retrieves in different areas of the lake. Still no action? Time to change flies. And, if I catch a foolish fish, and it is at least 10 inches

Once the fish are located and the depth and fly pattern are determined, the critical last piece of the puzzle is the appropriate retrieve of the fly. After you hook a fish, try to remember what you did.

long, I pump its stomach without fail, looking for preferred food items and the artificial flies to imitate them.

## Ignore This at Your Own Peril

There is one portion of the retrieve that can be effective but overlooked. This is during the lift of the rod tip to clear the line from the water for the next cast. There are occasions in which an interested fish is tracking the fly closely as it moves horizontally toward the angler but refuses to take it. However, once the line is short to the point the angler would lift it free of the water to cast, and the fly responds to the lift, moving vertically, this may act as a trigger for the following fish. If the line is lifted quickly, the fly may be pulled away from the fish before it can grab it. On the other hand, if the fly is lifted a bit slower, you may be pleasantly surprised by a tugging resistance.

If I get strikes consistently during the rod lift, I may incorporate this lift much earlier and throughout my retrieve. For instance, after I have made a cast and counted it down, I may start my retrieve by merely lifting my rod tip high. Assuming there is no strike, I drop the rod tip and strip in the slack line I have created by the lift. After letting the fly sink again, I list the rod tip a second time, repeating the procedures until the flies are near me, and I must cast again. At any time in the retrieval process, I may strip the fly for a distance before adding the rod lift. Here again, an endless combination of retrieves is possible. Just make sure you take note of what the fly is doing when the strike comes. Then, repeat it until it no longer induces strikes.

As I experiment with trying to discover the magic retrieve for the day, or the hour, I must remind myself to slow down. When the bite is slow, and when the bite is fast, the tendency for anglers is to pull the fly through the water too quickly. When the fish are striking only occasionally, or not at all, we can get anxious and frustrated. The result is to hurriedly cast and strip the flies in an attempt to find the effective flies and retrieves that appeal to the fish as soon as possible. In these times, catch yourself. Calm down and slow down. Sometimes the best retrieve is no retrieve. I wish I had a dime for every time I have made a cast, then laid my rod on my tube in order to free both hands to take a photo, only to watch my rod tip quiver and dip with a fish that picked up my fly as it sank or off the bottom.

## A Lesson on Edith Lake

My cousin John and I were on Edith Lake, BC, for the first time, in late spring 2010. My fish electronic depth finder secured on the side of my pontoon boat told me there were definitely fish in our vicinity. However, through the first few hours of fishing, I had managed only a few fish, and I was unable to discover any fly or technique that worked consistently. I watched other anglers on the lake, and spoke to a few, trying to glean any clues. Most had not landed a single fish, even those Canadians who lived near Edith and fished it regularly. Even though my fish-landed number was small—three—my observations and conversations put me at the top of the leader board.

My floating travels eventually took me back to the distant shallow end of the lake where we had launched our boats late morning. I watched as late arrivals launched their watercraft. I never know what I might hear or see as I try to assemble the puzzle pieces for successfully getting the fish to bite. Soon, I saw an angler in a cartop boat who launched and quickly anchored along a deep channel running parallel to the nearby run of shoreline. This guy knew exactly where he wanted to be, and what he wanted to do. The fact that he was a good caster also confirmed he was a man of experience. All these factors told me that I needed to watch this man fish.

After making his first cast, the one thing that caught my attention was his retrieve: short, quick strips. He never varied it. He was definitely not imitating the very slow movement of a chironomid pupa. These were the twitchy travels of the scuds that I knew to be abundant in the lake. However, because the stomach samples of the fish I had caught earlier contained nothing but chironomids, I'd ignored using a scud imitation. As I reviewed where I had caught my fish, it took only a couple of seconds to recall that they had been caught at the far end of the lake opposite from where I was now.

Sometimes a stomach sample and the day's champion fly may show little correlation. My #12 Beadhead Prince was not even close to the tiny olive chironomids on which the trout were gorging.

Unable to catch my chironomid-eating fish with a chironomid fly, I had actually landed them on a #12 Beadhead Prince Nymph, which was much, much larger than the miniscule olive chironomid pupae I found in the stomach samples. Go figure. I was still fishing the same as I watched the angler and his scud retrieve. And, even though I did not observe the scud angler hook a fish, I adopted his retrieve. Soon after quick-twitching my Woolly Bugger/Prince combo, I got a strike. Had the door been unlocked? Another few casts doing the same, I landed a good rainbow on the Prince. Ironically, though my luck had turned for the better, my oblivious mentor who had offered me the retrieving clue did not land a fish before he soon departed for a different location and a different method elsewhere on the lake.

With my stomach pump, I stole from the fish all that it had recently eaten. Though chironomid larvae were present, the majority of what my fish had eaten was scuds, in assorted shades of gold and olive. So, indeed, fish at the other end of the lake were focused on chironomid pupae, while the fish at this end were chowing down on scuds. I was proudly feeling a little like Sherlock Holmes.

If the Prince was getting me some fish-biting action, it only made sense that a scud fly fished with a scud retrieve would enhance my possibilities. So, I traded my Prince for a scud, high on optimism that non-stop action would soon follow. However, several different scud pattern changes later, I had only tallied one halfhearted strike, no landed fish. As a little consolation, no one I could see in my portion of the lake had landed a fish.

Reluctantly, I went back to my original dance partner, replacing the scud with the Prince. Roaming far and wide during my last hour on the lake, I got numerous strikes and managed to land two more rainbow trout on Edith Lake; all came on the Prince twitched like a scud. Go figure. My final count of six fish landed was three more than any fisherman I talked to or heard about that day. Interestingly, part of my success was due to an angler who may not have landed a single fish that day.

## Different Lake, Same Failure of Logic

On another springtime sojourn to eastern Washington, I fished Nunnally Lake for a day. It is located not too far from Lenice Lake, a short drive southeast of the town of Vantage, and south of George, Washington. (No, I'm not kidding.) Because of its near proximity to the popular and productive Lenice, for years I ignored Nunnally. Having heard good reports from other anglers, Dan Reynolds and I dragged our pontoon boats across the desert from our parked truck a good fraction of a mile to the lake. After launching, our strategy involved trolling the shoreline until we got a strike or two. Once a hotspot was located, we would sit stationary to cast and retrieve. We caught a few fish on assorted leech patterns, but the action was sporadic.

When Dan and I differed on where we wanted to be on the lake, he charted his own path, and I mine. In my solo travels, I soon encountered another angler who shared with me that he had some success on a black leech of his own design. After a little more chat, he traveled off in pursuit while I lingered in an area where I had just gotten a strike. Shortly, I landed a fish of about 14 inches. Its stomach contents revealed an abundance of emerald green chironomid pupae. This fish was being highly selective for only one food item, but in a foolish moment it had,

The Midnight Woolly Bugger, with or without a silver beadhead, is one of my All-Star flies. In shallow water, a metal beadhead may prove too heavy to keep the fly from fouling on the bottom vegetation or dragging through the silt.

apparently, deviated from its preference to eat my Midnight Woolly Bugger.

Therefore, of course, I did the logical thing, and changed flies immediately. I cut off the Bugger, changed to a lighter tippet, and began to fish an emerald green chironomid pupa. Even though I used a variety of presentations and both a sinking and floating fly line, my best efforts with the fly that very closely approximated the preferred food produced no strikes.

Once I resumed fishing my Midnight Leech with a quick, short twitch on a sinking line, I was back in the money. The fishing was not fast, but it was consistent. More stomach samples revealed the same green midge pupa, no leeches.

An explanation? My best guess is that the trout had fed upon the hatching chironomid pupa for as long as the hatch lasted and the pupae were readily available. Once the emergence had ended—before I arrived—the fish sought out other food sources and ignored the artificial imitations of the pupae that had ceased emerging. Though the stomach pump is invaluable, it is not a 100 percent predictor of what is guaranteed to work when it comes to fly selection.

## I Am Not Done Defying Common Sense

Many years ago, my friend Matt Ramsey was fishing Crane Prairie Reservoir with two companions. The damselflies were active, which always warms the core of any lake angler. Damselfly nymphs seem to be swimming candy. Fish love them!

Matt and his two friends had fair to good fishing as they cast and retrieved damsel imitations. However, sometime during their fishing they deviated from their casting and retrieving ways to suspending a damsel pattern underneath a floating indicator, and had good fishing results. For years prior to this event, Matt and I had become quite familiar and effective at suspending chironomid larvae and pupae under an indicator, but not a fly whose living counterparts are such capable and active swimmers. Though the damselfly nymph does pause in between its spurts of swimming, it is only a few seconds before it resumes its lateral wiggling swimming movement. Why would the fish be interested in the suspension of a damsel pattern under an indicator, imparting only occasional and slight movement of the fly?

Even after Matt's report of great success that day, I never tried this technique with any flies except midge pupae and larvae, which may wriggle in the real world, but are lousy swimmers. In retrospect, I am at a loss as I wonder why I never tried this. It was an "outside the box" method for flies other than chironomids. It wasn't until I started reading about lake fishing techniques used in British Columbia waters that my memories of Matt's damselfly fishing exploits on Crane Prairie were awakened anew.

As I read numerous Canadian fishing reports and blogs, I occasionally read a story about suspending non-chironomid flies underneath a small floating indicator. One of the more popular patterns mentioned was the Micro Leech. Yeow! Here we have an organism—the ubiquitous-in-most-stillwaters leech—with excellent swimming capabilities, suspended in the water column with very little movement compared to the activity of the real creature. Eventually, I focused specifically on searching specific references to fishing the Micro Leech. At least in the references I found, the Micro Leech was always discussed with the same presentation: suspended under an indicator.

Even those flies imitating aquatic organisms with good swimming abilities—like damselfly and mayfly nymphs, and leeches—are sometimes very effectively fished suspended under an indicator. Here, John Gorman awaits the strike.

On my very next stillwater expedition to a nearby pond, I tied on a black Micro Leech I had recently created at my fly-tying vise, suspended it about 3 feet under a pea-sized strike indicator. Bowing to my conventional wisdom, I paired it with

Micro Leeches and Halo Micro Leeches are effective and easy to tie. Black, claret, olive, brown, and rust are excellent colors. Match them with a variety of plastic and metal bead colors. The combinations are almost endless.

a chironomid pupa on the point, a couple of feet below the little leech pattern. Initially, I considered the ten fish I caught on the suspended Micro Leech in the next couple of hours to be suicidal misfits who would have eaten a paper clip or a shirt button threaded on a hook. I caught fish on the pupa, too, and accorded them much more respect than I did the Micro Leech eaters.

I replaced the black model with a claret Micro Leech. The trout liked it, too. Hmmm. Could there be something to this? On subsequent outings to this same location, and another pond, the suspended Micro Leech in any color I tried, including brown and olive versions, caught fish.

A few weeks after my initial trials with my new friend the Micro Leech, I arrived at our planned annual rendezvous with my sister Joann, her husband, Steve, and son Mark at a little desert lake we fish in the spring. Though we all caught fish on a broad variety of flies and methods that weekend, the Micro Leech fished with little or no movement under an indicator was one of the All-Star patterns of the event. Needless to say, this fly (and others, like the damselfly nymph) dangling below a strike indicator fished with a floating fly line, is a proven method for me, worthy of trying when others are not producing fishing action. However, like any other technique, there is no guarantee the indicator and suspended fly will catch fish on any given day. It is merely one more possibility in a successful fly angler's arsenal.

## Comic Relief

There are times—I cannot predict when—the fish will try to eat indicators. It was on my last steelhead trip a few days ago that my guest had a steelhead ignore his flies to come to the surface in an attempt to grab his indicator. What the fish thought the indicator represented I have no idea. It is fairly common for resident river trout to do this, too. On lakes, even though the trout

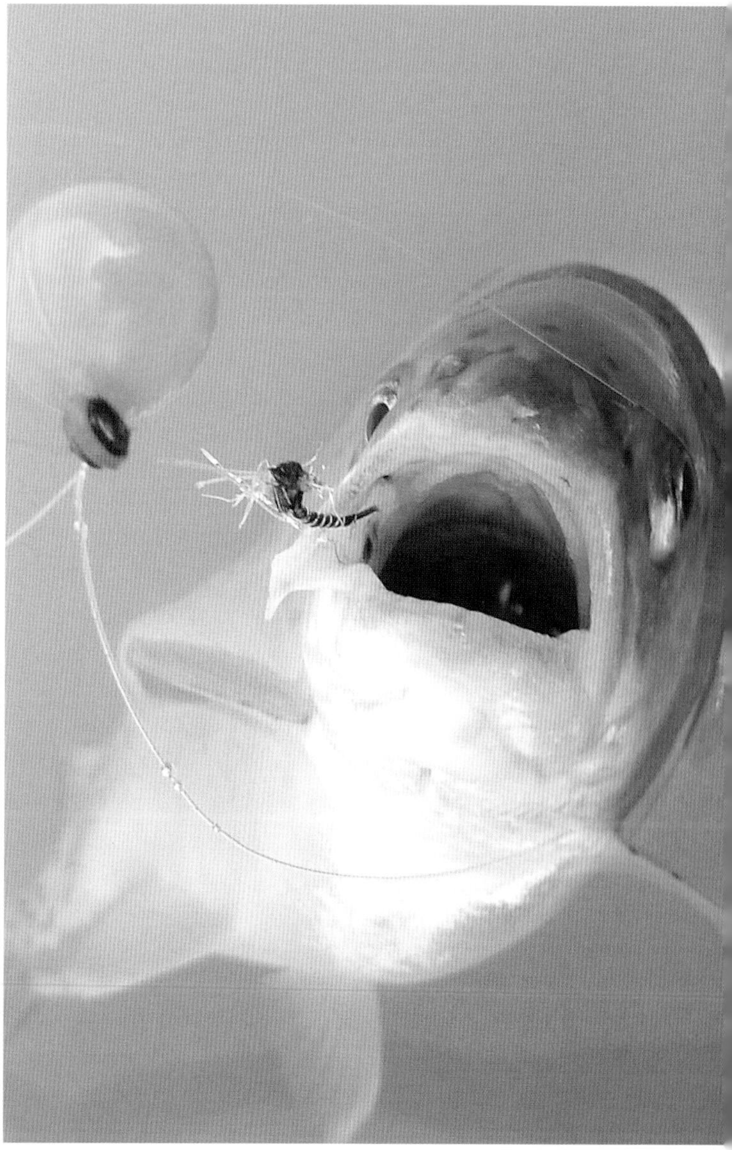

This is the comical result when the indicator-eating activity persists.

get a long hard look at the stationary float, they may decide to eat it. There are not too many brightly colored, spherical living food organisms floating or swimming on ponds and lakes, but occasionally fish want to dine on strike indicators. So, in such situations, I take what I am given. I stopped wishing my indicator had a hook on it every time a fish rose to it; I did something about it. The result makes for some entertaining photos.

## Anchors Aweigh, My Boys

When casting from a stationary position, and trying to maintain that specific position, the wind can move you off your mark. An anchor is very important, even if fishing in a float tube or a small pontoon boat. An anchor enables you to head off the effort and frustration of attempting to stay in one spot. For larger pontoons and boats, two anchors are much better than one. With a

Geese on the wing, Tunkwa Lake, BC. Tunkwa was a venue lake for the 1993 World Fly Fishing Championships.

solo anchor, a larger craft can be constantly swung or spun by the wind. Anchoring both the bow and stern means more fishing time and a better state of mind for the angler.

Casting and retrieving wet flies and nymphs in lakes and ponds can produce great fishing memories, even when only a few fish are brought to net. Most days, piecing the puzzle pieces correctly together—flies, location, depth, and retrieve—requires persistence and resourcefulness. The opportunities to learn the most come on days the fish challenge you to discover what it takes to catch them. Those who embrace and enjoy such challenges will be the consistent winners, while others go home to watch TV, content to watch fishing show hosts and their guests catch big fish with ease.

CHAPTER 8

# Effectively Fishing Chironomids

A big trout wears a little Turkey Tail Chironomid Pupa for the photo.
There is something special about the combination of a big fish and a tiny fly.

Chironomid fishing may be a lake angler's ultimate weapon of mass destruction. When it comes to cataclysmic fish-catching, an angler who masters chironomid fishing can rule a lake.

As you might remember from the chapter on aquatic organisms, the chironomid is a member of class Insecta (insects), order Diptera (flies), and family Chironomidae (midges). So, "midge" is a scientific, taxonomical name, not the generic term used by many people when describing "a tiny little bug I saw near the water that I could not possibly identify."

Perhaps the most deceptive thing about midges, and the reason too many fly anglers have ignored them, is the fact that some are quite small. Fishermen may assume that such a tiny morsel could not possibly interest a big fish. When I try to convey to my students why indeed midges do interest big fish, I ask them if they like popcorn. Of course, just about everyone does. A single piece of popcorn to a human might be the same size equivalent of a midge to a fish, even a large fish. Next, I enquire: "Do you sit down with a bowl of freshly-popped corn and eat only one or two kernels?" Heck no. The snacker will consume hundreds, even a thousand pieces of popcorn. It then follows that a fish will snack on many, many chironomids during a single feeding session. So, in order to be consistently effective, lake anglers cannot possibly ignore midges.

Midges are one of the few food sources available to fish year-round. Through stomach content samples taken from lake and pond fish throughout the calendar year, there are some days that stomach samples contain only midge larvae and pupae. It is not much of a stretch to assume that without the presence and availability of midges, some fish might not survive in their environment.

As you will recall from an earlier chapter, chironomids have a four-stage, or complete, life cycle. For the fly angler, three of the four stages are important to imitate: larva, pupa, and adult. And because midges can be active and hatching year-round, even during the dead of winter, they are definitely one of the go-to flies any time you launch your boat on a lake or pond.

## Pond Fishing on a Winter Day

In February of 2011, I took advantage of mild weather to do some pond fishing for trout. My plan was to check the fish activity on three different ponds. With a little luck, fish would be willing to bite in at least one of the three.

When I arrived early afternoon at Pond #1, I found its surface like glass, not a hint of a breeze. A quick scan revealed no rising fish. Water clarity was reasonable, with visibility into the depths at about 2 feet. The water temperature was typical for western Oregon in midwinter, about 42 degrees F. Examining the surface for insects or vacated midge pupae skins revealed nothing.

To make good use of my time and wait for the fish and insects to awaken, I began to stage some of my many fly boxes and gear for photographs I needed. There was a high overcast with the sun feebly trying to break through. The light was very good for the shots I wanted. As I went about my sorting and set up, I occasionally surveyed the pond for insects or rises. The quiet allowed me to listen for rises when my eyes were busy elsewhere. Shortly, I heard the familiar splash of a trout on the surface. I looked up to see an expanding ring, just out of casting range. Within a few minutes, there was another.

Since there were a few cruisers willing to come to the top, I readied my floating line rod. On the leader, I secured a strike indicator with two chironomid pupae flies, a dropper fly at 3 feet under the indicator, and the other 20 inches below the dropper. To add some visual attractiveness to my offerings, I selected flies with glitzy beads at the heads—one pearl orange, the other red. These flies were part impressionistic (shaped as chironomids) and part attractor (color and shine) and definitely bigger

Cool weather does not always deter the fish from eating. Snow and a little ice will definitely decrease—or eliminate—the crowds.

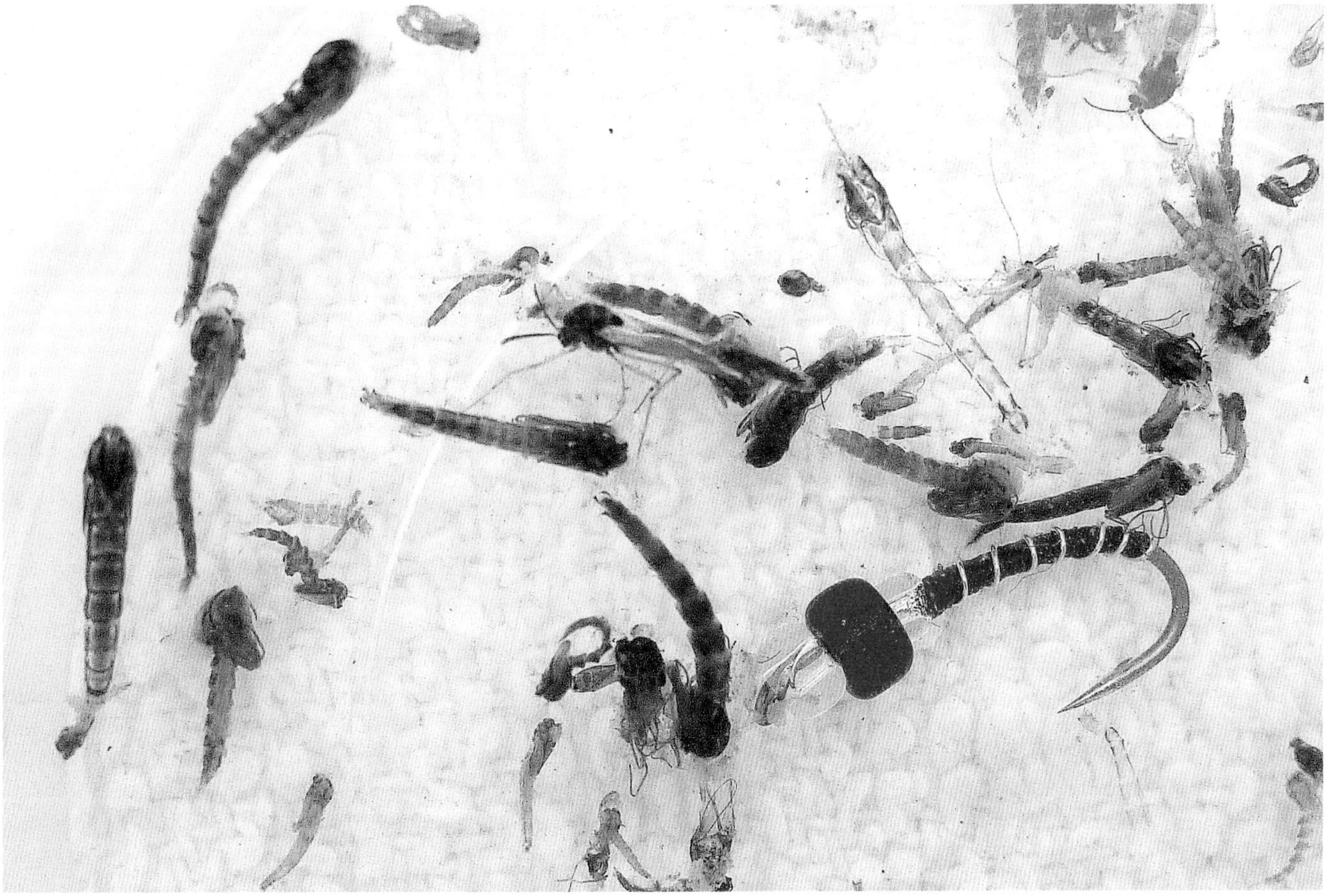

The Laser Beam Chironomid shines bright when it comes to catching fish, even if it's the wrong size and color. Pictured is the stomach sample from a fish that ate the Laser. A clear pupal shuck is visible just above the fly.

than the naturals. Sometimes the fish don't mind an oversized pattern, and a larger fly is easier to see. In limited visibility situations, this pair had served me well in the past.

I must admit that my focus was divided, which limited my fishing success. I made a few casts, then arranged my inanimate subjects and took photos. When my indicator went down on my first strike, I cleanly missed the hook up. When the second strike came twenty minutes later, I set the hook solidly into a 9-inch rainbow. The size of the fish was totally irrelevant to me. The important thing to me was actually fooling a fish. It took a silver-bodied fly with the orange bead.

The rises at Pond #1 were sporadic and spread out over a large area, but more frequent by midafternoon. This is reasonable since it was the warmest part of the day. Occasionally, I saw an airborne midge. It was these, I think, that encouraged a rise here and there. I was fascinated at how the rises were consistently beyond casting range. Since I was fishing on foot, no float tube, I could not get my flies to the red zone. I moved my casting positions to various points around the pond, managing to get one more strike, which I missed. Time to move on.

The conditions at Pond #2, about a mile away from the first, were exactly the same. I stayed with the same setup, two flies not too far below an indicator. As I walked toward the little bay I wanted to fish, I scanned the water for risers and insects—nothing.

Standing on a shoreline tree stump, I was in a position to cast to the water that had been productive for me previous springs and summers. My expectations were low, so any action would be a bonus. Lucky for me, my wait was a short one. Within ten minutes of my arrival, my indicator went down hard. As I raised my rod tip, I felt the solid resistance of a worthy trout. After an admirable struggle by the fish, I slid the rainbow into the shallows for a looked and a quick release. It had fallen for the red fly.

As I continued to fan my casts out in different directions, I found a scenic photo opportunity where the stumps in the lake and the trees were reflected in the pond's mirror surface. Being right-handed, I switched my rod to my left hand, to hold the camera in the favored one. As I raised the camera to look through the viewfinder, I simultaneously saw my indicator twitch. Instinctively, I raised the rod tip to feel that familiar thrashing resistance every angler loves. After a fine accounting of itself, actually pulling line from my fly reel several times during the battle, a solidly built 14-inch rainbow soon slid into the shallows for quick inspection and praise. After a few quick photos—which did not steal its spirit—I sent the fish back to his home.

During the next twenty-five minutes, I got one more strike. Missed it. It was getting late into the afternoon, so it was time to go to my last destination.

Pond #3 was lower than I had seen it months earlier. It is fed by many springs, so there is usually no shortage of water to fill the pond. However, excessive water had, at some point, breached part of the earthen berm that held water in the pond, decreasing its depth. Wandering the shoreline, I located the area of deepest water . . . and some rising fish!

The dimming light of evening was fast approaching as I made my first cast. As usual, the cruising risers were just out of reach, so I was never really able to put a cast onto the ring of a rise, but a few times I got close enough. During my brief stay, I got three strikes, landing one small rainbow on the red fly. As I headed to my car for my journey home, a few fish were still rising . . . as always, a little farther than I could realistically reach with limited backcast room.

In reflecting on my day to better ensure fishing success on a future trip to these ponds, I wished I had experimented more with fly patterns and depths at which they were fished. I never cast either of the two rods I had with me with sinking lines on them. There were additional locations at each pond I wished I had had time to fish. I wonder whether pursuing the fish in a float tube would have translated into more strikes? Probably.

One thing I noted was that strikes came within a minute of the cast. When I let the flies rest stationary for two to four minutes, the strike never came. With the in-water visibility limit of about 2 feet, I surmised that the flies had to land near a cruising fish by luck. There was a chance that the gentle splash-down of the flies and indicator drew the attention of the fish. I have certainly seen this reaction on excellent visibility days when I can watch cruising trout as I cast to them. It logically followed that I did not let my flies rest for more than a minute after the cast during the latter half of my fishing day.

Though I had some success, I know I can do better. I should have had two more floating line chironomid rods rigged and ready to cast before I went fishing. My float tube will be with me next time, as will my depth finder. Rather than take fish photos, I will use my stomach pump on them. Lastly, I will start a bit earlier. Review. Analyze. Plan. Go fishing.

## True Simpletons: Chironomid Larvae

If ever there was a commercial fly tier's "dream fly" as a moneymaker, it has to be midge larvae patterns. A skilled tier may be able to knock out a fly in forty-five seconds. If such a fly wholesaled at $10/dozen, that translates into $50/hour. Not bad. If you are a beginning fly-tier, this is an easy fly to start with that will catch fish . . . assuming you know the basics of how to fish it.

Chironomid larvae can be best described as "skinny little worms" that live in the mud, detritus, and vegetation on the lake bottom. Those residing in burrows or tubes in the substrate will leave these temporarily to feed on decomposing plant material or disintegrating organic matter. As they forage, fish will dine on the unprotected larvae. Other free-living, roaming

Even on a cold day chironomids may hatch, and when they do, some fish will look to eat them.

Though simpler fly patterns may work, sometimes a fly tier will tie for himself instead of the fish he will try to catch. Pictured is a glitzed up version of the San Juan Worm, the Turbo Worm. Yes, it does catch fish . . . and fishermen, too. Suspend it under a buoyant dry fly or indicator, and hold on tight.

sorts not residing in mud tubes are available to the fish on a continual basis.

It is logical, then, to fish chironomid larval imitations along the bottom. Though the shallower waters along the edges of the pond or lake can be very good locations to fish larvae flies, there are times that the fish may have retreated to deeper water, and midge larvae will be there. In fact, larvae may be found in water 50 feet deep. This is much deeper than most fly anglers are willing to fish. Count me among this group. Down-riggers and 8-ounce weights are too much for any fly rod I own, so I will max out my pursuits at about 30 feet.

Though the larvae wriggle, it's a stretch to call it swimming. So, when fishing a midge larva fly, get it near the bottom, and fish it with little or no movement. You can troll it as slow as possible for a short distance, then stop to let the fly settle and sit. If you choose to cast and retrieve, I suggest that all you do is attempt to keep your line tight by occasionally taking in the slack with a deathly-slow strip, or a creeping hand-twist retrieve.

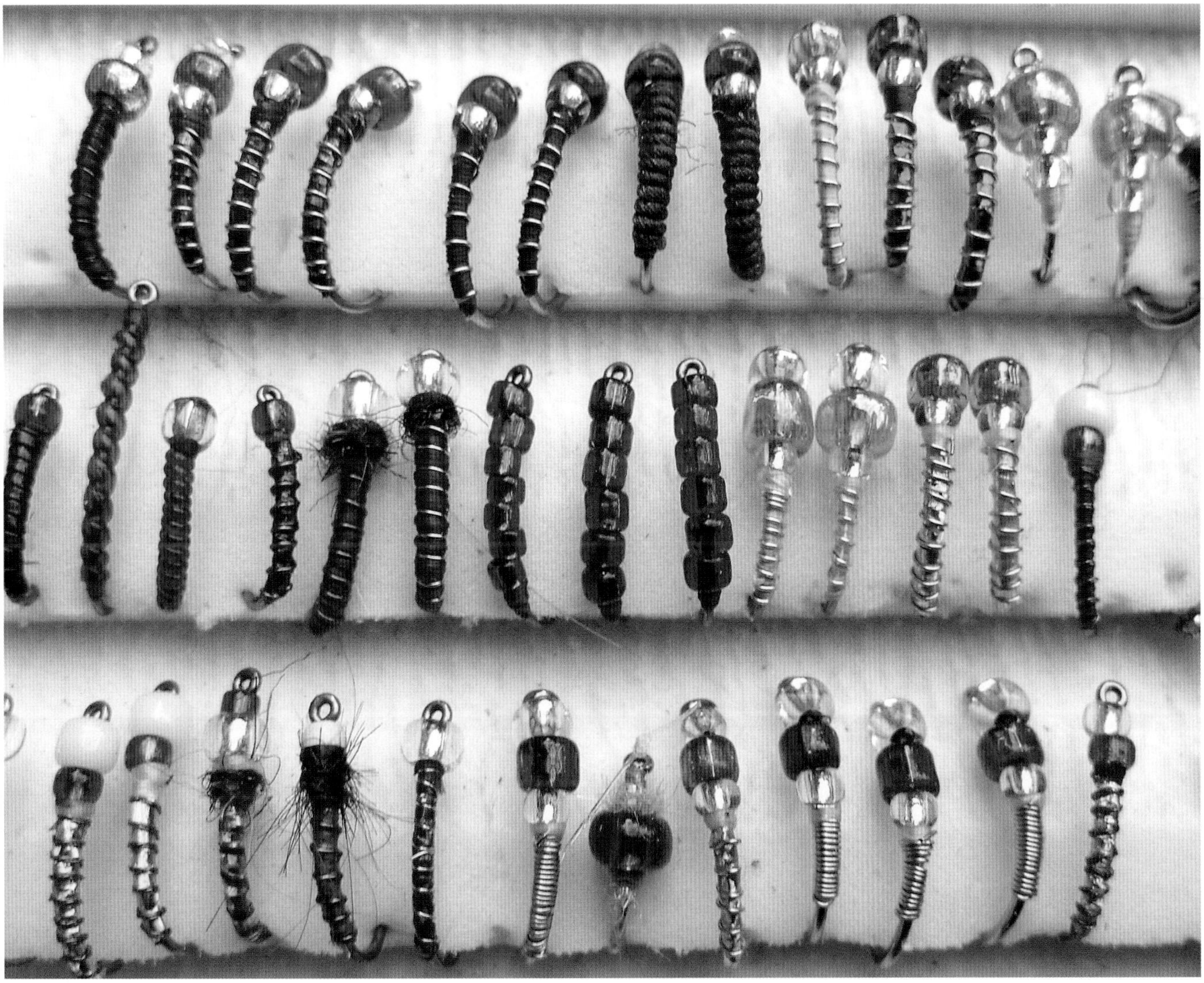

Beads add fun to tying chironomid patterns. I pair a crazy experimental fly with a proven fish-catcher pattern and see what happens. I have had many surprises.

## Hang 'Em Low

An effective method for fishing midge larvae is to suspend them under an indicator. The nearer the bottom, the better. If the bottom is friendly, having the fly sit on the substrate can be good. As the angler moves the fly occasionally, a little "dusty puff" disturbance of the mud or detritus may grab a fish's attention.

An electronic depth finder is indispensable to know precisely the length of leader and tippet needed under the indicator to put the flies near or on the bottom. If you do not have a depth finder, or don't want to hassle with it today, secure your forceps to your line or hook. Drop the system into the water from your watercraft, allowing the forceps to sink to the bottom. Once the system hits the bottom, make note of how much leader or leader and line is required to hit bottom.

I fish two larvae at a time, different colors. Brown, olive, amber, and red are my favorites. I separate the flies by about 18 inches on my leader. If the fish should show a color preference, then I will tie on two of the same.

It is amazing how subtle the fish strike can be. Even when the water's surface is still, a quiet interception of the fly may move the indicator so slightly that you may ignore it, or think it is your imagination. I cannot possibly recount how many times I have lifted my rod tip in response to an "imagined" strike to find a fish on the line. I try not to overreact on the strike, quickly lifting my rod tip a short distance to come tight. If it was truly my imagination, or I missed the strike, I merely drop the tip again, and let the flies settle toward the bottom to await another opportunity.

To visually enhance my larvae patterns, I sometimes incorporate a glass bead of matching color at the head of the fly. I have a few experimental patterns where the entire pattern is nothing but glass beads. However, to be able to slip glass beads onto a hook, their diameters must be much greater than that of the ultrathin midge larva. When I catch fish on such concoctions, I cannot help but wonder if fish really took the fly as a genuine larva, or took it because the fly merely looked interesting and edible.

## Bobbing the Midge

Fishing chironomid pupae under an indicator can make you feel guilty. Some fly anglers hesitate to do it, preferring instead to cast and slowly retrieve the fly. It is an interesting study in human behavior when I encounter those who turn up their noses at fishing a bobber. When their catch is minimal, those who disdain indicators can quickly lose their religion when anglers around them continue to sound off, "Yeehaw! I've got another one."

Fish cruise shorelines for food, making these good areas to dangle a chironomid under an indicator. Experiment to discover the right depth at which to suspend the fly. Often I will cruise directly over areas I will come back later to fish so that I have a very good feel for the depths I will be fishing my flies.

Blue skies can make for pleasant temperatures and beautiful photos, but not necessarily the best fishing conditions, especially when it's breezeless. If you can control the weather, or the timing of your trip, choose an overcast day with a hint of wind.

There is actually a simple solution, an alternative to standard strike indicators. In lieu of cork, foam, plastic, and yarn, use a dry fly. I often fish a *Callibaetis* dry fly as an indicator in late spring and summer. This is particularly effective when both mayflies and midges are available to the fish. I am sure the dry fly may be mistaken for either insect, even though there may be a size discrepancy. Fortunately for us, hungry fish are not always discriminating.

Even a fly that has no living counterpart can catch fish. If you tie a huge fluffy dry fly onto the upper portion of your tippet so it floats high and is easy to see at a great distance, a curious fish may impale itself on it.

There are some days when fish attack my indicator, trying to eat it. Go figure. I learned a long time ago that when this happens, attach a hook or fly to the indicator. On these special occasions, I typically land several fish on my indicator hook.

Good chironomid pupae fishing can be killer even if no hatch of the adults is occurring. Prior to their final ascent to the surface, midge pupae may emerge from the tubes or cases in the substrate where they transformed from larval to pupal form. They may be suspended in the first couple of feet off the bottom for a day or two, exposed and vulnerable to cruising fish. A fly suspended in this zone can be effective. The fishing can be so easy, you may go home early to do your laundry and clean the bathroom.

## It Isn't Always Easy

There are certainly those fishing days when lake fish do not go crazy for chironomids on your initial attempts. Fishing pupal flies near the bottom may only be the starting point for discovery. Because of nearby bottom contours, water temperatures at various depths, light intensity, water clarity, or the presence of flying predators, fish may choose a specific cruising and feeding level. If you get no action near the bottom, begin to experiment with suspending the flies at incrementally lesser depths. I gradually suspend my flies in 1-foot upward adjustments, moving them closer and closer to the surface. Of course, it could be the fly size and color that need adjustments. Carrying multiple rods onboard allows me to quickly switch up. Time is not only money; time is fish.

Even after experimenting with depth, presentation, size, and color, trout may ignore your chironomids. They may go off the bite for a time, or they may turn their focus to other food items. If the area I am fishing is confined, like a small bay, and shallow—10 feet or less—it is possible to spook the fish out of the area for a while. The flies, depth, and method may be correct, but the location to fish them must be changed. If good fishing action tapers off, my first tendency is to move to other locations before making adjustments to my gear or method. On waters I am familiar with, I make the rounds. I go from location A to B to C, and so on. Eventually I return to my starting point, to repeat my travels throughout the day. Fishing with companions can help you track the nomadic wanderings of the fish. With multiple companions, there are times I can accurately follow the movements of the fish moving along a shoreline, as fishing pressure moves from one area to another. The movements of the fish can be easily observed if they are feeding on pupae in or near the surface. Their rise activity will move from one location to another in response to fishing activities that disturb them.

## Fishing Naked

Sometimes, chironomid pupae must be fished in water deeper than 10 feet. With a fixed indicator, this presents an obvious difficulty. If an angler is using a standard 9-foot fly rod, a fish that has taken a fly 15 feet below an indicator that won't slide on the line is hard to land. Even when the angler reaches as high as possible with arms fully extended, the fish may still be under the surface, out of reach of a hand or the net. Imagine a depth of 25 feet with a fixed, non-sliding indicator!

There are a couple of solutions. One possibility involves a term I first heard coined in Canada: fishing naked. What is meant by this is fishing chironomid pupae on a l-o-n-g leader without the aid of an indicator. Fished with a floating fly line, a leader of up to 40 feet (!) is cast into depths of 25 to 30 feet.

Here's how you set up. After determining the depth, a leader that is approximately 25 percent longer than the depth is to be used. As an example, if the water is 20 feet deep, use a leader that measures 25 feet. For leaders of 20 feet or longer, I start with a butt section of monofilament line with a 0.025-inch constant diameter. To this I attach a store-bought 12-foot tapered leader with a butt diameter that measures 0.022 or 0.023 inch,

**25'–30' Leader**

I have found this very simple formula for constructing a l-o-n-g leader to be reasonably easy to cast and effective for fishing chironomids deep without the use of an indicator.

and an appropriate tippet diameter, typically 4X, 5X, or 6X, depending on the fly size and the fishing conditions. The length of the butt section is the difference between my overall desired leader length *minus* my 12-foot tapered leader. For instance, if I want an overall leader length of 30 feet, I will use a 0.025-inch butt section of 18 feet.

30' overall leader length – 12' tapered leader =
18' butt section of 0.025" diameter

I use a double surgeon's knot to secure the butt section and tapered leader.

Casting such a long leader can put immediate fear into the heart of any fly caster. Getting the system airborne and executing a cast where the line and leader land fully extended on the water can be a daunting task. It all starts with leader construction. Secondly, a certain amount of fly line must be left beyond the rod tip as the cast begins. I suggest a length of fly line approximately equal to the length of the leader. Finally, the sunken fly must be coaxed to the surface in a specific manner just prior to the beginning of the cast. This is most easily accomplished with a series of roll casts that extend the line and raise

When I am casting a 20- to 30-foot leader, any way to gain elevation for the cast will make it easier. Here, I am standing on the bow deck of my drift boat.

the leader and fly to the surface. After two or three roll casts to lift and extend the line/leader system, send the line overhead and to your rear into an initial backcast. With one or two false casts, send the fly to its destination.

A slightly weighted fly will make for a quicker descent. Chironomid patterns with a tungsten beadhead are a good solution. Experiment with a countdown before you commence to retrieve with a very slow strip or hand-twist retrieve. The descent to the bottom can take a couple of minutes. If your fly gets fowled with vegetation, shorten the countdown.

If you know you are fishing very near the bottom but not getting strikes, shorten the countdown systematically in 10-count increments. The fish may prefer intercepting chironomid pupae at level higher up in the water column.

As always, use the stomach pump on the first worthy fish you catch to make certain your fly closely approximates the naturals in size and color. If the water is extremely clear and the sun is high, it might be necessary to decrease the tippet size.

As with anything else worth doing, preparation and practice are the foundations. For those who want to be more proactively involved in their chironomid fishing, not relying on the much more passive endeavor of staring at an indicator, fishing naked is the solution.

## Deep Water Indicators

Another nifty piece of chironomid fishing equipment I saw for the first time in Canada is a slip strike indicator. This is the answer to fishing long leaders and indicators. The striking movement of the rod tip, or the subsequent pull on the line by a fleeing fish, disengages the indicator from its fixed position on the leader. This allows the indicator to slide freely up and down the leader while the fish is played.

A slip strike indicator is the best type to use when using leaders of 10 feet or more. It will break free and slide down the leader when a fish pulls hard against the rod.

Once you see how it is set up on the leader, the mechanics of the slip indicator are ingeniously simple. The indicator has two parts: a body of cork or buoyant foam with a hole bored through its center and a hollow peg that nestles into the hole. Before tying on a fly, slip the leader through the hollow peg, which is fitted into the hole in the indicator. Slide the pegged indicator to the desired location on the leader. Disengage the peg for a moment, pulling it up the leader a few inches toward the rod tip. Grab the leader immediately below the peg, and pull a small loop of line up to and alongside the peg. Slide the indicator up and onto the peg, wedging the small line loop between the indicator and peg. A tiny loop of line will be visible above the indicator.

Experiment with how snugly the peg is pushed into the hole of the indicator. It must be tight enough that the indicator does not disengage while casting, but not so snug that a quick lift of the rod tip against resistance or a fighting fish cannot free the peg from the indicator, allowing it to slide freely.

## Easy Peasy, Lemon Squeezy

I have saved the easiest chironomid fishing method for last. For maximum sinkage, string up the fly line with the fastest descent rating. Locate your fishing craft directly over the deep water (15 feet or more) that you want to fish. No cast required. Having determined the exact depth of the water, drop your fly/leader/line system off the side of the boat and start stripping line from the reel. Let out that length of leader and line so that your point fly is suspended barely above the bottom, directly below you. Next, wait for a cruising fish to bite your fly. If nothing happens, slowly lift your rod tip a few feet, then slowly lower the tip again. Repeat as needed. Easy and cheesy, but this can be deadly effective. If you doze off, don't drop your rod.

## Cast and Puff

A long time ago in a land far away (Idaho), my friends Jeff Hilden, Josh Cuperus, and I were fishing Henry's Lake. It was the first time for Josh and me; Jeff had fished it with a guide on a previous trip. By default, Jeff was now our guide. Fortunately, he has an excellent job outside the world of fly fishing to pay the bills and provide for his family.

After a fruitless morning of trying this and that, here and there, I pulled my float tube out of the water to wander the shoreline in search of hope. My plan was to watch for anglers who might offer me a clue about where the fish were and what fly they might eat. What I wanted to see more than anything was an angler with a bent rod. There was lots of chatter on the lake, but not the excited whooping associated with playing a fish. I had now wandered far away from Josh and Jeff, when I saw him.

Josh Cuperus displays a Henry's Lake cutthroat. Sometimes, a slow troll of a chironomid can be effective. Troll only as fast as you need to in order to keep the line tight.

There was an elderly man fishing solo in his pram, a little flat-bottom aluminum boat, a stone's throw from the shore. He was anchored with his back to me—perfect. I could watch him and not be watched. He eventually netted and released an excellent trout, then released it. In no obvious hurry, Pram Man lit a cigarette, settled himself, and made a cast. By the color of the line and the orientation it quickly assumed, I was positive he was using a sinking line. Once the line settled on the water, he sat down, still with his back to me. For the next couple of minutes he did nothing except sit and puff, absorbed in his waiting and his cigarette.

When he sensed the time was right, Pram Man made a couple of slow, short pulls on the fly line. By now, the line appeared to be almost straight down from his rod tip, almost below his boat. If he had chosen to, my man could have merely stripped line from his reel and let it sink straight down; it would have had exactly the same effect. He was obviously in deep water. Whereas we had been fishing all morning in water that was probably no more than 4 feet deep in most locations, this guy was parked over a hole. My bloodhound had sniffed out the spot I needed to know about. And to confirm it, he soon hooked another trout. Time for me to launch my tube for closer inspection . . . and some fishing.

As stealthy and as nonchalant as an excited fisherman can be, I kicked my craft out of the shallows. Not wanting to be perceived immediately as an intruder, my path was not directly toward Pram Man. I stayed well away from him, but always in position to watch him. Considerately, he was always fishing with his back to me. The fact he was always facing the same direction encouraged me to get a bit closer to his position. Approaching at a nonintrusive distance toward the rear of his boat, I made my first cast in his direction.

I was fishing a sparsely dressed Peacock Nymph. I was prompted to use this fly by a story someone had told me about his fishing day at Henry's Lake. Somewhere in the tale, a veteran angler had said the phrase "Thin is in!" making reference to his successful fly. Somehow, I had connected "thin is in" to a fly called the Skinny Minnie, a pattern with a slender thread or peacock body. Thus, my modified Prince Nymph with the skinny body was the fly of choice, in lieu of a more standard chironomid pupa pattern.

As I mirrored the cast, wait, and retrieve rhythm of Pram Man, hope was growing. The hole over which he and I were fishing had a circumference large enough that I could keep my distance. Since the angler was parked over the center of what must have been a large spring, I stayed on its edge, and continued to cast in his general direction. Just like in the movies, I was soon into my first Henry's Lake cutthroat. With the aid of my stomach pump, I quickly extracted numerous chironomid pupae the fish had eaten recently.

The pupae of some midge species have prominent white gill filaments protruding from the front side and dorsal part of the thorax. When present, this stark feature should be imitated in the design of the artificials.

Though my fly was not a perfect match for what the trout were consuming, I stayed with the peacock imitation and caught more fish, just as Pram Man did. The most important thing to the fish—besides this sweet location in deep water—was the manner in which the fly was fished: low and slow. As the fly was lifted vertically, straight up from the bottom, the strikes were most likely to occur.

Eventually, the action slowed as the sun got higher and the day grew warmer. As I went in search of greener pastures, I watched Pram Man lift his anchor and head for shore, confirming that the bite was off for now. For a while, the fishing had been easy peasy. And, later that evening it was again.

## Makes Little Sense, But . . .

Trolling chironomid pupae doesn't seem to make much sense on a couple of counts: one, they can barely move, wriggling instead of swimming, and two, their direction of movement is vertical, not horizontal. However, some of my angling friends and I have caught numerous fish over the years slowly pulling chironomids behind a float tube. It usually starts out as an accident. Moving from one location to another on a lake, the flies are left in the water, rather than reeling them up, as we travel from one spot to the next. Fish on! What worked on one fish will usually work on another.

Inquiring minds might want to know if the chironomid fly was taken because the fish actually thought it was a real chironomid, or if the fish ate it because they were willing to grab anything small and buggy that swam into their zone, not concerned about its exact identification. Whatever the motive for consumption in those wee little fish brains, trolling a chironomid will sometimes catch fish. During such times as these, the trout may seem like creatures of little discrimination. The trap for the stillwater angler, especially one with little experience,

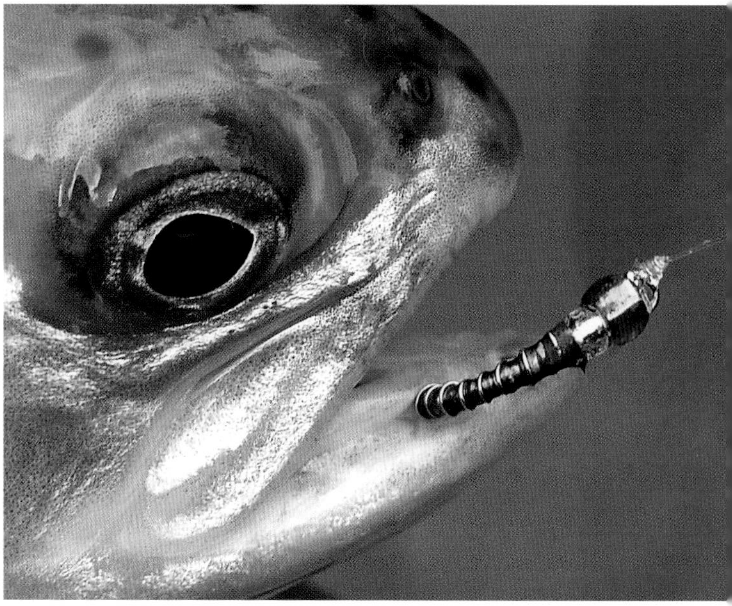

Chironomid patterns lend themselves to quick and simple experiments with colors and materials. Some experiments turn into fish-catching winners.

is to assume that trout can often be tricked into to doing something so illogical. If this is the assumption, humility and frustration are only one trip away. Enjoy trolling midges when you can, but don't underestimate a fish's intelligence, especially the bigger, older fish. They know how to survive, and long durations of gullibility are not likely.

## More Thoughts on Chironomid Flies

I enjoy tying simple flies. The simpler and faster the pattern, the more variations and experimental models I can tie. In a given fishing year, I tie more chironomid pupae than all other patterns combined. Fun colors such as red, purple, orange, blue, silver, gold, and kelly green are used in my fly tying. I had a couple of clients in my retail days who swore that a purple midge pupa was the Holy Grail of stillwater fishing.

The use of metal, plastic, and glass beads on some patterns can be very effective. Sometimes I wonder if the fish that bite flies with beads are biting the hook because they think they are eating an enticing mutant chironomid pupa, or they are merely attracted to the bead that happens to be attached to the body of the imitation. Previously, I had made mention of catching several trout one day when all that remained on the hook were some turns of thread and a glass bead. There are days when fly pattern is irrelevant. The fish are hungry and they just want something to eat. I remember to appreciate such days, especially those days when fish are hard to fool, even when I am using my best of the best flies.

The downside of having too many fish fall for my silly experimental flies is that I can lose a little respect for the fish. While it's fun for a while to catch fish on anything and everything, it is the challenge of successfully wooing difficult fish that gives me the most pleasure. Catching fish that others cannot is my personal ultimate achievement. I don't always win, but losing only makes me more determined. And, fortunately, I will never have the final answer. This is as it should be for me. There's always one more difficult fish to challenge me.

## Say It Again: Thin Is In!

It isn't just fashion models who know it. Chironomid larvae and pupae are thin. Your flies should be thin, too. When you look at the full length of your larvae flies, and the abdominal portion of your pupal patterns, if you ask yourself, "Is this body too thick, too rotund?" the answer is probably "Yes!" I know some very good chironomid anglers who fashion the main body of the fly out of fly-tying thread, or wrap the hook with a single strand of floss. Can't get much thinner than this until you fish a bare hook.

As I write this chapter, I am thinking of a new experimental pupa tied on a red anodized hook. I will secure some silver wire—without using thread—at the rear of the hook shank and spiral it onto the bare hook. I will secure the wire near the small bead at the hook eye. The only items on the hook will be six or seven turns of fine silver wire, a tiny bead, and a few turns of thread to secure everything at the head. Then, of course, I must do the same thing with a black hook and a bronze hook. By using different hook finishes, a variety of hook sizes and multiples of each, a range of wire colors, and all sorts of beads—glass, metal, plastic, lots of colors—all of a sudden I will have a hundred new chironomid pupae flies to try!

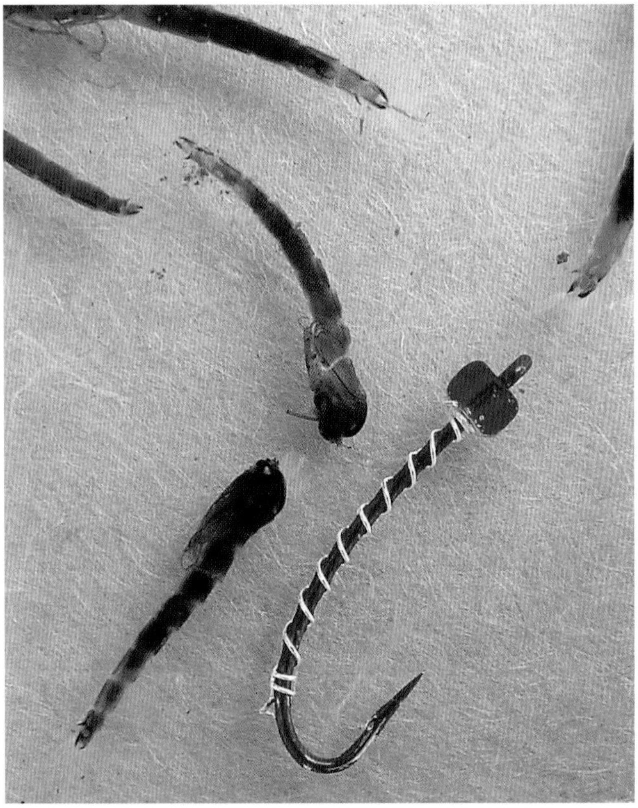

Taking thin to the extreme, wire can be spiraled onto a bare hook to create a chironomid pupa fly. Super glue holds the wire in place.

## Silver and Glass Mimic the Gas

As midge pupae prepare for their ascent to the surface, they are assisted in their upward journeys by the generation and trapping of gas bubbles beneath the skin. This buoyancy aid complements their feeble swimming efforts as they slowly float to the surface, where the thorax will split and the adult will emerge. The shiny, silvery appearance of the gas bubbles is an obvious attribute of the pupae as hungry fish intercept them. It only seems logical that this silvery sheen should be incorporated into some of the pupal fly patterns in your fly box.

Silver wire, silver and pearl tinsels, and clear glass, white and silver beads—either separately, or in concert—serve to enhance the gas bubble effect of attractive midge pupae patterns. I find that I tend to favor these flies, especially when the fish become more selective. And, of course, there are endless combinations of colors, finishes, and sizes that use these bubble-mimicking materials. My inclination at this very moment is to stop writing and start tying flies. I can't wait!

## Other Obvious Important Characteristics of Killer Pupae Patterns

Besides being very slim, the abdomen of the midge pupa is very obviously segmented. To maximize the authenticity of the artificial imitation, ribbing material, usually wire, creates the segmented look. Red and silver are the two most favored colors. Sometimes I use white thread.

Glass and silver beads can often enhance chironomid pupae patterns. The sheen created by these beads mimics the shiny appearance of gas-inflated insects as they drift toward the surface.

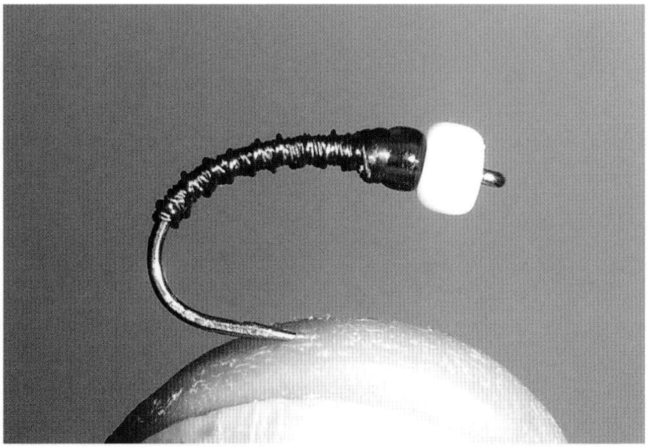

To simulate the prominent gill or respiration filaments found on some species of hatching chironomids, a small tuft of white Antron or polypropylene yarn, or a white bead, is placed near the hook eye.

The head and thorax appear fused, and distinctly larger than the abdomen, roughly twice the diameter. The head/thorax unit comprises about one quarter of the insect's total length and is often darker in coloration than the abdomen. Most good pupae patterns suggest these.

Prominent white respiration filaments on the top of the head/thorax region are very obvious to fish that eat them. A little tuft of white Antron or polypropylene yarn or ostrich herl simulates this feature. Some patterns, like the Ice Cream Cone Chironomid, use a white bead at the eye of the hook to simulate the filaments.

## It's a Team Effort

If my chironomid fishing efforts are sketchy, instead of fishing two midge patterns, I typically replace the point fly with a scud, Micro Leech, or damselfly nymph, additional members of my "A" Team. The point fly is easier and faster to switch than the dropper. Food preferences for stillwater fish can change hourly, it seems. Therefore, I experiment to discover what fish may want for the moment, the fly du jour. During this experimentation, the last fly to be replaced is the chironomid dropper. Because midges—particularly in the pupal stage—are so important in a lake fish's diet, this fly will always receive maximum playing time; it's only fitting for the "A" Team captain.

## Fishing Adult Chironomid Emerger Imitations

As the midge hatch progresses, and the bottom and midwater regions become less populated with pupae ascending toward the surface, the fish will eventually start to key on the struggling pupae at the water's surface trying to extricate themselves from their skins to make the final transition into winged adults.

A chironomid emerger fly with a body and "tail" of filoplume or marabou feathers simulates the ragged appearance of an adult midge squirming out of its pupal skin. This fly sits vertically on the surface.

Because feeding fish taking the surface pupae make a disturbance that looks like a rise to a floating adult, fishermen can be fooled and frustrated fishing adult imitations with minimal or no takes. Remember to look for the bubble that typically remains for a moment during the rise to a floating insect. No bubble, and no takes on your high-floating fly? Tie on an emerger.

Chironomid emerger patterns are fished on the surface, or barely beneath it. I particularly like flies that sit rather vertical on the water with the rear end subsurface and the forward half positioned above the waterline.

## Fishing Adult and Emerger Chironomid Imitations

When the chironomid hatch wanes, those fish with unsated appetites will turn to what remains: emergers at the surface and the winged adults. Here's a chance to strike to the rise. Most fly anglers relish surface opportunities because watching a trout revealing itself as it grabs the fly is always an adrenaline rush.

Midging trout can make for exciting surface fishing. Light tippets and adrenaline can be a dangerous mix.

Because fish as individuals may have particular food preferences at the surface—some taking only adults, some taking only emergers, and some taking both—the easy solution to make sure you get all comers is to fish both a dry fly and an emerger simultaneously. As to which fly goes where on the leader, I try to determine which fly I have the least certainty about. The fly that I anticipate needing to change the most often is the one I tie on the point because it is most easily switched out; the fly I am most confident in I tie on the dropper.

When fishing surface flies, I want to make sure the leader and tippet near the flies sink. A commercial wetting agent like Gehrke's Xink will enable the tippet and a few feet of leader nearest the dropper fly to break the surface film and sink. This is important because a floating leader and tippet create a slight depression as they lie on the water's surface. This, in turn, results in a shadow of the line, which may alarm wary trout. Too often I have watched cruising trout approach a surface fly only to reject it at the last second when they see the shadow cast by the leader that dimples the surface. Here's another little detail of importance. Unless an angler understands what actually caused the rejection of his fly, he may attribute the refusal to the wrong cause. It is not necessarily the fly pattern that caused the fish to flee, but possibly the shadow of the leader.

Some readers might have an obvious concern here: won't the sinking leader and tippet pull the dry fly and emerger underwater? Usually not. There is enough buoyancy in well designed and treated surface flies to resist being pulled under. With emergers that sit vertically in the water, I treat the front half of the fly with floatant, and dress the dry fly in its entirety. This retards the absorption of water and further aids in keeping the flies on top.

In lieu of a wetting agent, the use of fluorocarbon leaders and tippets aids in the solution of the sinkability problem. Compared to standard monofilament and copolymer materials, fluorocarbon is more inclined to sink of its own accord.

And be prepared with 6X or 7X tippets. It is common to fish adult midge patterns in sizes 18 and 20. If there is no breeze to riffle the surface, lengthening the leader to 14 to 16 feet may be the difference in enticing the fish.

## Heave It and Leave It?

It's definitely worth the effort to try to locate a concentration of rising chironomid-eating fish. This will maximize the chance a fish will find your surface flies. When the rises are sporadic and spread out, it's a lottery game that your flies will be seen. Take

If the fish are taking adult chironomids from the surface but refuse your stationary fly, skate it slowly for a short distance, wait for a count of 10, then repeat. Pictured is a Lady McConnell variation.

a few moments to scan for a small area where there may be a lot of rise activity.

As for presentation, make sure the flies are cast so that the leader extends fully above the water's surface and then gently falls, not splashing down hard. An errant cast can startle the fish and sink the flies, too. Once the flies have landed, prepare your patience. Heaving and leaving the flies can be tough on Type A personalities. I tend to count to myself so I get a true gauge of how long the flies have remained motionless. After about a minute, I will either pick it up to recast, or slowly lift my rod tip to reposition the flies closer to me by about 3 feet. The new location created by sliding the flies to me, or the waking movement of the flies, may trigger a response.

Some adult chironomids will "taxi" across the surface like a tiny float plane getting a running start on the water before takeoff. Fish recognize this commotion and the resulting wake, and may be enticed to take slowly skittering flies which imitate the "taxiing before takeoff" maneuver. The last time I fished surface chironomids, the rising fish I encountered and hooked were only interested in my flies as I gently lifted my rod tip to activate the flies.

The Griffith's Gnat is an effective imitation of an adult midge, fished both stationary and skated. It's an All-Star Team member.

For adult midge fly patterns, flies like the well-known Parachute Adams and Griffith's Gnat do an excellent job in the right sizes. The Parachute Adams, in particular, is easy to see because of its erect white post. I have also had good results with simple "buzz style" patterns. These have a simple prescription of hackle fibers tail, thin dubbed fur body, and a couple of turns of a high-quality rooster hackle at the front. No wing or rib. Simple. Cream, black, gray, tan, and olive adequately cover the spectrum. Sizes 14–20 are most useful.

CHAPTER 9

# Fishing Dry Flies and Emergers

This brown trout could not resist a Stimulator when caddisflies were on the water. Because the adult caddis flutters and skates as it tries to take off, it is best to mimic this same movement with your artificial.

Asked to pick the ultimate moment in a broad spectrum of fly-fishing experiences, it's safe to bet many anglers would choose the rise of a big trout to a dry fly. The thrill, the rush of watching the rise to a floating fly can linger in the mind's eye for a lifetime. As a kid, I watched an 11-inch cutthroat trout rise in the soft glare of a setting sun. I could see the dimpling silhouette of my fly as it sat on the water. The fish had risen a couple of times before I made my cast, and it was youthful hope and anticipation that excited me when my Adams landed in the trout's proximity. The rise was gentle but certain, and I raised my rod tip to secure the hook. I remember nothing about the ensuing fight other than the fact that I landed the magnificently-spotted cutthroat and made a quick measurement. What I will never forget, though, is the dimpling interception of my floating fly on that beautiful summer evening. The fish was not huge, and I only caught the one, but I will always be able to relive that shining moment of the strike. Even after a lifetime of subsequent fly fishing, I smile every time I recall the rise of that particular trout. This is the grip, the thrill, the potential of fishing dry flies.

With rare exception, I will see rising trout sometime during every fishing day on lakes and ponds. Often, the surface activity is sparse and sporadic, with no consistency in or concentration of the rising fish. As a consequence, there are many days on the water I never cast a dry fly or emerger. Because of my low expectations of finding and casting floating flies to rising fish, I have missed some good opportunities. My dry-fly rod is left in my 4Runner, parked too far for this lazy man to retrieve it. And I'm not willing to clip off the flies to re-rig my leader on one of the rods I have with me on my float tube or pontoon boat.

## *Iners:* Latin for Idle or Lazy

Isaac Newton was a smart guy. Besides being inspired by falling apples, he knew a lot about mathematics, physics, and human nature. In Newton's classic *Philosophiæ Naturalis Principia Mathematica*, we find his First Law of Physics, which addresses inertia. In part it states: "An object at rest remains at rest until acted upon by an external force." I think you can quickly see an application here to human nature, especially when you consider the Latin root of inertia, which is *iners*, meaning idle or lazy. In my particular case, a fisherman (idle, lazy) at rest tends to stay at rest (he thinks he's too far from his vehicle), sometimes even if acted upon by an external force (rising fish). That's right. I miss some dry-fly fishing opportunities because of Newton's First Law; I am overcome by inertia . . . unless I correct this shortcoming and act accordingly.

Even in late winter I can find trout rising to adult midges. As the numbers of ascending pupae diminish, and the hatch is winding down, hungry fish eat the adults because that's all that remains readily available. When it comes to dancing with fish, remember: the fish always lead. It is the fish that steer the fishing method. So, periodically I need to remind myself if the fish prefer dry flies, give 'em what they want. To this end I must be prepared with my dry-fly setup in advance. Before I get to my lake for the day, I want to have already prepared a dry-fly rod, guides strung and flies tied on the leader, ready to cast. I have done a preemptive strike on my inertia before it comes into play. And, my dry-fly rod is onboard with me, not snoozing quietly in my 4Runner.

## The Seasons of the Dry Fly Pattern Selection

Because my dry-fly rod is set up in advance of my next stillwater trip, I make my best guess as to what might be hatching. Late winter and early spring, I focus on midges. On my dry-fly rod you are most likely to find an emerger imitation on the dropper. Rising fish have usually learned it is easier to intercept a chironomid helplessly struggling to free itself from its straight jacket skin than an adult with wings ready to zoom off into the yonder just as an open mouth seeks to grab it. On the point, about 2 feet below the dropper fly, I tie on something generic like a Griffith's Gnat, Midge Sparkle Dun, or Parachute Adams. 6X and 7X fluorocarbon leaders are my usual choices.

Mating caddisflies, Scuitto Lake, BC. I am still working on the fly design to simulate two caddisflies in the throes of passion.

As late April and May arrive, I anticipate that certain lakes I fish will have *Callibaetis* mayflies beginning to emerge late morning through midafternoon. Quality central Washington lakes, like Dry Falls, Lenice, and Nunnally, have great hatches of these mayflies late April and early May. Here I will tie a Parachute Adams or tan Compara-dun or Sparkle Dun on the dropper. On the point, I secure an unweighted tan soft-hackle fly, an unweighted Pheasant Tail Nymph, or Filoplume Emerger. Because I may only occasionally change the dropper fly, and I will experiment more with unweighted nymphs and emergers, I put the latter flies on the point to facilitate a quick and easy change of the flies.

As the season progresses into late spring through midsummer, caddisflies and damselflies come into play. When caddisflies are hatching, I'm inclined to put the dry fly on the dropper

Caddisfly adults are very active as they try to fly from the surface after hatching. Twitching and skating the fly a short distance can prompt the fish to strike.

and the emerger imitation on the point. It is the emerging fly with which I will experiment most. When the fish are keying on adult damselflies it is one of those rare occasions when I will fish only one fly. These patterns tend to be big and air-resistant, making them harder to cast. For ease of casting, I don't pair up a second fly with adult damsels. Also, at this time of year, with the potential of dry-fly activity at its zenith, I may actually carry two rigged dry-fly rods on my watercraft. The additional rod will have *Callibaetis*, caddis, or midge adults and emergers already tied on and ready to rock.

## The Buffet Is Open

Late spring and summer, it's possible to have overlapping hatches of different insects on the water. As an example, it is not uncommon on a June day on many productive lakes to find emerging midges, mayflies, caddisflies, and damsels. At any given time during the day, the fish may focus on one particular group and ignore the rest. Then, rudely, they change their preference without announcement. You can bet I have my stomach/throat pump handy and in frequent use, as I try to stay with the current dietary focus of interest. And I know that the preferred buffet choices can vacillate between surface and subsurface items. When scuds and leeches are added to today's buffet menu, it can be quite challenging. This is why I am a big proponent of multiple rods all locked and loaded when I hit the water. At such times as these, I want a minimum of three, but four rods is significantly better. In my float tube, three rods elevated across my lap and one in my hand can be a little troublesome, but manageable. My suggestion is find a way to make this doable. Remember inertia.

## A Day on Blue Dun Lake

It was a stereotypical bluebird day in June on Blue Dun Lake. I launched midmorning under cloudless skies, with four rigged rods looking for fish trouble. I was fishing in a small pram by myself, so there was plenty of room for my rods, lined precisely like soldiers in a row. I anchored in what I thought to be a centralized location where I could cast 360 degrees into water deep enough for patrolling rainbows.

Since there was no surface activity, I began with my usual searching duo of a Bead Prince paired with a Midnight Bugger. Casting and varying the stripping length and speed, I picked up a couple of quality, hard-fighting trout to get the day started. There would be no skunk today.

Within the first thirty minutes of my launch, a few fish started to quietly break the surface. The rises were sporadic and not centralized. Also, I started to see a few chironomid adults pushed on the surface by a very gentle breeze that came and

A stomach sampling indicates the fish that gave up its lunch had a strong preference for *Callibaetis* mayfly nymphs. During emergence, the nymphs can hang in the surface, struggling to extricate themselves from their nymphal skins. A filoplume emerger fished as a dry fly is deadly in this situation.

went. Because the rises were soft and unhurried, I speculated that the trout were not taking adults, but, rather, helpless midge pupae just under or at the surface. Further, I could not detect a bubble inside the rise ring, another clue that the fish were feeding on something subsurface. Chironomid pupae under an indicator seemed a good choice. And it was, as I hooked and landed three or four fish in the next hour.

Then I started seeing a few splashy rises, different from the gentle types earlier. With a little focused looking on the lake's surface I spied a few *Callibaetis* mayfly duns. A few of these flies I was able to watch for several minutes before they drifted beyond my sight or flew off.

None that I watched were taken by a fish, even though rises happened around and near them. I had a rod set up with a floating line, and a tan Compara-dun on the dropper and an unweighted Epoxy Back Callibaetis Nymph on the point. A few casts into my new duo a 14-inch rainbow slammed my nymph as I slowly stripped back. Then another and another. Life was good. If the fish switched to the adult, I was already rigged. And, yes, the switch did come. For a brief spurt I had trout alternating back and forth between taking the nymph and taking the dry fly. And then it was over. The insects disappeared and the surface activity ceased.

I switched back to chironomids under a float, even though there were no chironomids on the surface. Nothing. So I picked up my leech and Prince rod on my clear intermediate line to cast and strip. The action was not fast in my last hour, but I managed to coax a couple more fish before packing it in for the day. The fishing had been changeable and a bit challenging—just the way I like it. To catch fish throughout the day as the buffet changes is always rewarding. The cerebral part of the sport of fly fishing speaks to me, as I am sure it does to many others who love some intrigue and puzzle-solving.

## Pass the Formic Acid, Please

For attack and defense ants use formic acid, which they can naturally produce. Fish may like—total speculation on my part—the flavoring effect of formic acid on ants they eat. Bottom line: fish love ants.

In the spring, when the temperature, humidity, and weather are just right, winged male ants and winged virgin queen ants leave their nests on mating flights. The females emit pheromones to attract the males, and mating commences. As their reward, the mated males soon die, while the mated females zoom off to try to establish a new colony. If successful, the queen will sire every individual in her colony for years to come. She may live for more than twenty years, never to fly again. She can tap into the sperm she has received and stored for the next two decades.

It is during these mating flights that ants can fall into lakes and ponds. Carry a few ants in your fly box. Ants have virtually no swimming ability because their legs are extremely skinny. The "heave it and leave it" fishing method seems to be best with ants.

## Additional Challenges to Be Met

A little breeze to ruffle the water's surface is a very good thing. From an underwater perspective, the light is dappled and a fly riding on the surface has a little bouncing movement. Both of these make the job of detecting an artificial fly a little harder. Additionally, a fly fisherman waving a rod back and forth, and a fly line that hits the water just a bit too forcefully, can be obscured with a little breeze. The bells and whistles of a fish's alarm system aren't as easily set off. A light breeze is always good.

If the air is dead still, an angler fishing a dry fly or emerger on the surface needs to understand the challenges of a delicate presentation coupled with minimal casting strokes. With a flat lake, an elevated-well-above-the-surface fly caster can be seen from a considerable distance. A fly line that splashes down hard will be both audible and visible to the fish. Even when the fly lands gently, it can be closely studied by any fish considering eating it. If the tippet attached to the fly is floating and creating a dimpled depression in the surface film, it will cast an alarming shadow. The shadow is particularly critical in shallow water where it is seen not only looking up, but also possibly in shadow on the lake bottom. Both can raise a red flag to experienced lunker fish, who became lunkers because they have finely tuned alarm systems. The less attuned, easily fooled fish have probably gone home in someone's cooler a few days ago, before you got there.

I remember fishing a desert lake one summer day a hundred years ago under a bright sun in dead-calm conditions. The visibility was excellent for both fishermen and cruising trout. The patrolling fish were searching in water that was no more than 30 inches deep. They were looking specifically for mayflies on the surface. My tan Compara-dun was a close match, and the fish were definitely attracted to my fly. So when I got refusal after refusal, I was confused. I soon discerned it was my tippet creating a crease in the surface film and a resulting shadow. Fortunately, I had a treatment in my vest to cause the tippet and the

When the surface of a lake or pond is dead calm, the fish get a very good look at what they might eat. If fish are being selective, envision what they are seeing.

A leader or tippet that floats casts a shadow that can startle fish. A wetting agent applied to the line will cause it to sink, effectively eliminating the shadow.

lower half of my leader to sink below the surface, while my fly stayed on top, refusing to let the sunken portion of the leader pull it down through the resistant surface film. Once I figured that out, catching the fish was no problem.

As an aside, to get a little understanding about the strength of the molecular bond of water molecules, conduct a little experiment in the kitchen. All you need is a full glass of water and a needle. Even though the needle is made of metal, with no inherent buoyancy, it will float. Hold the needle close to the water, and gently drop the needle sideways/broadside onto the water, and it will not sink. It will be supported by the surface tension inherent to water, based on the molecular bonding strength of the water molecules. Think of all those little molecules holding hands tightly enough to support that metal needle. If the needle is dropped on its end onto the water, it pierces the surface tension without hesitation. Think of a perfect vertical dive compared to a belly flop. Science class is adjourned now.

The resistance of the surface film to being too easily penetrated works in both directions. Little aquatic insects who reach the surface to hatch into adults must pierce the surface tension to get on top of the water. Some are unable to do so quickly

When exact color is important to selective fish, look at the underside of a floating insect to see what the fish sees. The belly color can definitely deviate in shade or color from the dorsal (top) side of the insect.

enough. Suddenly they are taken out of the gene pool by a merciless fish.

When I cast during dead-calm times, I do my best to cast to a point above the water's surface. That is, I want the line and leader to fully extend above the water and then softly fall—not splash—onto the water. I use a fluorocarbon tippet that has some degree of sinkablity, better than that of monofilament and copolymer types. Additionally, I will treat the last half of my leader, right up to the flies, with a potion to "wet" it and sink it, preventing the shadow. Fluorocarbon has also been proven more difficult for fish to see when compared to monofilament and copolymers of the same diameter.

As for leader length, think long when it's calm; 15 to 16 feet from fly line to the fly may be necessary. Put more distance between the flies and that splashing, shadow-casting fly line.

In calm conditions, the size shape and color of your flies might have to more closely approximate the naturals the fish are choosing. Focusing on color, sometimes the underside of an insect may be different from the topside, or dorsal view, of the bug. Typically the underside is a shade or three lighter. A brown insect can have a tan underside. If possible, inspect the belly of the naturals to determine the best color match for your artificial.

A strong wind will certainly disguise your presence and mediocre casting efforts, but it will also blow the little insect sailboats at a furious pace toward the shoreline. This is one environmental factor that can delay or end the day's fishing. If the wind is sporadic and manageable, and I want to continue fishing, anchoring is my immediate challenge. In my bigger boats, I must anchor both bow and stern. Casting is naturally downwind. It is because of the wind that I always check a weather report before I go fishing. If windy conditions are predicted, I may decide to go elsewhere or not go at all, tying flies, editing photos, or catching up on my writing instead.

## Add Some Action to Get Some Action

I mentioned earlier the technique of sometimes lifting the rod tip to gently skate imitations of adult midges; the same holds true for other insects that can buzz and whir on the surface. Specifically, I am talking about caddisflies and adult damselflies.

In Canada, you hear about some adult caddisflies referred to as "traveling sedges." These little buggers appear to run on the surface as if fleeing for their lives; and in many cases they truly are. These make lively and erratic targets for marauding trout. All this commotion also serves to draw the fishes' attention to these insects. It seems somewhat self-defeating. But since the species continues to survive and thrive, this evolutionary strategy is obviously effective. I'm sure it's a numbers game: enough targets survive to carry on the traveling sedge lineage. For an angler imitating these entertaining caddisflies, skating or skittering his fly is an effective presentation. There are times I may actually fish two dry caddisfly imitations at once. I vary the size and design of the patterns fished together, hoping one or the other has a special appeal to any one individual fish. Or one of the two flies may land or skitter into a fish's field of vision, getting its attention where a single fly might not.

Sometimes it can actually be beneficial to "splat" the fly onto the surface to draw a fish's attention to it. While I rarely do this with other flies imitating smaller fare, I will slam a damselfly adult. The real bugs can seem to crash land sometimes. They hit the deck hard. And once they are in the water, they taxi, flip and flop erratically, trying to get airborne again. Sometimes they make it; sometimes they sputter for a while before liftoff; sometimes they never fly again. The last will definitely be consumed if a trout or bass is nearby. It behooves the astute fly angler to imitate what the naturals do. Activate the fly, crash land it, and skate it, interspersed with pauses. Because the fish may miscalculate a bit, or you may zig the fly as the fish zags, expect some missed strikes. It's all part of the fun.

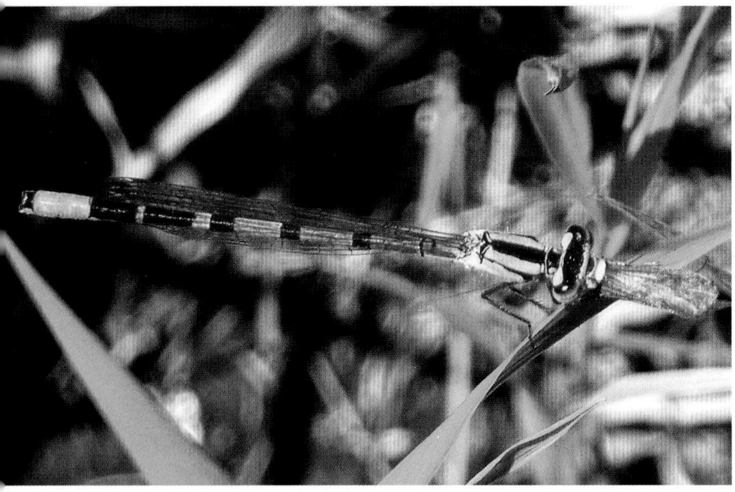

Pretty to the eye of a stillwater angler, damselflies are fast and maneuverable fliers, and very able predators who commonly dine on other insects.

As for locating the naturals and subsequently fishing the artificials, look for the caddisflies along the shallow perimeter of a lake or pond. Position yourself out from it, then cast toward the shoreline. As for the damsels, look near the water bordering areas of tall vegetation, like cattails. Damselflies are aerial predators. They dine on other insects, including mosquitoes. They hang in tall grass and shoreline growth looking to ambush their food. To ambush the trout, I position my boat a comfortable cast away from such shorelines, casting to the shore. Damselflies are bold fliers who can miscalculate the wind or fall asleep at the controls, ending up in the drink. A sudden breeze can also blow them into the water, too. Trout patrolling the edges of likely zones are on the lookout for damselflies. They are a big morsel, and they must taste good. Adult damsels can make for some frantic and memorable dry fly fishing in late spring and summer. Don't leave home without them.

CHAPTER 10

# Creating a Strategic Game Plan

Even when fishing in familiar territory, you should have a thoughtful game plan. My namesake, Gorman Lake, BC.

Just because I have fished a particular lake a number of times does not mean it is without challenges. On any given day the fish may not be easily caught. However, compared to a lake I am fishing for the first time, a body of water I am familiar with doesn't require that I learn the depths and contours of the bottom or the prevalent aquatic foods the fish are most likely to want. I already know these from previous trips here. Also, I have a good idea of specific locations in the lake where I can probably find fish. I am a little ahead on the necessary learning curve in figuring out how to catch fish today. I can dedicate most of my fishing time experimenting with fly patterns and the fishes' preference for the presentation of the flies.

There is a natural tendency to be complacent when fishing familiar territory, to go without a thoughtful game plan. The plan is particularly important when I know my actual fishing time will be short. If I have only three or four hours at the lake or pond—including time that will be specifically dedicated to photography and experimenting with new fly patterns—a specific plan is what gives me maximum opportunity to catch some fish in a short time period. A good plan also heads off bouts of impatience and frustration, so I can enjoy my fishing experience even if the fish are not very cooperative.

One of the significant aspects of all my game plans is to have my fly boxes sorted and ready and have all my rods strung the night before with flies tied on the leader, ready to cast. If my gear is not already in my 4Runner, I lay out all that I need to load the next morning in a specific staging area, usually my downstairs hallway. I don't want to deal with searching for a misplaced item when it's time to load up. Nor do I want to remember a forgotten fly box when I arrive at the lake. Good planning plus preparation equals maximum enjoyable fishing time.

## Once at the Lake or Pond

No matter where I am fishing, the first thing I do is look for rising fish. Even as I pass stillwaters along the highway, my eyes are scanning the surface for fish activity. It is a natural reaction, and I suspect most fly anglers do the same.

Rising, feeding fish provide me with important information as I prepare to fish: where on the lake feeding fish may be concentrated, a floating fly line is probably my best first choice, and dry flies and emergers on the surface or in the surface film will be the first type of flies I will use. Once I launch my pontoon or float tube, I will move to a stationary position and cast, not troll, to the risers.

Should I spy no rising fish, nor any evidence of activity near the lake's (or pond's) surface, I know I will start with a sinking line. Unless I observe particular aquatic insects flying, sitting in or on the surface, or resting on the shoreline vegetation, I start by trolling my Beadhead Midnight Bugger in tandem with a standard Prince or a beadhead model. My tendency is to troll parallel to the shoreline at a distance from the bank that has proved productive in the past. On all of the lakes with which I am familiar, I have a good feel for the depths and contours of the bottom, having used my electronic depth finder. It's in the channels, transition zones, and edges of drop-offs where I focus my efforts.

I don't leave the details of my trolling to chance; I am very aware of my trolling speed, my trolling path, and my line length. To start, I strip off 13 (my lucky number) lengths of fly line. For me, a "length" is the distance from my fly reel to the first guide on my rod. So, as I begin my fishing, I drop my leader and a tiny bit of fly line into the water in front of me, grab the fly line where it comes off my reel, and pull the line from the reel until I reach the first guide on my rod. The tip of my rod is within a few inches of the water so that as I start to kick my fins to move my pontoon or float tube, the line is pulled through the guides and into the water. If the line is a bit sticky in the guides, I shake the rod tip gently side to side, coaxing the fly line through the guides and into the water. Once 13 strips (or your favorite number) of fly line have put the fly about 40 feet (includes the rod length and 9 or 10 feet of leader) from me, I begin a slow troll. When I say "slow," I mean I am barely moving. With the exception of small fish, most aquatic organisms move slowly. Something that is less than an inch long is not moving very quickly.

This tactic cost me. In British Columbia a stillwater angler fishing alone may fish two fly rods at once. As the fisherman tends one rod in order to cast or change flies, I highly recommend he strap the unattended rod to the boat. I wish I had!

Once I locate the fish, I prefer to cast from a fixed position. Trolling through the "fish zone" may cause the fish to scatter, especially in shallow water. Good casting skills enhance a stillwater angler's chances of enticing wary fish, which cannot be closely approached without alarming them.

In addition, swimming creatures usually don't swim an extended period without stopping for a bit. Therefore, I troll 10 to 20 feet, then slow down or stop. As I do so, the fly line sinks, and the flies descend in the water column. As I resume the troll, the line tightens and the flies ascend a bit. The drop of the flies as I slow or stop, and the rise of the flies as I resume trolling, can be triggers for a following fish. I pay close attention to such clues, and then repeat those movements and manipulations of the flies that prompt the fish to bite them.

The advantage of fishing with a companion is the opportunity to try different flies, different methods, in different locations. And, for some of us, much of the pleasure in a fishing adventure is the camaraderie, as I often find with my cousin John Gorman.

Part of the successful puzzle-solving while fishing is noting the areas of the lake that produce strikes as I troll. I make references about exactly where I am on the lake, such as what I am near or across from on the lakeshore and how far I am from the bank. Inevitably, I will find a certain area where I consistently get strikes. Once out of the area, the red zone, I no longer get any more strikes. So, I turn my float tube or boat around to troll back through the red zone, or stop to cast and retrieve until the action stops. At all times, I am paying attention to my trolling speed, how much line I pull from my reel to begin trolling, and what my flies are doing, or not doing, as I troll.

Since I will feel the strike of a fish while trolling, watching my line as I fish this method is not necessary. I am free to survey other portions of the lake. Rising fish or other anglers catching fish in a particular location may tip me off to move to a new location.

## The Man in the Baby Blue Pontoon Boat

Some fishing friends and I were fishing Clark Canyon Reservoir in southwest Montana on a July morning. The three of us had had fabulous fishing the day before, trolling and casting damselfly nymphs on a slow sinking fly line. The large maniac rainbows had struck our flies viciously the previous morning, and we landed more than our share until a tremendous west wind turned the lake into high waves and whitecaps that seriously threatened our safety.

But this day, trolling through familiar areas that had produced so many fun memories yesterday did not yield any strikes for my friends or me. Nor for any of the other dozen fly anglers in our immediate area whom we watched as we trolled in all different directions, varying our speed, line lengths, and fly patterns. Everyone in my group changed flies multiple times, to no avail. We searched for bent rods, and saw one very occasionally. It seemed the fish were not in a biting mood.

I decided to separate myself from my comrades a bit, kicking my float tube toward a bay just off the mouth of a small inlet stream. We had caught some fish in this zone the day before, but had not fished it because it was so crowded today. Because discouraged anglers had begun to leave, there was now more room to freely fish in the bay without encroaching on some angler's personal fishing space.

Shortly, I spied a fisherman in a baby blue pontoon boat near the edge of the bay. His rod was bent hard against a hooked trout. Was he lucky, or was he on to something? I continued to slowly troll my damselfly nymph on my clear, slow-sinking line. When the subject soon hooked a second fish, he had my complete attention. Since he was stationary, casting repeatedly in one direction, I moved to a position behind him to observe. Since successful anglers can also be secretive, I preferred that he not be concerned with the fact that I was "going to school" on him.

Unlike everyone else on the lake who was trolling, Baby Blue was in a fixed position and casting. I quickly perceived he was casting parallel to the edge of a bare-submerged weed bed, so I positioned myself to do the same. Then I mirrored everything he did. He would cast; I would cast. He allowed his line and fly to sink and sit for a very long time; I did the same. When he made a single slow strip retrieve of the fly, I mimicked his move. Then, he would patiently pause before making another slow strip of the line. I did the same. He'd stop. I'd stop. He'd strip. I'd strip. Bam! Fish on! Now, there were two anglers on Clark Canyon Reservoir who had the combination to the safe.

The fish did not want a trolled fly that day, at least not when I fished it. The natural tendency while trolling a fly is to swim it too quickly, and move it consistently without significant pauses. Additionally, trollers tend to patrol open water, away from weed beds that may catch their lines and flies. Baby Blue and I were in a maze of elodea beds separated by narrow chan-

Thanks to the man in the baby blue pontoon, I was able to catch and release some fish of my own that challenging day on Clark Canyon Reservoir.

Not all experimental flies turn out to be champion flies, but occasionally one will tempt a fish that proven flies have failed to entice.

nels of open water. It was in these channels that the trout roamed in search of swimming damselfly nymphs, safe from the scores of fly anglers pulling flies behind themselves futilely in search of a biter.

Even on familiar lakes there are lessons to be learned. Observation of successful anglers who are catching fish when others are not can offer you clues about how to do the same. This strategy has paid big dividends for me many times.

## Poor Man's GPS

As I move around a larger lake, I may discover an area far from the shoreline where biting fish are concentrated. If I am several hundred feet or more from the lake's edge, I need to triangulate my position in order stay in it, or come back to this same area on a future trip. Once I have zeroed in on the specific area, I stop in the middle of this red zone and pick three reference points in the direction I am facing as I troll. Examples would be two treetops and a distant mountain peak. When the mountaintop is between

When all the landmark reference points are properly aligned, I can get close to a specific location on a lake that has proven productive in the past. These specific points on Diamond Lake help me locate a prominent submerged log that has been an epicenter of good fishing for me.

tree #1 and tree #2, I know I am in alignment with the zone. As I troll toward or away from the mountaintop and it stays between my two trees, like situating the front post on a rifle barrel between the two sides of V-shaped rear notch near your eye while aiming at a target, I am aligned with the red zone fishing area.

However, I could be too far, one way or the other, from the red zone; I can be too close or too far from the mountaintop, which would take me out of the zone. So when I am—as best as I can determine while I am catching fish—in the middle of the red zone, I must also select three reference points on my right or left when the mountaintop is between tree #1 and tree #2. For instance, when the mountaintop is situated perfectly, I look to my left and spy a camper's tent that sits well behind and between two large rocks. If I move too far left or right out of the red zone, I notice that I can no longer see the tent because it is now hidden behind one of the rocks. As I troll in and around the zone, once I am not catching fish, I return to my original location on the lake where I can see both the mountaintop and the tent in their centered positions. I may decide to stay relatively stationary, even anchor my floating craft, and cast in all directions to retrieve my flies instead of troll them.

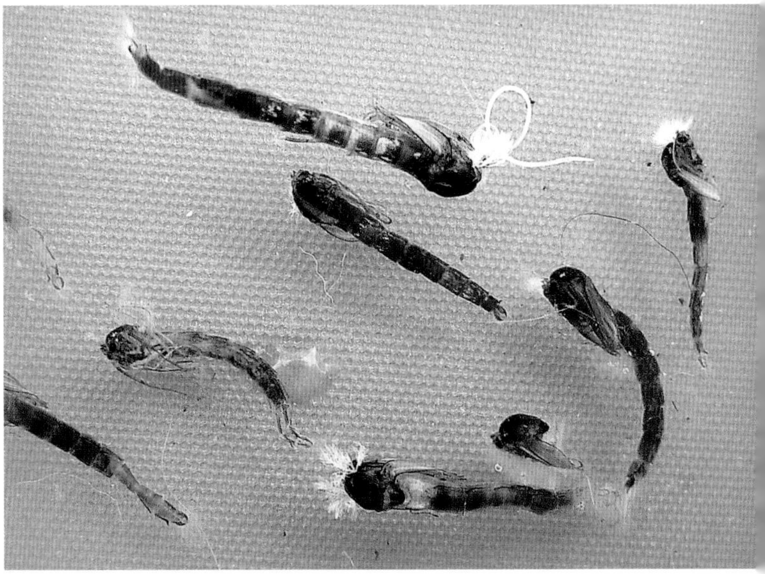

Chironomid pupae are common fare when examining a trout's stomach contents any time of year. Carry a wide variety of pupal patterns.

## Insects as Clues

Knowing that food preferences and feeding locations typically change throughout the fishing day on stillwaters, I am always vigilant for clues that a change is coming. The presence of swimming or flying insects is such a clue.

Because my lake fishing here in Western Oregon begins in earnest in March, I will use midges as one example of an insect that I look for and often discover to be active at some point in the day. In fact, I can expect to see midges throughout the year on stillwaters. In spite of their small size, because of their abundance and year-round availability, they are a staple fish food in virtually all lakes and ponds. Readers may find the terms midge and chironomid used interchangeably. (For taxonomy details check http://bugguide.net/node/view/55/tree/all.)

As you will recall, midges have four life stages: egg, larva, pupa, and adult. The egg stage is of no importance to a fly tier who would create artificials to imitate the chironomid, but larva, pupa, and adult patterns are important additions to have in every stillwater angler's fly box.

If I see midge pupae at water's surface when I did not discover any earlier in the day, I know the midges are active, and a hatch is beginning. I make note of the color and size of the pupae. If the fish are not rising, I am going to fish a larva pattern with a pupa just off the bottom in those parts of the lake that have produced fish for me in the past. I will suspend them underneath a small indicator. An alternative would to be to retrieve the flies as slow as I can stand it with a sinking fly line. If the water is less than 15 feet deep, my choice will be a slow-sinking or intermediate fly line; deeper than this, I employ a Type III density-compensated sinker that descends and fishes in a straight line configuration. If the line is not density-compensated, it tends to sink in a "U" shape, whereby I am out of touch with my flies if the fish take is gentle. I may never know a fish has intercepted my fly before it discerns it as a fake, and releases it.

If I land several fish, and they measure between 10 and 18 inches, I will use my stomach pump on them to discover what they are eating. If they have recently eaten chironomid larvae or pupae, I will get a good gauge on the exact sizes and colors. The other food items in the contents can offer clues for effective flies to use when the midges are not hatching. For instance, if I should find water boatmen and scuds in the stomach, these are good patterns to try when the fish are not selective for something else. Once the chironomid hatch fades, and the fish stop striking my chironomid flies, you can bet I will pair a scud and water boatman to troll or cast in likely areas.

## Invite a Research Team

When the fishing is moody and answers to solving the bite puzzle are hard to come by, if you fish with a capable companion or two, you have two more heads trying to crack the code. Multiple parties trying different flies, fishing different methods, and patrolling different areas make for quicker solutions when the fishing is tough. When the information is shared by the successful angler, make sure you get the entire solution: exact fly patterns, leader length, tippet diameter, line length trolled or cast, sink rate if a sinking line is used, distance between the indicator and flies if a floating line and indicator are the ticket, and the exact retrieve or trolling details. Success is made up of *all* these details. Think of a completed puzzle assembled on a card table. For the picture to be complete, all pieces must be in place. Same way with successful fishing.

Another big plus of fishing with friends is photo opportunities. I have had some great fish-catching experiences by myself on lakes. However, it is difficult to play a worthy fish and get photos of the action and a "hero shot" without help. I remind my companions to bring their cameras for our trip. Inevitably, someone's camera will have dead batteries, or it will be raining and the camera owner is concerned about damaging it. For these reasons, I bring two waterproof point-and-shoot cameras, one of which I give to one of my friends for the fishing day. It does not take long to realize the benefits of a camera strap, even if you have to fashion one with a piece of fishing line. My cameras are waterproof, but that does not matter if they sink to bottom in 20 feet of water.

Companions might very well split the cost of your trip. If it is a distant fishing trip, fuel and accommodation expenses can be shared. Additionally, it's great to have a spare driver or two when distance and driving fatigue take their toll.

Lastly, there is the safety issue. Accidents happen. I will not belabor the safety issues that are obvious whenever you are in, on, or around water. Companions can watch after each other. Even though it may not be required, a floating device or inflatable fishing vest on you or your watercraft is smart.

## The Natural Progression of Events

If I put in a full 8- to 12-hour fishing day on a lake, I usually witness many changes in the necessary successful angling strategies. It is uncommon on most lakes, especially public, heavily fished lakes, for any one combination of flies, retrieve, depth, and location to work the entire day. Something is going to change. Therefore, when the bite fades and the catching slows or stops, a change is necessary. My first inclination is to move elsewhere on the lake. There's a chance that fisherman activity—casting, splashy movement, reeling in thrashing fish, and so on—has forced the fish to move elsewhere. They may still be interested in taking the same proven flies, fished in the same manner, but they have relocated in a quieter location. Or the willing fish in the immediate area of my fishing reach have been hooked and/or landed, and are not willing to bite again. Either way, it's time to move.

If it is a short distance to my next location, I will kick (with fins) or row there without fishing on the way. If it is a long distance, I may troll flies as I go, assuming the flies I am trolling are not ones I normally fish without much movement, such as chironomids under an indicator and dry flies. I am not saying that fish cannot be enticed trolling these, but I would rather troll flies that imitate naturally swimming fare, like damselflies, dragonflies, leeches, mayfly nymphs, scuds, and small fish. If there is any doubt, I will troll my Prince and Midnight Bugger.

If I am fishing chironomids under an indicator, and the fishing has slowed, I may choose to cast to likely areas not too far from the shore or off the edges of lily pads or beds of elodea, likely cruising areas for fish looking for a snack. Once in position to reach likely water, I fan five or six casts at different

This rainbow ate a Halo Micro Leech paired on the leader with a chironomid pupa. This combination is an excellent choice under an indicator when prospecting a shoreline.

angles from a fixed position. If nothing happens, I move 20 or 30 feet farther along my course, and repeat my casting routine. If I should get a few strikes, I linger and make more casts until the action dies. Then I move again. When I halt my casting to move a short distance to cast again, I scan my surroundings, always searching for rising fish, hatching insects, or an angler with a fish on. If this strategy does not produce enough action to keep me satisfied, it is time for me to move to very specific locations where I have caught fish when most areas on the lake fail to produce.

On familiar waters, experience has shown me where fish tend to linger even if they are not actively feeding. If the area—often a little bay—is small, like on a pond, I will station myself to cast, rather than troll. If I have not fished this location earlier, or I fished it with flies that were not my last effective flies that the fish grabbed the previous couple of hours, I will use the flies that served me so well recently. I know fish are in this particular spot because past fishing has told me so, or, more likely, my depth finder electronics reads "Fish!" If these flies fail to produce as I cover the area and use a variety of retrieves, if appropriate, then I change flies. I am assuming, of course, that lake fish can be tempted to eat if I discover the right flies enticingly retrieved at the correct depth. Just like people at the all-you-can-eat buffet, even when we are stuffed, there is always room for dessert.

A good psychological strategy to pursue when the fishing is tough is to take a shore break. Head off frustration before it saps the joy out of your day. It can happen. Taking a break will recharge your emotions positively, enable you to relax, discuss victories with your friends, maybe talk to anglers not in your circle who are willing to give you some cheap advice, and gather yourself for the next round of fishing.

Check your fly periodically for vegetation or debris that may have fouled the hook. When you feel a little resistance during the retrieve or troll of the fly, check it.

Many Glacier Hotel on Swiftcurrent Lake, Glacier National Park, MT. If you haven't been here, put this park on your bucket list.

## Take Heart

Even lakes and ponds that I may fish three or four consecutive days can treat me cruelly the day after an outstanding fish-catching one. I have to remind myself, just as you need to remind yourself, that it is on challenging days I have the best chance to learn something of value. When the fishing action is nonstop, there is little to be learned. On days when the fish-catching is relentless, I usually quit early to look for interesting photography opportunities, and may not care to fish the balance of my day. If I am by myself, I often choose to go to another lake or pond within easy walking or driving distance. Sometimes, I just go home. Even a hungry person can only eat dessert for so long before it is no longer appealing.

So take heart when lake fishing frustrates you. Calm yourself, let the frustration pass, and start formulating a game plan for the rest of the day's fishing, or for your next trip. A true puzzle solver welcomes the opportunity to discover the riddle's answer that others cannot or will not find. It is through defeat on lake fishing days that creative strategies are born—strategies that, when successful, magnify the enjoyment of your angling victories when you can consistently trick lake fish into biting your fly.

## Too Many Lakes, Too Little Time

Every year I like to add a few new lakes to my angling experience. With thousands of potentially good choices in western North America alone, I must methodically narrow my scope. What about a lake might excite me (or you), and how much will my enjoyment of it be tempered by the time and effort it takes to fish there? In answering this question I factor in things like a

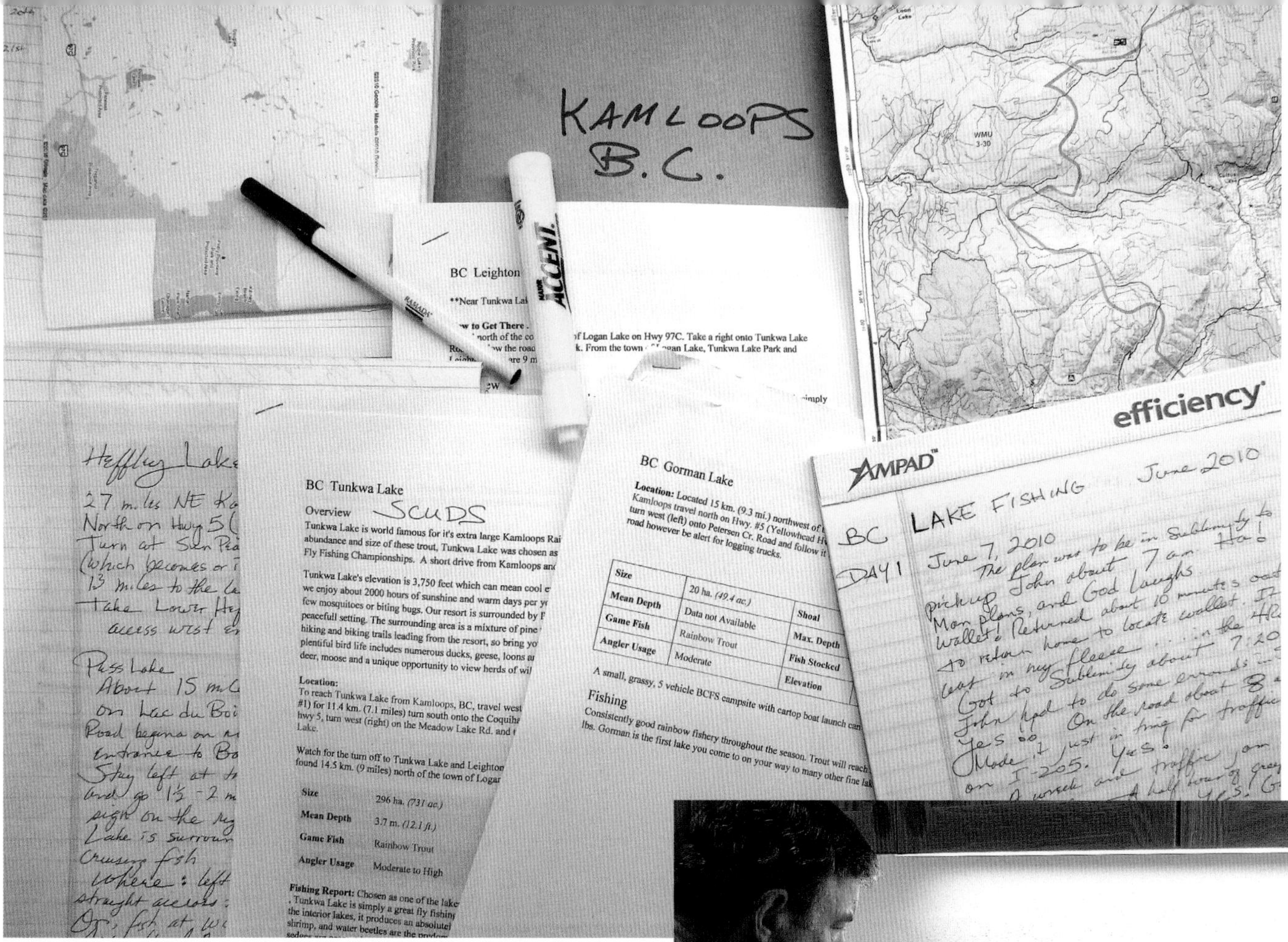


I keep a folder of documents for each lake or group of lakes to which I will be traveling. I try to leave very little to chance; it will cost me valuable fishing time if I forget or overlook details. Write it down.

For some of us, part of the pleasure of fishing a new lake is the research and planning—the formation of strategic game plan. It's somewhat like a treasure hunt, with maps, documents, and the necessary equipment to locate the gold.

beautiful setting, accessibility, quality of the fish (numbers, size, species), the specific timeframe I have available to fish, distance from home, availability of research information, lake fishing alternatives in the immediate area of my chosen lake, and the availability of accommodations, supplies, and amenities where I may set up my home base nearest the lake or lakes I may want to fish. These considerations may only be the starting point for you, but they are a start nonetheless.

My lake information is organized in a file or folder on my computer. While I am in the info gathering stage, I store all that I have learned and wish to retain for further review. I want to know about the numbers and quality of fish in a lake I am considering. The opportunity for fish exceeding 20 inches is always intriguing, but I also want reasonable driving distance from my home base along with reasonable access. If a helicopter or mountain climbing gear is needed, I usually pass. I get written access directions and maps of every lake I will visit. If there are particular portions of the lake someone has referenced in an article or blog, I make note. Of course I write down any fly patterns and specific angling techniques I discover.

If I have a week or so, I want to be based where I can sample a number of lakes. I am a gadabout, and I like variety. Even if I have excellent fishing at a new lake, I usually do not fish it a second time on the same trip. A campsite on Oregon's Century Drive, south of Bend, or a motel in Kamloops, BC, are a couple of examples of "home bases" which give me many stillwater choices in all directions of the compass. If I choose—and sometimes I do—I can easily fish two different lakes in a day.

I like the adventure, the newness, and the challenge of unfamiliar waters. It can be very exhilarating to successfully catch at least a handful of trout on a lake I have never seen. And, yes, I am very aware of the possibility of being skunked. That's why I leave very little to chance and rely on a thoughtful plan. Within my plan there are always contingencies. So my plan takes on the look of a flow chart. If this, then this; if not this, then that. If neither, then this is what I will do.

The chance to release a big rainbow trout is confirmation that my planning was good and that my treasure hunt has been successful.

## Researching New Waters

Once I have targeted a new lake for exploration, long before my actual fishing day, it's time to prepare. Preparation and research before I ever go to the lake can save me frustration and time, and translate into increased fishing success. Research can truly add to the overall pleasure of fishing new waters, too.

I welcome on-water instruction from a knowledgeable acquaintance on my new lake, but this does not preclude me from thinking for myself as I try to trick the fish. An experienced friend can give me tips, but it is no guarantee of future success on this particular lake. Conditions change, and intelligent adjustments must be made. Don't become dependent on anyone except the man in the mirror.

The first thing I need to do is answer the question: Where are the fish? Possible helpful answers to this question will start long before I launch my float tube or boat on a new lake. First-hand, trusted sources are the best. When my friends tantalize me with stories about their successful stillwater fishing adventures, if I am even the slightest bit interested in possibly fishing that lake some day, the first question I pose is exactly where on the lake I need to focus my fishing efforts. What is nearby, and what are some easily recognizable landmarks? I will inquire about flies and methods, too, but I need to know where to be on the lake. If I don't remember all the details, I eventually follow up with an email or phone call. The info goes into a written file.

In addition to my maps, I carry equipment to search and communicate as I fish. And I record some of the memories with my cameras.

Some easily accessible and productive lakes will always be crowded when the fishing is good. No secrets there. However, if you find a gem off the beaten path where you enjoy a modicum of solitude, seriously think about who you want to share your fish stories with—perhaps not the outdoor editor of your local newspaper.

However, for many bodies of water of interest to me, I have no personal sources I can tap. I must resort to other means.

A quick Internet search can reveal a lot. Fly fishing research immediately offers blogs, chat rooms, and fishing forums. Unless I get better information, these may be the only clues to the "where" that I will have. Big lakes can be overwhelming when it comes to randomly picking a location at which to begin exploring it, so any information is better than none.

If fishing photos are posted with the blogs, chat, and advertisements, landmarks may be noticed. When viewing photos and videos, I have referenced specific boat launches, resorts, rock outcroppings, creek mouths, cliffs, and rockslides on the waters I intend to visit.

Some online sources have something to sell you: a guided fishing trip, a map of good fishing locations, a DVD or book detailing your lake of interest. Although it is not in the best financial interest of the sellers to tell you everything you need to know, you may discover information about specific flies, methods, and best times of year to fish there.

The second source of useful information when searching fishing reports—sometimes including information about location—are state departments of fish and wildlife. Check out the fishing reports published frequently by state or province (Canada) fisheries agencies.

You can also try searching for bathymetric maps of the lake you're planning to fish. These maps show the depths and contours of the lake bottom. Knowing where the areas of 15 feet or shallower are located is important. The best weed growth and food production in a lake will be in shallow water. I scan the shoreline of the map for references to creeks, well-known points or bays, a lodge, resort, or campground, and boat launches. The accompanying text may make reference to a general compass portion of the lake as productive, for instance "the south end" or "the northeast corner." I print out these maps for my files.

You may even find useful information about fishing your lake of interest on YouTube. Recently, I viewed a video of Roche Lake, where I plan to go again this spring. I recognized the specific boat launch the angler/cameraman was near. I recalled the landmark near which he fished and, of course, filmed his fight with a Kamloops rainbow trout.

Magazine articles detailing lakes and pertinent fishing information for them is a double-edged sword. While the article can be very useful as I read about a new lake, I know that I will not be the lone reader. Other anglers looking for the same information will read it, too, and may plan a trip to the featured water just as I do. Or I may be very familiar with the lake of the article's focus and have appreciated the welcome solitude offered by its relative obscurity, which now may be lost because of the newly written story.

## Equipment and Supplies

For an experienced lake angler, there are usually not too many surprises as far as equipment and supplies needed for a fishing expedition, even to a new body of water. The one exception is fly patterns. Once I find the fish on my new lake, I need to have the flies that the fish want. Though I have, literally, thousands of stillwater flies, I may not have exactly the flies I need. Each lake can have its fly pattern idiosyncrasies. Proven flies that are

Roche Lake, near Kamloops, BC, is full of fabulous rainbow trout, some of whom have a cruel streak in their personality. I learned to embrace the challenge. It's the only lake I have ever fished where the trout will forcefully slam a stationary fly dangled under an indicator.

killers on one lake or region of lakes may be the wrong size, color, or design to imitate exactly the same insect in another lake or another geographical region. Fish in clear-water lakes, especially wary due to high angling pressure, often have the desire to study an artificial fly before they decide to bite it. Having a more exacting imitation for today's lake can be pivotal to success. As a result, as I prepare to fish a new lake, I gather as much information as I can about flies that may be specific to it. As a fly tier, part of my gathering preparation is to tie new flies I have learned about. And, even though I may have tied a good supply of new patterns, I still plan to take my fly-tying kit with me in case I need to tie more than I realized I needed, or in case I discover new necessary flies I did not know about during my pretrip research.

During the days leading up to my trip to a new lake, I like to stage all my gear, accessories, and materials in a specific area of my hallway or garage. When departure time for my trip arrives, everything is in one spot, ready to be loaded, saving me time and frustration: toilet tissue, headache medication, sunscreen, lip balm with sunscreen, a bottle of water, and a granola bar. Forgetting even a single one of these little "necessities" as you launch your boat can color your fishing day, whether the fish are biting or not.

I prefer to shop at my local grocery outlet so I know I have the food and drink basics I want with me. Shopping before I leave home assures me I will always have what I like and will pay the prices I expect.

A checklist can seem a bit extreme, especially for those of us who trend toward the lazy. But a Microsoft Word document, once created, is easily modified and printed out for your lazy convenience. This is a piece of cheap insurance to make sure that you have—as best you can—remembered all you may need on your planned fishing expedition, especially those far from home. I hate to overlook little items like batteries for my electronic depth finder or my wader repair kit when I spring a leak.

## Unexpected Travel Challenges

My friend Jeff Hilden had three flat tires simultaneously on a nasty gravel road along the Deschutes River, at least 15 miles from the nearest town. In such places, because of the topography, there may be no cell phone reception. If there is little traffic to assist with a ride, it's a long walk. Needless to say, such situations can seriously alter fishing plans.

Another tire story: I flew to eastern Oregon in his small plane with Jackson Cooper to fish Mann Lake. Adjacent to Mann is a long, long, straight stretch of gravel road. This was our landing strip. Because this area is sparsely populated and traffic is light, there would be no difficulty for Jackson in sticking the landing. However, as we touched down, one of the tires blew out and was damaged beyond repair. We were a long way from a town that might have an airplane tire, more than an hour's drive by car. Fortunately, one of Jackson's pilot friends had accompanied us in his own plane. The friend consented to fly to Ontario to pick up a new tire for us while Jackson and I grabbed our gear and headed for the lake a few hundred yards away. Besides the good luck that we had an escort, the fishing was most excellent.

This remote road near Mann Lake has other stories to tell. Besides numerous flat tires on my vehicles and those of my fishing friends, I was in a serious automobile crash there in 1994, after which the driver of the other vehicle had to be life-flighted out by helicopter. In another incident, friend Alex Barkume also had a serious vehicle crash. What some of us won't risk for lake fishing!

Even in popularly fished lakes that see a lot of fishing traffic, I may need to rely on my 4-wheel drive capability to get in and out of boat launch areas. If I should park a little off the beaten path, conditions may warrant all-wheel drive to return to the roadway. Even in primitive campgrounds or parking access areas on lakes, a snow or a heavy rain can turn driving into a carnival ride. The high road clearance of recreational vehicles can be important, too. While he could be catching fish and having a memorable day, a driver may instead be working to get his passenger car unstuck using fallen tree limbs and a makeshift shovel. What looked like a reasonably good road on the map can be a muddy, sticky quagmire. If it's not rain and mud, higher elevation lakes can get snow any time of year. I have driven while it's snowing in August in Yellowstone Park.

## Once at My Destination

If there is a local sporting goods store or fly shop near my destination lake (or lakes), I will stop to visit and inquire about the fishing conditions, my chances of success, and specific flies. Besides possibly buying my fishing license there if I am out of state or in a foreign country, I always make it a point to buy something else. Even if there may be nothing I need right now, I know I will always use leaders, tippet material, and indicators eventually. None of these spoil. Retailers stay in business to help you and me when customers support them with dollars. Good information is usually worth much more than the goods purchased. I am happy to support them.

On extended trips where I have traveled hundreds of miles, I usually spend what remains of my arrival day sorting gear and fly boxes, and readying my rods, which will be assembled and

Cousin John Gorman is ready to launch on Tunkwa Lake, BC. Tunkwa is a large lake, with large fish, and large challenges for first time visiting anglers.

Precious fishing time can be saved by stringing fly rods the night before. With my 4Runner, I can carry my 9-foot and 9½-foot rods full-length inside the vehicle.

rigged when I head for the lake. When I hit the water no fishing time will be foregone to ready all my rods. Doing it in advance can save me most of an hour. Time is fish.

Since my days of camping in the mud and rainstorm are behind me, I will check the weather forecast for the immediate area on my computer in my motel room. Knowing what weather to expect can alter my decision about what specific lake I will fish tomorrow or influence the time of day I plan to begin my fishing. Wind is a huge factor, especially on large bodies of water. It is the single biggest detrimental factor influencing lake fishing. I can deal easily with cold, rain, and snow, but a howling wind can make fishing impossible, in addition to being dangerous for small floating craft. This is one of the reasons it is important to have alternative lakes to fish nearby, if there are any. This is one thing I like about the Kamloops, BC, region. If I get blown off one lake, I can usually find a smaller or more sheltered lake within a half hour. The same is true of Oregon's Century Drive lakes, south of Bend. Alternative waters are a crucial part of most of my fishing plans. Many of the new lakes I choose to fish are those that have other quality lakes near them.

## Survey the Scene and Let's Launch

There is a large advantage to launching at popular boat landings on your lake: this is where boat fishermen will concentrate as they come and go. It's like the water cooler gathering spot in the office or the lunchroom. There is always talk. Anglers like to chat about their successes.

Besides the prelaunch conversations with other fishermen, I try to restrain my urge to paddle out and start fishing long

This is the launch at Diamond Lake's south end. Launches can be gathering spots where anglers chat about their successes.

enough to make a mental check of what I have packed on my person and my boat. If I have to postpone or disturb my fishing to paddle or kick a half mile back to my 4Runner, having forgotten to change the batteries in my depth finder, or having left my stomach pump in my other fishing vest, it can be a bit upsetting. A few minutes spent making sure all I need is onboard is an excellent use of those seconds. It's all part of an effective strategy.

While I am waiting to launch at a busy ramp, I take the time to double check that I have all my equipment onboard once I am on the lake. Forgetting that special box of new chironomid flies, the rod with the necessary fly line, or the toilet tissue can be hard lessons.

Once on the water, I start pulling line from the reel of my trolling rod. Unless I have good reason to change my decision, I will fish the leech pattern du jour on a short dropper about 30 inches above a Beadhead Prince on the point, assuming it is legal to fish multiple flies. (It's one fly in British Columbia.) My fly line is my slow-sinking, clear intermediate, 13 strips to start. I'm in no hurry as I troll. Once settled in, flies trailing me, I pan my surroundings to see what I might see.

I might spy some rising fish. And I listen. Could it be slurping fish, or maybe some conversations worth monitoring? Sound carries so well across a lake!

Besides trying to view all directions at once for clues about the fish or fishing, I watch the screen of my electronic tool for bottom structure, depth, temperature, and fish. I constantly adjust my trolling speed, accelerating a little, slowing a little, then stopping for a few moments. Maybe I change direction, even do a figure eight, trying in all of these to elicit a strike. If nothing happens, I may extend my line length by another two or three strips to get the flies deeper. If fishing with a friend or two, I look their way to see if they might have hooked a fish.

If I get no strikes, or a few sporadically, and I see a cluster of boats somewhere on the lake, I will most likely move in their direction. On large lakes, binoculars are a great visual aid. If the gathering is more than a few hundred yards away, I reel in my flies and paddle or motor hard to get to them. Once within

If there is one thing all stillwater fly anglers look for throughout their fishing day, it is rising fish.

In addition to the equipment basics, I am never on a new lake without my electronic depth finder.

a few hundred feet of the pack, I pull line from my trolling rod, and begin fishing again. I do not charge into the herd. Instead, I begin to circle, making sure I do not move into someone's personal fishing space. My visual attention is on both anglers and my electronic screen. Being this close, I can watch the screen while listening for fishermen's chatter or the distinctive sounds of a good fish pulling line from a fly reel and jumping to throw the hook. If I can discern experienced anglers, generally typified by good casting skills, I pay particular attention to how they are retrieving or fishing their flies, and the type of fly line—floating or sinking—being used. Of course, it could be that some or all of the fishermen are trolling the area in which they are concentrated, and there is no casting.

However those in the immediate vicinity are fishing, I am looking for the guy in the group who is hooking fish. I want to do what he is doing. He trolls; I troll. He casts and retrieves; I cast and retrieve, mirroring his every move. If he is fishing a dry fly, pupa, or nymph under an indicator, that's what I do. My rods are all rigged and ready if I need to change to a no-retrieve method.

Watching and imitating the technique employed by Mr. Success is no guarantee of my success. His location, or his specific fly, also come into play. If I hook and land a fish, you can bet I will pump its stomach (or throat) in an attempt to discover if the fish might be selective for one or two food items in particular.

Sometimes I can locate willing fish on the distant perimeter of the grouped anglers. No need for me to attempt to crash the party. The fish are spread out enough that I need get no closer. However, if I can find no action, and I'm not getting significant readings on my fish finder, I will try to get closer without intruding. This a much easier proposition if most or all are trolling.

Moving into the traffic flow is a simple, nonthreatening matter. If everyone is on anchor, then it gets trickier. Most male anglers are territorial. So my general rule of courtesy is that if an angler casts directly at me, and I at him, our lines will not meet. This guideline has never gotten me into trouble. And there is always a chance that someone in the group will get restless to move elsewhere, or head to shore for a dining or bathroom

Sometimes on a crowded lake positioning is like a slow-moving game of chess as the board pieces move themselves around, hoping to slide into a strategic vacancy. This game is not for everyone.

break. I am always looking for preliminary clues as someone is preparing to leave so that I am moving into position, ready to slide in before some other outsider preempts me.

If I join the group, I have a better chance to determine the depth of submerged features that have apparently drawn the fish to this area. They could be sitting over a spring, or an old river channel, a weed bed, a shoal, or a hole. Just knowing the depth of the red zone is very important. It gives me a starting point. My first inclination is to fish a specific depth, just off the bottom. If fishing a floating line and nymphs or pupae under an indicator, I know at what length I need to separate my indicator and flies.

If there are friends in the group, in different boats, they will talk to each other. Should key fishing information be exchanged between parties, it's laid out there for all and any to hear and use. Too, there are times a friendly fisherman will generously offer tips to those who are struggling. If I am one of the strugglers, you can bet I will take his suggestion to heart. In return, I may very well offer up tips of my own should I discover a better fly or method. It can work both ways.

## Nothing Lasts Forever

If I have found nothing useful where other anglers are fishing, and we are not getting any strikes, it's time for me to move on. I may return to an area I had previously fished with some success, and troll my way in that direction, watching for clues as I go.

When it's time to hit the beach, pack up, and head out, I may have another opportunity to chat with other fishermen as they launch or prepare to load their boats for home. Helpful information may very well be gleaned for the next time I fish this lake, and maybe I've given something helpful to the other angler, too.

## Journaling

Once back at my motel, campsite, or home, I will write an entry in my fishing log before I forget the details and lessons of my fishing day. On future trips, of course, I can refer back to my notes to heed my insights and reminders that will move me toward catching fish the next time I visit.

Making a daily diary entry sounds tedious to many. And, it can be, especially if you are tired at the end of a long fishing day. But keeping a daily fishing journal facilitates my learning, saves me a truckload of time, and catches me more fish.

A journal doesn't have to be a masterpiece of grammar and spelling. You may be the only one to ever read it. So scratch out the bare essentials of what must be remembered, then call it finished. Be disciplined enough to do it before the day ends and you turn out the lights. Even overnight a few key things will be forgotten or overlooked. Write while the day's experience is fresh.

### What to Include

- Travel directions, distance, estimated travel time, border crossing info (for Canada, for instance)
- Licensing costs and purchasing locations, and fishing regulations on the waters to be fished
- Accommodations, supplies, fuel, food
- Contact info for fly shops or sporting goods store for fishing reports and flies
- What I forgot on last trip, or mistakes made, and things I got right and need to remember. What would I do differently next time?
- If it's a return trip, flies, including sizes and colors, where to fish specifically, what I observed, what stomach samples revealed, what other anglers had to say—all these details need to be recorded.

One hazard of which I must constantly remind myself is that if I wait until bedtime to write my thoughts, I may well not turn out the lights until after midnight. Thus it makes it difficult to get up early. An early start to a fishing day on a lake can be crucial to success. Too often I have regretted arriving to fish after the action is over or is waning quickly. Because it is in my nature to stay up late, I must recognize that this one significant detail can nullify the entirety of my strategic planning. Though an early start is no guarantee of success, I do not ever want to look back on a mediocre or fruitless fishing day to wonder if my tardy arrival was a key factor. It's early to bed for Michael.

CHAPTER 11

# Pay-for-Play Stillwaters

For those with the financial mean and the desire, pay-for-play lakes can offer privacy, solitude, and some very good fishing.

For those anglers with the financial means or who know the right people, lakes where you a pay a fee for the opportunity to catch trophy fish or large quantities of fish—pay-for-play lakes and ponds—can be well worth the price of admission. Sometimes the fishing can be outrageously easy, kind of like fishing in Disneyland or heaven. For newbie anglers, this can jumpstart their skills and determination to continue to fish stillwaters, both private and public. For those who don't have the chance to fish very often, pay-for-play places can maximize catching opportunities in the precious little time that these poor souls can commit to fly fishing in a year. And, though it may not be true of all private waters, most have a limited number of anglers on any given day; some allow you the exclusive rights for a day reserved solely for you and your guests. One can enjoy time with his friends, uninterrupted by the great unwashed angling hordes and obnoxious guys like me.

When I read a magazine article or book about the best trout lakes on Earth, I always look to separate pay-for-play lakes from public lakes. Comparing fishing public lakes to private waters—in some instances—may be comparable to contrasting hunting for big game in the public forest or desert to hunting them in a game preserve or private property where the animals are released in and confined to specific small areas. Private waters and preserves serve as means to a successful end—often a trophy captured or killed—but sometimes the effort, skill, and lessons learned may be, too often, not quite as valuable, especially for a skilled, experienced fisherman. Conversely, I am also aware that freshly planted public lakes can make for gullible fish, easily caught, too. And, in either case, for the veteran, sometimes when the fish are naïve and suicidal there is not much of value learned to carry forward to the next fishing outing where there are serious puzzles to solve. As it is with most of life's learning, the best lessons often come with struggle, experimentation, thought, and perseverance. This said, sometimes it just feels good to go out and tally some crazy numbers as an end in itself. How many fish can I catch and release in an hour, or before lunch, or casting and fishing left-handed? How many different and silly flies will catch fish for me today? Without setting the hook, how many strikes can I get on a single cast and retrieve of the flies?

Personally, I have fished dozens of private lakes over the course of my career. They can provide entertaining fishing, and are a source of much positive reinforcement when experimenting with new fishing techniques and flies. Besides providing anglers with the opportunity to find a trophy catch, private lakes can provide a fisherman—especially a newbie—with some useful fishing lessons: hooking, playing, landing big fish, and experimentation with a variety of presentations, retrieves, and fly patterns. For those who have only trolled for fish in lakes, casting and retrieving flies, or fishing an artificial under an indicator successfully, can hone these new skills in a hurry when plenty of foolish fish, especially big ones, are very cooperative. When the challenge of catching fish disappears, so does much of the enjoyment. I have occasions each season when I end up on a lake, either private or public, and the fishing presents no mystery. This is when I realize how much of my angling pleasure is derived from meeting the challenges. At this point in my fishing life, I no longer have a pressing need or desire for easy fishing; I've had enough of this dessert that it rarely tastes good for long. A few bites, and I'm sated. Then, I prefer to focus (pardon the pun) on taking photos. What I can also enjoy in these situations is watching and helping my fishing companions enjoy the fast action. It's important for me to remember that newbies or occasional anglers can have a great time reeling in a hundred fish during the fishing day. Their pleasure truly becomes my pleasure. This can make for great conversation on the way home and create fond memories of a successful fishing trip. These are worthy outcomes.

For consistently successful efforts when pursuing fish in competitive public waters, pay-for-play stillwaters are not always fertile ground for developing the mental toughness and persistence necessary for the development of the Lake Fishing Assassin. Pay-for-play fish can be too easy, especially if fishing pressure is low and infrequent. The exception would be when popular, reasonably priced private waters receive a lot of angling pressure. Fish that are caught and released many times eventually become wary and demand better angling skills, more precise techniques, and more exacting fly patterns to be fooled again. Knowing the value of uneducated trophy fish, savvy property owners may limit the days available to fish during the week or month, giving the fish time to recover from and forget the trauma of being caught. Big, naïve fish can equal significant income.

## Challenging Conditions at Pay-for-Play Lakes

There are pay lakes where the fishing can definitely evolve into being challenging. If a private lake or pond is reasonably priced and a short drive from a high-population urban area, many anglers will frequent it. If the lake is designated catch-and-release, the fish can become shy and discriminating as they are captured and released multiple times. In this case, those fly fisherman seeking puzzle-solving challenges can often find them. And the visiting angler can be sure there are indeed fish in the pay lake, not having to wonder if the lake has been "fished out," or if a wintertime event, such as a sustained period of freezing temperatures, killed all the fish. The lake's caretaker will make sure there are fish to be caught so paying customers continue to pony up.

## The Downside

No two anglers stand at exactly the same spot on their fly fishing journeys. What each wants is shaped by personality, values, and experiences. Those who have the financial means may be perfectly happy to catch many and large fish in private stillwaters until the day they make their last cast. The challenge of joining and competing with the general public on public waters for, perhaps, fewer and smaller fish is of no interest. The opportunity to potentially catch many and larger fish in a private setting in solitude, or with a few companions, has much allure. Having had such experiences many times, I can recommend

Anglers risk being jaded by catching large fish—sometimes many of them—in private waters. Then, fishing public stillwaters where the fish may not be as easy, numerous, or large can be a disappointment if expectations are not adjusted.

them. However, if an angler is driven to test his skills against all comers "in the arena," he must eventually go to the arena. In many competitions, there are multiple rounds (golf), multiple games and sets (tennis), multiple innings (baseball), or multiple periods or quarters (basketball and football). So, fishing in the arena should realistically be viewed as a longer-term, multiple-session competition. Everyone has an off day. Even the best hitter in major league baseball can go hitless on any given day, but over the course of a 162-game season, he will rise to the top of the pack. The same holds true in fishing. A champion stillwater angler is destined to lose a few, but win many, many more than the vast majority—maybe all—of the competition.

Not every angler is driven by competition against other anglers. In fact, it can be very unhealthy. If it becomes an obsession to win at all costs, antisocial, rude behavior could be the logical result. As soon as we go there, enjoyment of the fishing experience is destined to disappear, especially on those days when other fishermen are catching fish and the obsessive personality is not. I have made a lot of friends over the years meeting new people while fishing, friends who became my fishing companions. We may compete with others as team members and each other, too, but such competitions can be friendly and enjoyable even in a "loss." If I am outplayed, I will figure out how to win next time. It's a long season, a long journey. Just like fresh milk in a bucket, the cream will eventually rise to the top.

Big fish can spoil an angler. For some of us who have been fortunate enough to catch many lunkers over the years, it's catching the *challenging* fish where satisfaction is found, whether big or small.

## The Big Fish Syndrome

Getting a taste of catching the larger fish, trophy fish, available in many private lake fish experiences can jade an angler. Some anglers will be disappointed when they are unable to catch what they consider "big" fish in public lakes. Such a disappointment can overwhelm the beauty of a lake, the companionship, the fishing lessons that could have been learned, and the overall enjoyment of the fishing day. We can all get stuck in the gotta-catch-a-big-fish stage of our journey. I've been there. Who doesn't like to catch big fish?

I remember when I knew that big no longer mattered so much to me. It was back in the late 1980s. Some of my fishing friends discovered an area below a private dam owned by a rancher where many large rainbow trout were stranded. When the river flow below the dam was dropped to an extremely low level, the fish had to remain in the deeper water within a mile or so of the dam in order to survive. If they should leave this portion of the river and head downstream, they would have to negotiate extremely shallow water, so shallow that their backs might not be covered as they sought a new home. The fish were obviously not willing to risk the journey, so they stayed put. My friends caught truckloads of big fish with nowhere to go, and the circus fishing persisted over a course of several months. Though invited several times to experience this fishery, I had no desire to do so. Where was the challenge? Where was the sport? I realized then that numbers and size held little appeal for me if there were few challenges to meet or puzzles to solve.

I still fish private lakes and ponds. Because other skilled anglers have access too, the fish can become wary after being caught and released multiple times. Most pay-for-play waters are strictly catch-and-release because fish—especially BIG fish—are expensive. So fishing with some challenging aspects is often the case even in private waters. I like that. If I want to experiment with new flies, fine-tune a fishing technique, try new equipment, capture aquatic organisms, or take stillwater photos, I can rely on my stable of private lakes and ponds. There are days when I have only a few short hours to fish, collect, or photograph. Fortunately, a few places I have access to allow me to travel only a short way to get what I want or need. Such convenience is well worth the cost. But in all of this, I know the real tests, the confirmation of the skills I hope I possess, and the truer confirmation of new flies I hope will be champions, lie in the public realm. Here all comers are welcome, and some proficient anglers will bring with them their talents and their champion flies, against which I will match mine.

When I find easy fishing on private waters, it is a good time for me to treat a friend or family member to a fishing trip. Perhaps my favorite thing about private waters is that I can often invite someone to a fun day of schooling about the fly fishing skills necessary to catch fish in stillwaters. The environment will be safe and relatively quiet. And I know there are fish to be caught. I can teach them about assembling the equipment, knots, casting, fly selection, effective fishing techniques, and hooking, playing, and landing fish. My role on the lake is coach and mentor. I am happy to tie on the flies, undo tangles, net the fish, and take the photos to commemorate the day. For me, fishing doesn't get much better this.

If there is something interesting about a shoreline area—exact location, depth, wind protection, or a PowerPoint slide presentation for my students—I will photograph it and add it to my files on that particular lake. For instance, in this photo from Pass Lake, BC, a shoreline of cattails will often have trout cruising near the vegetation where insects live or crawl upon when hatching. A natural cove in the cattails can sometimes serve as a wind break.

## Lake Journal Entries from Familiar Lakes and Ponds

***May 15, 2010. Big Lake.***

I fished Big Lake for the second time ever today. When Marcy and I fished it for the first time two weeks ago, our success was too sporadic, in my thinking. Besides a few new experimental flies, I took my electronic depth finder. It was essential for me to understand the underwater topography of the lake. The water is too murky for me to see more than 30 inches, even with the aid of high sun and polarized glasses.

I crisscrossed the eastern two-thirds of the lake, making mental notes and triangulating areas of the deepest water. I found distinct holes and channels, with depths up to 11 feet.

I took three rods onto the lake with me: two with floating lines armed with Micro Leeches—claret and claret/black—Hare Scuds and assorted chironomids, and a clear sink-tip with my usual Bead Prince and Midnight Bugger. Early in my first mapping run I trolled and retrieved the Bugger/Prince combo. I caught a small largemouth bass that

In heavily fished waters where the fish are released, the fish can become educated, wary. So it is quite important to jot some notes about specific flies, specific techniques, and productive locations, and helpful hints learned that day about dealing with other anglers who want to catch the same fish you do, such as times of day or days of the week to avoid.

Bluegills are bushwhacking opportunists. They lie near or under cover waiting for food to swim or crawl near their position. Shorelines and weed beds are productive locations. As for flies, standard trout patterns will do just fine.

took the Bugger. Then, nothing, not even a strike for the next twenty minutes.

There were four other anglers on the lake during my patrol. Before my day ended, six other anglers tried their luck.

Shortly, I started plying deeper water—6 to 10 feet—with Hare Scuds, Micro Leeches, and chironomids. My attention was split between watching my strike indicator and the display on my Buddy depth finder. It would also indicate the presence of nearby fish, but no concentration of fish. They were spread out and cruising at all depths. During the first hour I tallied only a couple of additional strikes, but no hookups. A float tuber with a spinning rod landed two before I could finally land a trout. He never tallied a third fish before he left.

There was very little rise activity, so I decided to concentrate on transition zones where shallow water quickly descended into deeper and on boundaries at the edges of vegetation. I discovered a number of these types along the far (northern) shoreline. Fishing a glass bead/black body/red rib chironomid on the point, 4 feet under the indicator, and a claret Micro Leech on the dropper, I finally got a solid hookup and landed a 10-inch trout. I pumped its stomach, and found a couple of tiny, tiny chironomid pupae. A few casts later, I landed another trout of about the same size when it took the Micro Leech. Had the "bite" turned on? I fished and mapped farther along the shoreline. It was in this same general area that Marcy and I had our best fishing on our initial foray. Within 15 minutes I had a third fish. I did my best to steal this fish's breakfast too with my stomach pump. Again, just a couple of extremely small midge pupae. So for the next hour I weaved in and out along this same shoreline, fishing and making a mental map of the lake bottom as I watched both my electronic screen and my strike indicator. Occasionally, I would get a strike and land another 3 or 4 fish. I pumped a third stomach, finding exactly what I had found in the other two stomachs: a pair of micro pupae. All landed fish took the same size 12 chironomid.

I needed a bathroom and lunch break. So, I mapped my route back to the launch site. As I lunched at the water's edge, I watched some bluegill on patrol in a jungle of "floating hearts." I caught two in two casts, watching a small pack follow the Hare Scud until the leader of the pack sucked it in. I got a few photos.

When I returned to the lake, I kicked my pontoon boat to the far shore. As I headed out, another angler with a spinning rod landed a small trout. It would be the last one caught by an angler other than me.

I patrolled and mentally mapped depths as I went. I started casting to the likely boundaries and transition zones, catching the occasional fish. On three occasions a fish would rise, I would cast my fly to the ring of the rise, and I caught a fish. This worked maybe one out of four times, but it was well worth it. I landed my largest rainbow of the day—about 16"—by casting to a rise. I did not land the largest trout I briefly hooked. I had cast into a deep, narrow channel, as I was traveling near it. I saw a big flash as I turned the fish before it expelled my fly.

All totaled, I landed more than a dozen fish before I quit just before 3 p.m. All landed trout except one, ate the chironomid, glass bead/black body/red wire rib. Ten other anglers landed but three fish that I know about. I did not feel badly about my performance, however I wonder if I could have done better by changing flies or methods. There is never enough time, it seems, to find the Holy Grail combination of method, fly, depth, and location to catch a fish on every other cast. Before I return to Big Lake I will formulate a little different game plan, once I have had more time to process today's events. I *know* I can get more strikes and land more fish per hour next time. As with every stream and lake I fish, this is my goal, and this is my pleasure: crack the code, open the safe, catch the fish that others cannot.

***March 5, 2012. Little and Big Lakes.***

Ground frozen, frosty when I arrived at 10 a.m. Forecast was for warming into 50s. Water temp upper 40s. Occasional rising fish, too far to cast. Fishing a Laser Beam size 10 and 12 maroon Micro Leech at Little Tree. 4½ feet from

This albino rainbow trout can be easily seen as it swims in relatively clear water, providing the angler with an opportunity for sight fishing. In addition to watching an albino intercept my well-placed cast, I also had numerous chances to watch these fish reject my fly.

Hareline Dubbin distributes some beautiful and durable anodized metallic beads. This fish took a claret Micro Leech with a blood red bead at the head.

indicator to Leech, 6 feet to Laser. Water over 10 feet deep. Second cast an 18-inch football. Casted toward rises, but too far. Presentation: Cast and let it sit, wait 30 seconds, short pull. Caught 3 fish. All took within 30 seconds of cast. No response to retrieve and let sit. Apparently, the 3 successful casts put the flies near cruising fish. All on Laser Beam. Did not experiment with different flies or different depths, nor launch boat.

Launched Hobie on Big. Depth finder battery dead. Doh! Decided to troll stillwater line with Black Micro and Prince. Found fish in deeper part of lake from island to far dock. 6 to 9 feet of water. Nothing in deepest area. Caught 3 rainbows, then an albino rainbow.

Pumped stomachs, only chironomids from size 30 to size 18. Dark olive and a few brown. No adults ingested, but adults hatched as I photoed the pupae. Another rainbow and two more albinos. Most took Prince. Best presentation. Troll a ways, then retrieve the fly. Took on retrieve. Went back to Laser Beam and Micro. Caught 4 more trout, including a 4th albino. Laser took all but one fish. Tried a Black Micro with a black chironomid for a short while. Had larger indicator, too much splash? Out of small indicators. No strikes.

Two guys at Little casting from bank. One guy hooked and landed a fish. Thought the albinos were golden trout. Big Tree one guy casting from docks. No fish landed that I saw. Two guys in pontoon boats trolling and casting got no fish that I saw.

***March 17, 2012. Big and Little Lakes.***

Erin go bragh! Air temp 36 degrees. Patrick and I arrived after 10 a.m., sat in 4Runner, and watched rain mixed with snow. Inflow streams high and murky. Little seemed too murky to fish.

Launched in Big after 11 a.m. Trolled and cast Micro Leech and Prince. Patrick trolled red body/brown hackle/black tail with a little maroon mixed in tail, and olive Hares's Ear. Patrick got 3 or 4 on Woolly Bugger before he broke it off during the release of a fish. I got one on Micro Leech and missed a couple others. Switched to Black Micro and various chironomids under an indicator. Fish took Micro.

Trout were rising in spurts for pupae in surface film. I had left my emerger box at home. Switched to a variety of buggers. Missed some strikes. Eventually stayed with Micro

There can be a huge advantage for late winter or early spring stillwater fly anglers: many anglers are unwilling to brave the weather.

and chironomid. Pumped some stomachs. All chironomid pupae, olive, reddish brown, and metallic. Best chironomid: Laser Beam. Landed one fish that had a Snow Cone pattern broken off in its jaw. Fly body red/black/silver wire.

I missed many more strikes than usual. Can't explain why. Cold water/hesitant fish? Caught 2 albinos, my last 2 fish of the day. Patrick's last two strikes were from albino, one of which he watched chase the fly; pulled it away before fish could be solidly hooked. Then landed one albino.

We landed 8 or 9 fish each. Saw one other angler fish Big from dock nearest Little. Nothing.

***March 22, 2012. Mountain Lake.***

On way to Seattle, arrived about 10 a.m., 36 degrees, snow on the ground. Overcast, no wind. Two guys launching tubes to troll. I fished dock. Chironos hatching. A few rises. Started casting stillwater line with Olive/Black Bugger, no bead, on dropper line. No point fly. I was in a hurry to make sure tubers did not fish from or near dock. I landed a couple of smaller fish immediately. One of the tubers got a fish just off boat launch. I landed a 21- to 22-inch football on Bugger. Landed an albino.

Circled back to 4Runner to get other rods and flies. Did not fish indicator at all, not wanting to show the tubers. Fished "naked,"chironos on floating line. Cast out, counted to 10, then slow retrieve, both hand-twist and pulls. Interspersed with lifts. A slow lift was often productive. Some hits light, saw only a slight straightening of kink in fly line. Fun.

Best flies: Son 2 of Laser Beam (red metal bead, gunmetal body, red wire rib) and two new unnamed patterns, the first consisting of a black bead, gunmetal body, copper rib, and the second a black bead, silver holographic body, and small fl. orange wool rib. Pumped 6 or 7 fish, not many in each fish, but all chironomid pupae. Many adults on surface. Landed 15 fish by 12:15 and took 80 photos. Lots of snowy scenic photos.

Sometimes fishing is a bit too easy. Hard to believe with the air temperature in the 30s. I am sure the water was much warmer. The days immediately preceding the snow were in the 50s, and it takes a long while to change the water temperature even a single degree. A big hatch of chironomids and the fish ate 'em with enthusiasm. Simple formula for crazy fishing. I left totally satisfied. Didn't need to catch another fish. May not see another day like this for a while, and that's okay.

***March 26, 2012. Mountain Lake with Mark and Joann.***

Joann and I drove from Seattle to Mark's home. Mark took drift boat, as Joann drove with me. Arrived at lake about noon. Logging activities, gate was left open as we came and went. At the lake, a hunter on an ATV shouting boat driving directions. One fisherman on dock who soon left to fish middle lake. Float tuber above the lake outlet stream. I made a few casts from dock with indicator while Mark launched boat. Nothing. Nothing on retrieve. Tuber seemed to get a few missed strikes, but never saw a fish.

Day was bright sun, 54 degrees, and very windy at times. Much different from March 22—overcast and windless. Hard to know how much fishing pressure on the weekend before us. Anchored boat just off dock. Slow. Joann and Mark each got a strike, but nothing else there. I was casting naked, but no strike. Cast bugger and large mayfly nymph on sinking line. Nothing. Eventually settled almost straight out a very long cast from the outlet. Mark had good number of strikes on a *beadless* black Micro Leech. Joann got several, including an albino on Black Micro with silver bead. Mark got a couple of albinos and an 18-incher plus smaller ones. Moved around here and there and got a few.

Moved near distant bay across from outlet. Casting toward outlet and casting toward lake center were best. Sporadically lots of action. Mark swithched to Turkey Chirono Pupa—best chirono imitation of the day. I switched Joann over to Turkey and a red metal bead/rusty brown Micro Leech she had tied the day before at Mark's. Her Micro was deadly, but the Turkey caught some, too.

As the action would fade, I moved the boat farther from the bay toward the lake middle. After every move we had a flurry of action. I landed a couple on an Ice Cream Cone. Good fishing.

After 4:30 p.m. I made the last move much closer to the shoreline opposite the bay, an area that had produced for me on previous trips in 2010 and 2011. Joann had three fish on, landing 2, on her first 3 casts. Rusty Micro Leech, red bead. Two casts later she hooked a bigger fish that broke her off on a submerged stump. Mark landed a fish on his last

Mother Joann and son Mark Severson. This was a family fishing outing. Interestingly, all anglers this day were happiest when someone else caught a good fish. That's true love!

cast, so we headed to the launch site for departure. We landed 25–30 fish, and lost that many, too. Very few chironomid adults on surface, and few risers, though the rise activity was best after 3:30 in the center of the lake.

***April 13, 2012. Mountain Lake with Joann.***

Had high hopes after our last outing. Met in Kelso, ate at Denny's. Left Joann's Camry in Denny's parking lot. Oops.

Made Mountain Lake by late morning. One other angler. Fishing was slow. Trolling no good. Finally settled on chironomids. Okay results, especially on Turkey Noid and shiny black body, silver rib, silver bead. No monsters. Moved much eventually, and caught a few after each move. One albino. Other guy got very few fish that we saw. As we were in out last half hour (4–4:30 p.m.), another guy showed up who fished chironomids under an indicator in the center of the lake. He did well as we were winding down. Weather may have been too nice through most of day, though rain was beginning as we left. New guy had it dialed. One possibility—the bite was coming on as we were beginning to leave.

All stomachs I pumped had the usual size 16 chironomid pupae.

***April 14, 2012. Mountain Lake with Mark Severson.***

Spent the night in Kelso at the Super 8, $53 + taxes. Remember: Exit 39. Mark arrived about 8:30, and we were fishing by 10 a.m. Slow, especially for Mark. He landed two by 4:30 p.m. I did much better, even with identical flies. Don't know why. The older guy from yesterday was leaving as we came in. He said he destroyed the fish until 9 a.m., then it slowed greatly. Early arrival could be the key. Seen that before!

Some flies just look "right." This tri-color-tail Bugger with a peacock body is such a fly and a member of my All-Star Team.

We moved around, we changed flies, but no super secret found. Best flies: same as day before. Fished naked, floating line, longer leader, no indicator. Worked okay, but using indicator was better. Saw lots of cruising albinos, but fish were moody. We missed many, many strikes. Don't know why. I went to 5X just to be sure tippet wasn't an issue. Mark fished 4X, and this could have been the problem in clear water, spooky fish. Micro Leech—zilch, the same for buggers and Prince.

***April 27, 2012. Apple Pond.***

Rain on forecast for p.m. I arrived by 10:30 a.m. Water clarity poor, maybe 2 feet. Pond looked low, too. Initially took photos of some flies, overrun reel, fly lines. Started to rain. Ended photo session. Time to fish. Launched Hobie—two rods, floater, and indicator and clear sink-tip. On sink tip—the only line I used today—I had a #6 Peacock Bugger, with a few strands of Mylar in the tail, and black hackle, gold bead. On point I had a red bead, black & claret hackle over black dubbed body and rabbit tail black.

Within a few minutes of launch hooked a good fish (15 inches) while stripping a bit during troll. Fought surprisingly hard! Pumped stomach—nothing. Hooked another soon, about 12 inches. Pumped—nothing. Both had taken the Peacock . . . in the library . . . with the candlestick. Soon a few more, all on Peacock, liked a lift or strip better than troll. Had one fish follow the lift right to the surface. As I roll cast to lift the line for a recast, the fish swirled and grabbed the fly. My roll cast hooked it. Eventually switched our black Rabbit Bugger for a Black Micro Leech silver bead. Made my way around most of the pond. Best action was in middle and far half across from boat launch, no surprise. Landed 9 fair-hooked fish. Only one took the Micro Leech; 8 of 9 took Peacock on the dropper. The gold bead? Don't know, but preference was quite obvious. Ran out of time just after 1 p.m. Fairly good fishing. Did not try indicator rod. All fish fought extra hard. Peculiar. Smallest fish about 12 inches, largest maybe 16 inches.

***April 29, 2012. Apple Pond.***

My primary goal is photos I need for the book. Fishing will be incidental, but I am curious after last trip. Must resist temptation to fish until some serious attention to photography.

Lots of fly shots. Good. Not much insect activity, though there is an occasional rise. Random, unpredictable. Some photos in direct sunlight; some in shadow. Bright light makes it hard to see LCD screen. Took lots of shots, hoping I could get one good one of each subject.

Sometimes a lucky photo shot happens as an angler holds the rod in one hand and the camera in the other.

Finally took a little time to fish. Did not try chironos under indicator on last trip. Did today. Pair of flies: glass bead Pheasant Tail and Snow Cone black body. First cast got a spunky 13-inch rainbow on Pheasant. Then, nothing and more nothing for the next 15 minutes. Moved all over the near half of the pond to spots which have historically been productive. Time for more photos while the breeze stays down.

Sporadic splashy rises made me look hard at the pond surface. I saw a curious little beetle with pink markings on its head drift by. On Macro setting, I shot some pics with arm extended, poor vision on screen because of bright light. Hoped I could get one in focus. Saw nothing else on surface. More photos of flies from my box.

Decided to cast Beadhead Peacock Bugger that had produced so well a couple days earlier. Fish on first cast, about same size as the other. What is it about the first cast? And, just as before with the chironos, nothing more except a half-hearted tug which I couldn't bury the hook point. So, it's back to the chironos. A couple of swings and misses. Went to the most distant point in the pond and fished around the lily pads. Not many pads on the surface, and the leaves were small this early in the spring. A strike and a miss. A second takedown of the indicator—same result. Finally hooked and landed an 11-inch rainbow. Stomach pump showed only a few small chironomid pupae. Glass Bead Pheasant, silver rib. Two more strikes, and lost one as I reached to grab it. Then, nothing, nothing, nothing, and I made my way back to the 4Runner. It was a short day, mediocre catching, but I got my photos. Mission accomplished.

The alderfly looks like a caddisfly with armor. I have never witnessed a hatch of these insects, just the occasional individual.

As I was loading my gear I found a little alderfly—about a size 12—crawling on the truck. I wonder if these were the focus of interest for the rising fish today. If so, they were not so numerous I could actually find one on the pond's surface. It might have been worth a little effort to fish a dark caddis imitation which would have been a good match for this bug. I will make sure I have one in my box next time I launch.

## Lake Journal Entries from Trips to New Lakes

***June 8, 2010. Edith Lake.***

Weather looked promising, fluffy clouds and blue skies. Edith lake is beautiful country. Rolling hills, variety of trees, looks like central Oregon in many ways. The lake is like a squared off "W." Parked at the far end of the lake. Took a half hour or more to get John set up to launch his Hobie (pontoon boat). Another half hour for me to set up and finally get into the water. I kicked off from the shore just about 1 p.m. The water at the launch site was shallow near the shoreline, so we pushed well away before fishing. We both started with sinking lines; John with a Type III, me with the clear stillwater slow-sinking line. John reported

Edith Lake is an easy 15 minute drive south of Kamloops, British Columbia. If an angler based in Kamloops has only a few hours to fish, Edith is an excellent choice. It's mostly rainbows, but there are a few brook trout in the lake, too.

a strike while trolling within the first few minutes of his launch. We were both armed with leech patterns. John black, me an olive Bugger.

The Buddy (depth finder) registered fish in the shallow bay. I soon resorted to a floating line and indicator. Tried a burgundy Micro Leech, then a Hare Scud. Nothing. John continued to troll, and I went back to trolling the maroon Micro near the shore parallel to the road on the west side of the lake. This portion of the lake sloped to deep water quickly, over 20 feet in a reasonable cast from the bank. Tried a Half-Back Nymph, too. Nothing. Shortly, I spoke to a guy rowing a canoe who said he was trolling a black Micro Leech. He had one strike, and suggested I try an olive

I don't see it often, but occasionally I see a canoe set up for rowing. I used to own one myself, but I sold it years ago. I have never missed it—not once.

leech of some sort. He was a local who had obviously fished Edith before. A nearby bank angler offered he had landed a two-pounder on Power Bait. Another pontooner said he had landed a rainbow as he had trolled away from the NW corner boat launch. Then, nothing since.

As I trolled out of casting range of a second bank angler, I finally got a strike. Missed it. So, there were fish around that might bite. I caught up with John. He thought maybe he had another strike. The puzzle continued. I got a second strike and a miss, and John broke off a fish on a hard strike combined with an overly enthusiastic response with the rod tip.

After 3 o'clock a guy with a cartop boat launched where we were parked. As I had hoped, this guy seemed to know exactly what he was doing to catch fish at Edith. I got into position to watch him. He did not go far, going immediately to a position not far from the shore in the SW corner of the lake. He patrolled it back and forth, casting a sinking line. He trolled a short distance, then would stop to retrieve his line for a few strips, though never the full length of line he trailed behind his boat. I was interested in his retrieve—short and fast like a scud swimming action, or a dragonfly nymph. I was fishing a skinny damsel nymph, then a Bead Prince, while mirroring his retrieve. I got a strike. Yes! Then, nothing. Not catching anything, the newly arrived expert moved to the eastern shoreline and started trolling along it just a few rod lengths out from the bank. As I continued to

This Edith Lake rainbow tried to destroy my Beadhead Prince Nymph. The rod and reel I am holding were pulled off my boat by a nasty fish on a subsequent trip to British Columbia, never to be seen again as it sank into 20 feet of water.

troll and watch him, I got a strike. This 13-inch rainbow stayed on the hook. Time for the stomach pump. Quite revealing. Packed with food, predominantly scuds, with lots of chironomid larvae in the mix. Got some good photos. Got the fish on my #12 Bead Prince. After the pumping I switched to a dark olive green scud pattern with a gold bead at the head.

Thought I was on to something now. Fished the scud for perhaps 30 minutes without a sniff. Changed back to the Prince, following John up the same shoreline as the expert, who had disappeared around the corner toward the north end of the lake. I wanted to find him again to discover specifically where he was fishing. John got another strike. I got nothing until I was near a shallow shoal, trolling just off the edge of it. I had cast from shallow water into the deep and used a short quick retrieve of the fly, just like the expert had demonstrated. Bang. Soon I cradled a 13 to 14-inch rainbow that had eaten my Prince. Hard-fighting fish, just like the first. Impressive. John took some photos of me and my fish, then floated away. I continued my pursuit of the expert, whom I now spied perhaps 200 yards away. Soon I had another strike. Missed. Then another rainbow, which I landed. A clone of the others, about 14 inches. Canoe Man happened by just after my release, wanting to know if the fish was a rainbow. I asked him what other species were present in the lake. Brook trout. I decided to try an Olive Willy, a fly I had never tried.

As I got nearer the Expert, I heard him tell another fisherman that he was fishing a dragonfly nymph, not the scud I had originally suspected. Thus, the short, fast retrieve. A few minutes later I landed a 9-inch brookie on the Willy. Then resumed my pursuit of the expert, trolling, watching, and listening as I went. Got another couple of strikes and misses.

Two boys in a cartopper chugged out into my course, dropped anchor, and proceeded to fish chironomids under indicators, not too far from where I caught the brook trout. I trolled on a course that allowed me to watch them. They had obviously fished here before. Later, as I passed near them, they told me they were fishing 18 feet from the indicator to the fly in 19 feet of water. Between them they had tallied one strike.

Eventually I caught up with the expert as he was talking with Canoe Man. Expert had landed a 3-pounder. No one here talks about length, only pounds. Caught it on a yellow damsel nymph. As the pair trolled together back toward the main body of the lake, I ventured part way into the distant arm of the lake to check out the area and chart its depth where I had observed the Expert fishing before he left. After doing so, and no strikes, I too began to fish my way back to the main body of the lake. I had a strike and miss, then got slammed by a hard fighter. During the battle the rainbow jumped higher than my head! Some serious air. He shook loose as I eventually brought him near my boat. Bead Prince again.

As I trolled near the shallow shoal where I had gotten a fish earlier, I had a hard strike, and the hook point held. The fish almost got me into my backing and never jumped. Another great fight. 16-inch rainbow. Pumped its stomach. One scud and a hundred tiny olive chironomid pupae. Bead Prince scored another trout eating something much different from my fly.

One more strike as I made my way to the 4Runner. Total for me: 5 rainbows landed, 1 brookie, and 10 missed strikes. Most on troll. Did not witness any fish landed by others throughout the day. Canoe Man related he had caught two rainbows and two brookies, while the Expert got one fish that I had heard about. Power Bait had accounted for one fish from the bank. Boaters and bankers came and went all afternoon. My 6 fish landed was respectable, I guess, along with 10 other chances. Not too bad for the first time at Edith.

Another Edith Lake rainbow. Having to take a photo of the fish without help, I slid it onto my extended legs near my feet. I put the rod into the photo for perspective.

Learned lessons:

- Always observe other anglers, especially those who seem to be fishing with definite purpose in specific areas.
- Retrieve and location can be much more important than the fly pattern. When in doubt, use a Bead Prince.
- Stomach pump and Buddy electronics are invaluable on new waters.
- Remember the binoculars left in the truck.
- I fished a 5X tippet. This may have been significant in Edith's clear water.
- Persist to finally solve the puzzle. Today was tough at times, but rewarding.
- I got vastly different food preferences in different portions of the lake. When the fish are being more selective, different flies for different locations will likely be the difference between success and failure.
- Always consider doing reconnaissance on local anglers on the lake.
- Persist. Persist some more.

***June 16, 2011. Heffley Lake with Jeff Hilden.***

Got to have Plan A, B, and C. Jeff Hilden and I thought we might try out Black Lake in the general vicinity of Roche Lake today. I had studied a map online and had a clear understanding of the route. We had heard the road in was nasty, but I had 4-wheel drive if needed, and reasonable clearance. Once to the turnoff for the final leg into the lake, we found the road was not only nasty, but downright hideous. If I started down what was a narrow boulder-filled track, I might not have enough room to turnaround to reverse our course. I don't know if any tow truck operator in the western world would venture onto this forsaken "road" to rescue us. Fortunately, we had options.

On the way back to the main highway, we stopped at Tulip Lake. Once we made it to a parking area at lakeside, we walked out onto a large dock to survey the scene. Standing in a cold, cold breeze, we saw no other anglers and no rising fish. We had heard no encouraging reports about the lake from the local fishing store in Kamloops. We left.

Jeff had fished Heffley Lake with a guide on a previous trip a few years earlier. Even though he had only caught two fish all day on the lake, we thought it had potential. I had researched directions to the lake the night before, so we were set to go.

I burned up a half hour of travel when I took a wrong turn. My directions were good. I just need to follow them. Doh!

On the map I had looked at the night before, I located an apparent access on Lower Heffley Road. After locating this access point, I quickly realized the "launch area" was not a totally simple matter there. There is one small slide-in point along the road before it dead-ends at a couple of homes. With preliminary scouting accomplished, we decided the best place to start was at the resort farther up the main road. We could possibly get more information and a better launch site. And Jeff was keen on the possibility of renting a boat with a motor at the resort.

Once at the resort, we talked to the man behind the counter, who indicated that we could not rent a boat there because we did not have Canadian driving licenses. As for launching our boats nearby at a public site, he indicated that vandalism to my vehicle was a definite possibility. As for the fishing potential, his assessment was sketchy and vague. Additionally, we saw no other boats on the lake in the area of the resort. We figured if the fishing was good, word would be out and anglers would flock to this lake. So we circled back to Lower Heffley Road and readied our pontoon boats and gear for launching.

During preparations Jeff found a dragonfly nymph walking on the roadway. It's a great clue when the insect trout food comes to you. The insect made for some good photos.

Because of the dragonfly nymph's distinctive jet propulsion swimming movement, the artificial imitation is most effectively fished with short pulls of the fly line. As in the adult stage, dragonfly nymphs are predators.

Jeff slid into the water long before I did. He trolled directly toward the far side of the lake. Once I launched, it was not long before I got a strike trolling a Prince parallel to the near shore, headed west. Missed. It was the only attention my fly got as I paralleled the shoreline, which eventually turned south. I was slowly making my way to Jeff's distant location. Much of the water near the shoreline measured 9 to 12 feet deep, quickly sloping to 30 feet out toward the open water. In certain areas I located a good number of fish on my Buddy, but they were not enthusiastic, easily fooled biters.

We finally set up our stations in a large shallow bay at the west end of the lake. Our electronics indicated there were some fish around.

In early afternoon there was a steady hatch of *Callibaetis* mayflies. I caught the first fish of the day—a 14-inch rainbow—by casting and retrieving an unnamed (to me) Callibaetis Nymph that had been sitting in my fly box for years into about 20 feet of water from my shallower water position over a depth of about 9 to 11 feet.

I was casting my Type III sinker, wishing I had not left my clear slower-sinking line in the 4Runner. The Type III had too much sink when I was fishing shallower water with a slow retrieve. I got a couple more halfhearted strikes, but the fish were not committed to what we were doing.

Though the *Callibaetis* adults were on the water, it was the nymph imitation that caught my first Heffley Lake fish.

As the afternoon advanced, Jeff was getting bored, so he decided to troll his way back to the truck. Fishing in about 9 feet of water across the bay, Jeff got hit hard by a fish he landed on a sparse, beadless black Micro Leech. This was the beginning. I switched to a black Micro Leech with a silver beadhead. The fishing was not fast, but it was consistent for the next 40 minutes. I landed a good trout and broke off another. Jeff landed two or three more, then I got a third and missed some additional strikes, all while fishing the shallow water of the bay. Some fish had come in from the depths and were cruising for food. Then it turned off. The weather had turned sunny and the breeze had lain down. We trolled and talked our way back to the launch site. Not another nibble.

Lessons learned:

- Next time, take the Sun Peaks Resort Exit off Hwy 1 to get to Hwy 5.
- Always bring the clear stillwater fly line, even if it is just the reel and no rod. I needed it today.
- Tie up some Micro Leech patterns with a much sparser body.
- It would have probably been better fishing if we had gotten here much earlier. This is a recurring theme.
- I should have given more play to fishing dragonfly patterns than I did today.
- Next time, consider fishing deeper water, and cover more ground. There are shoals toward the resort that Jeff's guide had focused their fishing efforts on. Though Jeff had mediocre fishing results at that time, the guide obviously knew that the shoals were the place to be.
- Bring an anchor for the other Hobie boat.
- Use the stomach pump even if I think I know what the fish are preferring, like the mayfly hatch. In retrospect, I cannot reason why I did not use my stomach pump on my fish or one of Jeff's.

***June 17, 2012. Heffley Lake with Chuck Wagner.***

Slept in, getting up at 7:28 a.m. Made Heffley Lake by about 9:00. Overcast, no rain, no wind. No action until about 10:30.

Chuck got things started by landing a couple fish on the troll. Black bead/black body Micro Leech. I got a fish about 15 inches by casting and stripping. Pumped stomach—more than a dozen partially digested leeches, one scud. Choice of fly became obvious. Decided to fish balanced leech under indicator. Landed a small fish on a brown one. Then, got broken off by big trout, over 20 inches, that jumped, then dived into weeds. Had one more balanced claret leech. It, too, got broken off in the weeds by a fish. A 7-pound tippet strength is not adequate sometimes.

Experimented with a slip knot to secure tippet to body of Micro Leech to create a balanced fly. It worked acceptably well, and the fish liked it.

When will I learn? As I suspended leech under indicator, I fished my intermediate sink-tip casting and stripping while watching the indicator. I missed 10–12 strikes on indicator rod because I was to slow to pick it up as I fished the other rod. So, periodically, I would just fish the indicator rod solo. Of course, the fish would NEVER bite with my full attention on the indicator rod. Once as I missed another on the suspended leech as I stripped the sinking line rod, I started to reel in the sink tip to again focus just on the indicator rod. As I reeled in, the biggest fish I saw all day grabbed my fly and jumped. Then it dove into the weeds and broke me off.

Fishing was definitely better during a breeze.

Even the best flies will produce mediocre results if an angler is not on the lake during "the bite." I must remind myself to put my journaling aside at night so I can get a reasonably early start the next morning.

A "balanced" Micro Leech presents a more realistic *horizontal* profile of the fly. Virtually any nymph or leech pattern suspended under an indicator can be tied in this manner.

A large caddisfly adult entered my no-fly zone so I shot it down to get a closer look. What fish would not be excited to see this B-52 morsel!

New plan: Fish two indicator rods so I could have a hand on each rod. When I did, of course the fish would not bite. The opportunity to fish two rods on British Columbia lakes offers the potential for frustration because most anglers have only two hands.

Hooked another fish while stripping the fly. When the fish was nearing exhaustion under my rod tip, I saw a high-speed underwater streak in pursuit of my panicked trout. It was a loon. Another National Geographic moment. The bird took my fish, but I got my flies back.

Earlier, I had watched two adult loons with one little chick loon. Most entertaining as little loon stayed close at all times. One time an adult loon lifted itself erect on the water to flap its wings, as if stretching or drying its wings. Immediately, the tiny bird did exactly the same thing. Amusing.

Soon, all three birds crawled out on a partially submerged log nearby and were, apparently, dining on my stolen fish. The loon family stayed in our little bay at all times. One of the adults surfaced within a couple of rod lengths from me, having little fear.

Captured a *large* caddisfly when I knocked it out of the air with my hand. It crawled onto my boat so I got some good pics. About 1½ inches long, gray-brown wing, dark olive body, about the same size as an October caddis. Definitely the largest lake caddisfly I have ever seen. Captured it for more photos, and then put it into my little lidded container for future observation. Posed it with a Stimulator, then it plopped into the water and paddled off to—hopefully—complete its life's mission.

Decided to tie on a large modified Carey Bugger to perhaps imitate a large Caddis pupa. Tied it on the tippet of my clear line spooled on my Lamson reel on my Sage RPL 4-piece. Started to slowly kick toward deeper water and the lake outflow where I had many strikes yesterday. Once I had my usual 13 strips of line out, I picked up the intermediate sink-tip and began stripping out line to troll both rods. After a few strips, my unattended trolling rod got yanked hard and was pulled from the boat! And the rod kept moving farther from me as the fish continued to run. I immediately reversed course to chase the rod. As the reel sank, the rod tip came up, extending straight vertically a couple of feet above the water before it slowly sank out of sight. My efforts to snag the rod or the line by dredging the bottom with a couple of flies and 4 or 5 split shot on the leader were futile. About $600 (retail) of equipment—and the *big* fish which I did not see—were lost. When will I learn? Am I totally incorrigible? I was lucky 2 days ago to get back my rod and reel after it was pulled into the water by a Roche Lake fish. Apparently, I had used up all my rod-saving luck on Friday. No such luck today. The fish had the last laugh.

As we kicked toward the takeout, Chuck landed his fifth fish on a #14 tan LaFontaine Sparkle Pupa. I got a couple of soft strikes trolling but no more hookups. I will always remember my last hookup on Heffley Lake.

I have not missed so many strikes in a single fishing day in recent memory . . . maybe ever. I was totally out of sync. As soon as I put down one rod to tend the second, the fish seemed to ALWAYS strike the fly on the unattended rod. Unbelievable! I would have been way ahead to fish only one rod.

The suspended Balance Micro Leech can be an extremely effective technique, and leeches are definitely used as a main food source in Heffley. Midge hatch was quite sparse compared to other British Columbia lakes I have fished. Major bite period was supposedly 11:40 to 1:40. Bite started earlier, but a good portion definitely fell into this time slot.

Reminders:

- I am sorely lacking in beadless Micro Leeches. Fish may prefer them, and in shallow water they won't get caught in weeds or drag the bottom.
- The Cortland green-blue intermediate sink-tip is a great line, and casts much better than my clear sink-tip. It casts extremely well on my Sage 389LL. What a sweet rod, which was patiently awaiting my return after so many years of being ignored. Never again.
- Forgot two-way radios. Bring GPS. Make sure depth finder works. Totally blind on new waters. The importance of it was learned *again* at Jacko Lake.
- Reconsider the wisdom of two rods.

CHAPTER 12

# Fishing Under the Stars

Fishing beneath a moonlit night sky is a mix of romance, intrigue, Loch Ness, and vampire bats. It also offers the chance to catch trophy fish.

How would you like a shot at landing a true trophy lake fish, maybe the biggest your lake of choice holds? Is solitude on a busy lake, the opportunity to fish anywhere you choose with no one else around, an attractive thought? How about living a fly-fishing experience that few other anglers will ever have? If you answered "Tell me more!" to any or all of these, then plan on fishing stillwaters in the heart of the night.

If you have never fished on a lake or pond at night, sensations can be mixed: eerie, tantalizingly dangerous, exhilarating. You may experience fear of the dark, Loch Ness, Jaws, the Creature from the Black Lagoon, gators and crocs, river monsters. I guarantee at least one fleeting thought of "Will something silent and evil grab my legs and pull me under, just like in the movies?" But this will fade into the distant dark when you get a massive strike that pulls your rod down hard, taking the tip to the water's surface. All in all, it's a thrilling adventure.

## My Introduction to the Night

My introduction to fishing under the stars was on a private lake in eastern Oregon. Since public trout waters in Oregon cannot be legally fished at night (Miller Lake in south central Oregon is an exception), the fact that Grindstone Lake is on the heart of a large ranch allowed us to stay on the good side of the law.

Brian O'Keefe had graciously invited Don Roberts and me to join him in pursuit of some huge rainbows that lived in this lake. It was August. In Oregon's high desert at summer's zenith, the temperatures can routinely exceed 100 degrees F. Our first day made the mark, and the fish were not enthusiastic about eating our artificial flies, which can be quite typical for lake fish during the dog days of summer. However, we did fool a few lunkers into eating our leeches. None of the landed fish I remember were smaller than 24 inches, and they all had profiles of dirigibles.

My 4-weight rod was put to the test, bending almost all the way back to my white knuckles. The advantage of such a full-flexing, light-tipped fly rod was that it was difficult for a hard pulling trout to break my tippet. Think of trying to break a bungee cord: it can't be done. The same thing is true for a forgiving fly rod. And if you are questioning whether a fish is played to irrecoverable exhaustion, I don't believe so. Like a runner sprinting up a hill, who will tire and stop before his heart actually explodes, a tired fish that can be brought to hand after a hard fight can be held in the water and revived before release by any angler with common sense.

After dinner and some fishing conversation, night had fully fallen. A partial moon provided enough light for us to find our way as we slipped our float tubes into the lake again. High on anticipation, we began our night patrol to discover whether the big rainbows could track down our leeches in the night.

Besides excellent vision, fish have a sensory organ, the lateral line, that runs parallel to its sides. Just like ears, the lateral line picks up vibrations and movements in the fish's environment. Vibrations and sounds travel a long way underwater—much better than in air. Water is a denser medium. Even if a fish cannot initially see the fly in the dark, the splash when it lands after the cast and the vibrations created as it is stripped or trolled through the water alert the fish in proximity. Big fish—survivors who lived long enough to grow large—are usually discerning when it comes to distinguishing the sound of a potentially edible morsel from the vibration created by a big and threatening creature that might dine on them. Bottom line: a fish is capable of finding and grabbing your fly in the dark.

The excitement of the grab and fight of a big fish in the dark is magnified because the angler relies on feel and sound, with little or no aid from the eyes. The senses of hearing and touch are ramped up a notch to compensate for the loss of sight. In normal light, we can watch and anticipate what a trout will do during the fight and react instantly to thwart the fish's efforts. In the darkness, it is possible to get disoriented, like spinning briefly on a merry-go-round with your eyes closed, then imme-

As the sun starts to set it's time for final preparations while there is still adequate light to ready fly rods, organize equipment, and prepare the boat or float tube. These tasks will take at least twice the time doing them in the dark.

Casting a large black Bunny Leech into the darkness in response to a nearby, unseen splash was occasionally rewarded with a big tug.

diately going for a walk with the eyes still shut. All these add to the fun and unique nature of the night fishing experience.

Most anglers find it easiest and most effective to troll a fly at night. But I had my most productive efforts by casting my black Bunny Leech and retrieving it at a medium-fast pace in one-foot strips. From my position I would cast alternately toward all points on the compass and many points in between. Whenever I heard a fish splash in the dark I would swivel to cast generally in its direction. This strategy was reinforced when I was occasionally rewarded with a strike. During the next couple of hours, I landed five rainbows between 6 and 8 pounds.

Fatigue eventually won out. I was thoroughly soaked from trying to corral thrashing fish that doused me as I tried to hold them long enough to remove the fly and revive them a bit before they swam into the darkness. We had endured very warm temperatures during the day, adding to our fatigue, and we would be up relatively early in the morning to launch our float tubes in the morning light. It had been a memorable experience in the dark.

## Don't Have Night Vision Goggles? Then, Prepare.

If you have an extra thousand dollars, you can buy one of the premiere visual tools for fishing at night. Tying knots and undoing tangles in the dark will not be problems. Navigating precisely to that weed bed or drop-off where the lunkers lurk is no challenge. However, until you save enough scratch to buy such a device, you need to do some basic preparation before you launch your tube or pontoon boat to kick blindly into the black in pursuit of trophy trout.

Let's start with lighting fixtures. There are several possibilities. You may want a miniature waterproof flashlight (that will ultimately be held in your mouth in order for you to use both hands), or a headlamp. There are also small gooseneck lights that can be clipped into to a fishing vest or shirt pocket.

Some anglers are concerned that night fish can be put off by a bright light at night. Because it has the longest, least-penetrating wavelength, red light is best for not alarming the fish. In lieu of red light bulbs, which could be hard to find, consider putting some type of red plastic wrap over the lens, secured with a rubber band.

## Before I Launch

When I slip into the water in the dead of night in my pontoon boat, I have three rods all rigged and ready to cast. All this has been done long before the daylight fades. If I tangle a line or break off a fly in the dark it is much easier for me to reach for another rod that is ready to cast than mess with a bird's nest or tie on a replacement fly. I have three rods onboard even though I am capable of carrying five ready-to-cast rods. If I carry two additional rods in the rod holders on the right side of my boat there is a chance—since I am a right-handed caster—that I will wrap the fly line I am casting around one or both of the elevated rod tips mounted on that side of my boat. It only takes one lapse of awareness for this to happen. The risk of this aggravation is not worth it to me. As an added prep move, I have a fly already tied to the end of the tippet on my tippet spool. With little difficulty I can pull and cut the needed tippet from the spool with the fly already attached. A surgeon's knot is much more easily tied in poor light than the clinch knot required to tie on a fly.

Since the fish are not leader shy in the night, I use a 2X or 1X tippet. Besides the added strength of a larger diameter, I get an easier turnover of the leader and fly, and a decreased chance of tangling on the cast or hitting myself.

## Fly Choice

A large Woolly Bugger or Bunny Leech are popular and effective night-fishing flies. As for color, it seems to make little difference. Silhouette as seen against the night sky and lively movement seem to be the two most important considerations in fly design and selection. Though I have not tried it, some anglers will incorporate a head or body that has a small bead within it that rattles. The audible element of the rattle serves to bring additional attention to the fly for the hungry trophy on the prowl. For audible attraction, I am inclined to "splat" my fly hard onto the surface when I cast it. The crash landing can definitely get a nearby trout's attention.

Too much weight in the fly or the use of a very fast-sinking line can be counterproductive. Decreased is the ease of a fish

As I ready for a night fishing adventure, I want to survey in daylight the lake I will fish. I make mental notes about my options for entering and exiting the lake in relation to those locations in the lake I will patrol in the dark and about specific shoreline areas where I might want to cast from the bank.

seeing the fly from below, silhouetted against the lighter background of the night sky. A floating line can be a better choice for a couple of reasons. First, the angler is less likely to snag in shallow water as the fly is retrieved and trolled. Second, a floating line is easier to pick up off the water and cast than a sinking one.

Especially in shallow water, let's say six feet or less, a floating fly, such as a deer hair mouse or a deer hair popper, can produce some exciting action. The flat face of a popper will produce an audible "pop" as it is stripped. No, poppers are not just for bass; a predacious trout will jump on these at night.

## Reconnaissance in Daylight

For the sake of safety and fish-catching potential, scout the body of water you choose for venturing onto at night. If there are surface logs, fallen trees, or surface weed beds to negotiate, you want to know where those obstacles are located. If there is a treacherous or brushy shoreline to deal with when launching or landing your craft, a smart angler will have these mentally marked. If you need a visual reference on a dark night, consider using glow sticks. A glow stick is a plastic tube containing chemicals which, when mixed by breaking the internal barrier in the tube that separates them, provides a glowing light through chemiluminescence. Often used as party favors, glow sticks are inexpensive and found in many retail outlets and general merchandise stores. Those producing a color closest to white are most easily seen in the dark. They can be situated at strategic locations, such as a launch or landing site on the shoreline, or to reference key fishing spots. The glow sticks can be placed and activated during evening daylight, providing illumination hours into the night.

If a very exact location is necessary for fishing success, a portable GPS unit with predetermined waypoints on the lake can be used. Some models come with a lighted display screen and can easily be read in the dark.

## Troll or Cast?

There are some nights when there are frequent fishy splashes in the immediate area where I am fishing. I've had good success in these situations with casting to the splash. There's a fish near the splash, no doubt. When I send my fly to the general vicinity of the commotion, I am sure that most of the time I have missed the center of the resulting watery rings. Anyway, the fish is not stationary after the splash, moving in some ran-

Launch sites on some lakes are challenging during the day. Getting in and out of the lake in the dark can present safety issues.

dom direction I have to guess about. So, there is an element of luck involved when my fly lands near the moving fish. I can compensate a little for a miss by the fact that my fly will make a noisy "splat" as I purposely crash land it on the surface. This can get an aggressive fish's attention, causing it to turn to investigate my fly. As soon as the fly is on the water, I'm stripping it. The swimming movement of the fly is picked by the fish's lateral line, pinpointing its position. If the fish is well below the fly as it approaches, the predator may visually pick up the fly's swimming silhouette against the background of the lighter night sky. Visibility is enhanced when the night is illuminated by the moon.

Casting the fly to the fish cruising in the night has a couple of attractive advantages. The hard landing of the fly splashing down can audibly get a fish's attention, and the angler can put the fly immediately in the vicinity of a fish that has revealed itself by breaking the surface. Additionally, for those anglers who prefer to be more proactively involved in the exercise of fly fishing, casting and stripping is definitely less passive than trolling.

Because my flies can be large, and heavy when waterlogged, a 6- or 7-weight fly rod may be the best choice to propel my offering. I prefer rods with a soft, forgiving tip action. I can better feel such a rod flex when casting in the darkness, so I can more easily control the timing of my casting stroke. If you are new to casting with no visual reference, practice during daylight with your eyes closed. And use the largest fly that you plan to throw during your nighttime fishing to simulate as best as you can what you will have to cast in the dark.

A note of caution: When fly-casting there is always a risk of being struck by the hook, whether night or day. The obvious concern is being struck in the eye. When it's light, you can often see trouble coming at your face and react accordingly. An errant casting stroke in the dark can be dangerous. This is why practicing with your rod of choice and a big fly if you will use one, is important. As you might guess, windy nights are the worst. It may not be smart to venture forth on a breezy night. You can always wear glasses with un-tinted lenses.

On those nights when the fish are not inclined to splash to reveal their whereabouts, trolling allows for covering a lot of area in a short time compared to casting from a stationary position. If trolling results in a significant number of strikes in a specific spot, you can halt your craft and cast "around the clock." That is, casting progressively in a clockwise or counterclockwise position. For instance, if the first cast is made at an arbitrary 12 o'clock direction, the second cast is directed at 1 o'clock, the third at 2 o'clock, and so on, until you arrive back at the 12 o'clock direction. If during the casting progression around the clock a fish should splash within casting range, immediately turn and make the cast toward the splash.

It will be a great aid to your trolling cause if you have familiarized yourself in daylight with the area you plan to troll in the dark. Submerged wood, shallow weed beds, and shallow shoal areas can all grab your fly. There's always a chance the fly will be lost when you attempt to break it free. Replacing a section of tippet and tying on a fresh fly can be a tedious aggravation. This is why I carry ready two rods in reserve on my boat. Besides dodging the aggravation of nighttime knot tying, I save valuable fishing time by quickly changing rods.

If you should feel a slight "pluck" on your fly while trolling or stripping your fly in the dark, make sure you immediately check the fly for debris—usually vegetation—that may be attached to and trailing on your hook. It can adversely alter the silhouette of the fly, or if the light is good enough, the fish will see the vegetation trailing the fly. In either case, a potentially interested fish may refuse the fouled fly. Periodically check your fly if you are not getting any fishing action. You don't want to troll for hours to no fish-catching avail only to find that you have some green "mermaid hair" on your hook.

## Moon Phase

With a little hunting on the Internet, it is possible to find good lunar information. I want to know how much potential illumination the moon will provide, so I try to find out where it is in its phase, what time it rises, and what time it drops below the horizon again. If the lake—or the portion I want to fish—is lined with tall trees or is bordered by a cliff or steep hill that can block the light of a moon near the horizon, I also want to know when the moon will be at its zenith to provide maximum candle power. Do not leave the moon phase and the timing of its position in the sky to chance. Be prepared, and if you can, plan the timing of your night fishing trip accordingly.

These things being said, some anglers want to fish during the dark phase of the moon or at that time of night when the moon is near or below the horizon. I have had good (and poor) fishing under both bright moonlight and moonless conditions.

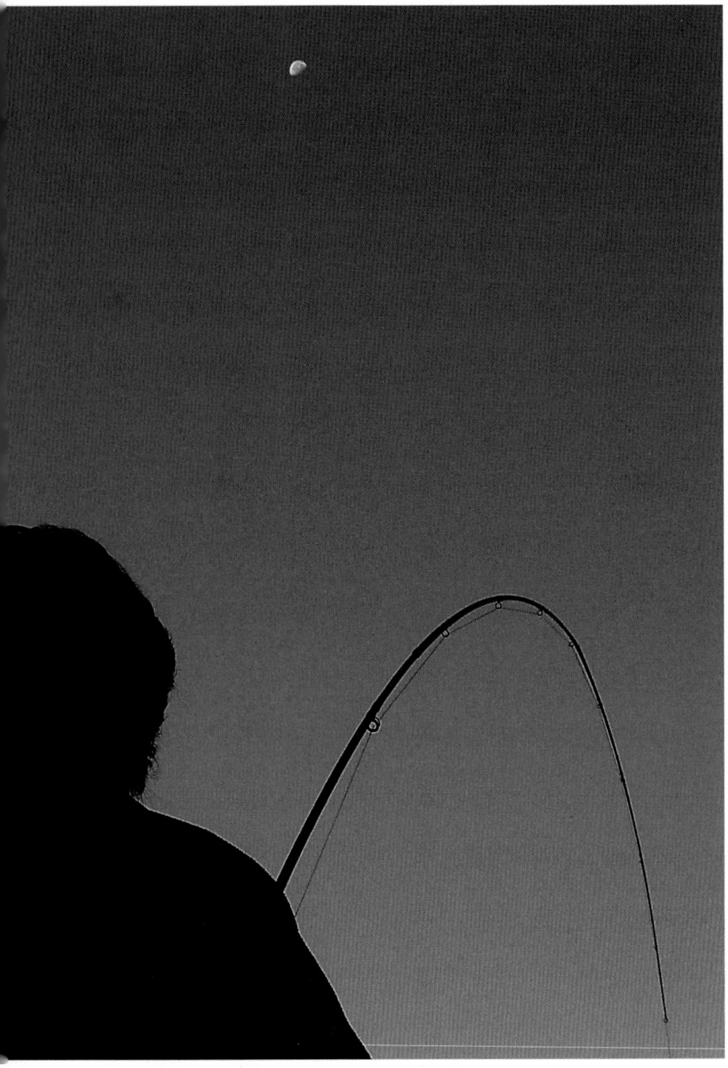

Moon phase and moon position during the night can have a bearing on the timing of your fishing and your fishing success. Check the solunar table as part of night fishing planning.

For those brand new to night fishing, I would strongly suggest venturing out with a bright moon. The added illumination makes negotiating the lake and dealing with rods and lines in the dark a little easier.

## Small Desert Lakes and Ponds

If you know of, or have access to, productive waters with a minimum of tall vegetation along the shoreline, there may be no need to launch a boat or inflatable craft at night. I have fished some high desert lakes in Oregon (no legal problems on private waters) and Washington where I can roam and cast at the water's edge with minimal interference from trees and brush. Usually all I have to contend with is low-growing sagebrush. As long as I keep my backcast elevated, my casting difficulties are minimal. On the other hand, those lakes and ponds in rainy, temperate areas tend to be rimmed with high trees and brush, making shoreline casting difficult or impossible. The other big plus of high desert lakes is that the water chemistry tends toward the alkaline end of the pH scale. This often translates into better growing conditions for more and bigger fish. Add to this the fact that desert lakes typically receive more sunshine, resulting in enhanced photosynthesis, and you have the potential for more insect and crustacean habitats. More fish food can translate into more and faster-growing fish. So, if more fish and bigger fish have appeal for you, head for those lakes where the water chemistry and sunshine are optimal. In the Pacific Northwest this means getting into and east of the Cascade Mountains.

## Pick Your Season

Some night-fishing anglers are so into nocturnal adventuring they may fish under the stars any season of the year. As for myself, I do it most often during the dog days of summer, in July, August, and early September. Fishing success during daylight hours can be minimal in these as lakes and ponds are warm to the point that trout are uncomfortable and lethargic. My nighttime efforts can produce good results on a lake or pond where no fish can be caught during the sunlight hours of a scorching summer day. Additionally, in popular lakes that get a lot of fishing pressure, the fish that have eluded anglers' efforts to throw them in the boat cooler in earlier months may have become educated and wary. They have somehow come to learn that daytime feeding is much more hazardous than dining at night. Again, my best chance is to trick them while the stars shine.

During the dog days, specific locations in a lake where cooler water temperatures are found can find the fish concentrated. Inlet stream mouths and underwater springs are a couple of good examples here. Because springs can be hard to locate in the midst of a lake, especially a larger one, a GPS device with an illuminated screen and specific waypoints programmed into it with can be invaluable.

## Confusion Countered by Experience

As I read about or talk with other anglers who fish stillwaters at night, I find a broad range of experiences and opinions about flies, moon phase, intensity or lack of moonlight, leader length, fly patterns, and all manner of things that alarm the fish. Know that you will discover "expert" opinions that will contradict the dos and don'ts of other night fishing experts. Ultimately it is up to you, reader, to do some research and planning, and venture forth into the night to formulate your own opinions. Here I have relayed what has worked for me on the waters I have fished. Geographical regions, time of year, moon phase and moonlight available, weather and water conditions, and the particular fish species you target all have a bearing on your equipment, flies, techniques, and the degree of stealth required. You are dealing with a system in flux with many variables in it. As one variable is changed, other elements in the success formula are altered, too. This is why a game plan with contingencies is so important. On any given night, a resourceful angler may have to resort to Plan B, C, or D.

Productive high desert lakes may have few trees to interfere with your fishing at night. Do some reconnaissance during the day, noting anything in the terrain that could pose a problem in the dark, especially if casting from the shore. Keep the rod tip and fly line high on the backcast to prevent a break-off of the fly, saving time and frustration.

## My Guideline Suggestions for Night Fishing

In spite of the array of varied opinions by nighttime fly anglers, I will finish here by summarizing some additional guidelines to get you started if you wish to venture into the dark.

1. For fly selection it is difficult to go wrong in choosing a Woolly Bugger or Rabbit Strip Leech. Both designs have good movement and a broad silhouette. Use sizes 2, 4, and 6. I have used dark colors with good success. Know that other good night anglers will use much smaller flies, especially if they hit the lake just at dusk when the light intensity is in transition. There are many aquatic insects that can hatch at dusk, and into the early darkness, where size 10, 12, and 14 hooks are best. If the lake you fish in late summer has a population of *Hexagenia* mayflies, such as Washington's Merrill Lake, this is the absolute best time to fish these large insects. The fish will go bonkers on the surface at dusk in frenzied pursuit. For big flies I will use a 1X or 2X tippet, in hopes a trophy will grab me hard. About 6 or 7 feet of leader is adequate, and it's easier than a standard 9-footer to cast. Night fish are not leader shy.

Timing is important for catching the *Hexagenia* mayfly hatch at dusk; it may last for less than an hour. Be on the water as the sun sets, ready to cast. Rather than try to tie on a new fly in the event of a break-off, have a second rod rigged in advance. Pictured is an Extended-Body Big Yellow May.

2. Consider having multiple rods rigged and ready to cast. If you don't want the hassle of tying knots or undoing tangles in the dark, merely reach for a fresh rod. Six- and 7-weight rods have the backbone to cast big or waterlogged flies.
3. For the combination of effectiveness and ease of casting, a floating fly line may be all that you need.
4. If fish are rolling and splashing near me, I will stop moving to cast from a stationary position. I have had good results when I immediately pick up my line to cast in the direction of a rolling fish. As for the specific retrieve, it always involves experimentation. Sometimes long strips work; sometimes short strips work. Sometimes fast strips work; sometimes slow strips work. Know that a fish can grab your fly just as you are about to lift it out of the water for another cast.
5. A couple of safety precautions: Consider wearing eyewear to protect your eyes from a hook. Consider fishing with a friend, especially where alligators, snapping turtles, water moccasins, and assorted underwater beasts are present. A friend may not be able to help you, but he can tell your family and the authorities how and where you died.

Summer night. Moonlight. Big fish. And maybe a werewolf encounter if you are lucky. Even though you may not be able to pinpoint a splashing or rising fish in the dark, I have found it surprisingly productive to cast in the general direction of the noise. Perhaps it is the splash of my big fly in its general vicinity that gets the fish's attention and draws it to my fly.

# CHAPTER 13

# The Making of Champion Lake Flies

Not all champion lake flies look like anything fish commonly (or ever) see. Sometimes it pays to experiment.

Before I get into specific stillwater fly patterns, here is an overview of what goes into the creation of effective flies, how they come into being, and some of the fly-tying materials that collaborate to produce a champion lake fly. For those readers who tie flies, what follows may give you some ideas for creating your own effective pattern designs and your own champions. And, if you are not a fly tier, you may find the information useful the next time you select finished flies from the bins of your local fly shop or sporting goods retailer.

## Selecting My All-Star Team

As a professional fishing guide, I know the importance of enabling my clients to catch fish. They need to have a good time with me, tell their friends, and come back—hopefully—to fish with me again. Part of the successful formula that enables them to catch fish with me are the flies I choose. On rivers, fly selection is a much simpler matter than it is on lakes and ponds. Whereas I can carry my stream fly selection in a

A stillwater fly angler who is also a fly tier can create and discover his own champion flies.

single box, I will have a dozen boxes, or more, on any day fishing stillwaters.

One of the challenges for the fly angler fishing lakes and ponds is that the fish usually get a long, hard look at an artificial before they decide to eat it . . . or not eat it. In the moving waters of streams and rivers, the fish are often forced to make a rash decision as a morsel is carried past them by the current. If they hesitate, the drifting snack may be gone forever. Another factor in forcing the fish into a bad decision to eat a fake with a hook in it is that choppy, broken surface currents distort its vision. Light penetrating a river's riffly surface is refracted, reflected, and bounced, similar to the effect created by a kaleidoscope. On top of the fact that the fly is moving with the current, the light to illuminate it is ever changing.

On a windless day on a lake, when the surface is flat, and the sun high, even the best anglers can be hard-pressed to get a strike. Visibility for the fish as they inspect an artificial fly is just too good. Any experienced stillwater fisherman will tell you the fishing improves when there's a little breeze. The riffled surface creates enough light distortion that the fish are more prone to mistaking a fly for something alive and edible. In spite of decreased visibility, the one viewing advantage that stillwater fish retain is inspecting a slow-moving object. They can pursue and study the fly in a much more casual manner than a stream fish before making the decision to bite it. For this reason, lake flies must be more exacting in their design, materials, and color than patterns fished in a moving water environment.

Whereas river flies are swept along by the currents, it is the angler who must create the swimming locomotion when imitating organisms on the move in lakes and ponds. Some creatures have very distinctive swimming movements. For instance, a dragonfly nymph propels itself in spurts. Damselfly nymphs wiggle laterally through the water. Leeches contract and extend, undulating as they swim. Obviously, an effective stillwater fisherman has learned about these creatures and their peculiar movements so that he may not only have flies that look similar to the real thing, but also mimic as best he can the actual swimming movements of these creatures. A well-designed fly may be totally ineffective if it is not moved through the water in a convincing manner.

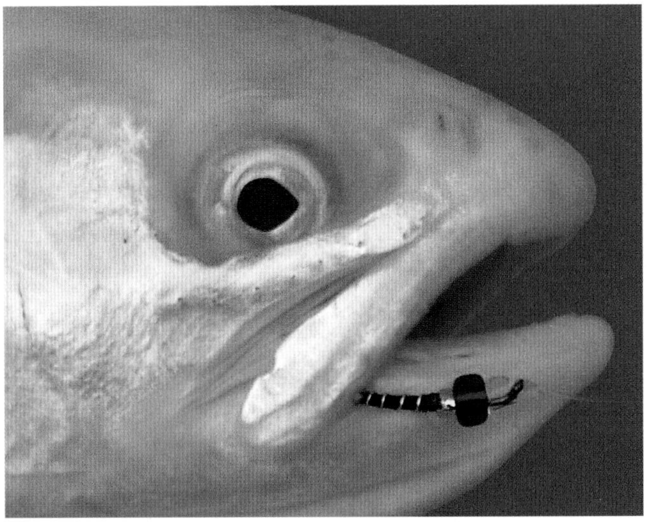

This albino rainbow trout could not resist one of my All-Star Team members, the Laser Beam Chironomid.

## There Will Always Be One More Undiscovered All-Star

Fortunately for me, the Holy Grail of stillwater flies will never be discovered. At such a statement you might ask, "Why wouldn't it be great to discover the one holy fly pattern, that Champion of Champions that never fails, one that always catches the fish?"

In my infant years of fly fishing, I sought that Holy Grail, the Ultimate Fly. During my time of enthusiastic ignorance, I very much enjoyed the search. It was like trying to capture an elusive leprechaun who would reward me with a pot of gold for his release. Once the Ultimate Fly was found I would never have another fishless day; all that swims would succumb to my every cast.

As the years passed and my fly-fishing experience grew, I came to a couple of important realizations: 1. There is no Holy Grail fly. 2. Even if there were a Holy Grail, it would take away the joy of the search, the joy of the effort. Gone would be the striving for better skills and contemplative solutions in attempting to catch challenging stillwater fish. There would be no challenge, no striving, and little or no enjoyment.

## Not All Are Created Equal

A small minority of stillwater fly patterns are definitely superior to the worldwide population of flies cast by lake and pond anglers. In the unjust world of fly fishing, all flies are not created equal; some catch fish on a consistent basis, while others do not. Consistency is the operative word. If fish are in a suicidal mood, a fly made from the threads of an old sock, cat whiskers, and a rubber band can catch fish—but chances are it would be the fishing world's one-hit wonder with success never to be repeated. So just what keeps a lake or pond fly out of the bargain bin and moves it to the top of the classics chart?

Superior flies attain their status when they have proven themselves over and over in the arena, just like a gladiator who slays his competitors and lives to fight another day. When called upon to catch fish in the right circumstances, and presented properly by the angler, the champion fly pattern fools wary fish when other flies—some near-clones—fail.

On any given day on any given stillwater, the majority of fish will fall into three main degrees of selectivity: some may be easily fooled, others slightly more wary, and some very difficult to catch. The overall catching success will often be determined by the level of expertise of the angler and superiority of his fly patterns. At one extreme, we have suicidal fish that will eat everything, no exceptions ever. These can be caught by just about any angler, regardless of skill, using just about any fly with any method. It is suicidal fish that may encourage the beginner to continue his fly-fishing endeavors, which is good. However, it usually does little to aid you in your search for superior stillwater flies. Also, on the downside, such easy fishing will give a mediocre fly angler an inflated assessment of his skills. We have all been there, or will be.

The second rank of relatively easy-to-catch fish dine indiscriminately on most flies. They require a little coaxing when it comes to biting the fly. The right retrieve at the right depth is

The cutthroat trout of Henry's Lake show a distinct preference for the Beadhead Midnight Bugger fished on a slow-sinking intermediate fly line.

To maximize the fishing time for trying out experimental flies, consider fishing two at once on the same leader.

much more important than the particular fly. This situation can be confirmed when many anglers are catching fish on many different fly patterns but are employing the same fishing method. Or it can be confirmed by a single angler willing to experiment with a variety of fly patterns fished with the one particular retrieve at a specific depth. If flies of vastly different designs and sizes, such as a Woolly Bugger, a scud, a Prince Nymph, and a damselfly nymph all catch fish, it seems reasonable the fish are not being too selective for pattern.

The third rank of difficulty and selectivity for stillwater fish is pickier fish. These require a specific one or two retrievals at a specific depth, with a few (usually not just one) specific flies. As for fly size and color, there is some leeway, too. Here we have the need for more specific fly patterns, a narrower range than those demanded by the others, but not just one fly pattern in only one size and one particular color. Especially in quality public lakes, this probably constitutes the degree of challenge presented by most of the fish most of the time, assuming that hatchery fish have not been planted in the lake during the last week. Many quality lakes have regular plants of hatchery trout. Before these acclimate, learning to find the natural foods of their new home, introduced fish may be among the suicidal ranks for a time.

Those fish offering the highest level of education demand a specific fly—size, shape, color, and materials. These fish are very selective. The correct fly fishing method and the correct depth are also necessary parts of the fish-catching solution. Through experience and trial and error, the successful stillwater angler may very well be one of the elite few on the lake catching any fish. In fact, he or she may be the *only* one. This is a heady situation, and pride may precede your next defeat (or mine). Just as the easiest-to-catch fish can inflate your judgment of your actual talents, the hardest-to-catch can do the same on steroids.

Lastly, there are the Nope/No Not Now fish. They care not about your mad skills or past victories. Superior flies with superior techniques are useless. Environmental conditions and mysterious moods put the fish off the bite. Though hope and pride may cause you to persist, sometimes it's better to gather up your toys and go home. Factors like a full moon or prolonged hot weather can thwart even the best anglers. There can be unknown factors in play that put fish off the bite, or you may run out of time to test enough flies and methods. Nightfall or a deadline arrives before everything can be tried. Temporary defeat—even the best must learn to deal with it.

On those waters where the hatchery truck has just recently departed, or at remote lakes where the fish are starving or completely naïve, the average angler can look like a champ. For beginners, the casting, experimenting with retrieves, detecting the strike, setting the hook, and playing fish correctly are all good for experience-building. For intermediate and accomplished lake anglers, the pickier fish provide challenge and learning at a much higher level. They will help you discover your All-Star flies. The Nope/No Not Now's can get inside your head, because there is no way to know for sure that you cannot coax a Nope/No Not Now's into to saying "yes, yes" to the next new fly you put in front of it.

## Test in the Arena

Perhaps the best arena in which to test for superior gladiator flies is an easily accessible public lake with big fish in it. Such lakes receive much fishing pressure, and the bigger fish are usually older, "wiser" fish. If Arena Lake is a catch-and-release water, so much the better. A fish that has been caught and released a number of times over several years learns to be wary about eating just any old thing that swims through its visual zone.

On popular, heavily fished stillwaters, it can be fruitful to fish something out of the ordinary. Give wary fish a fly they haven't seen and pique their curiosity.

The angler's obvious advantage lies in the fact that fish need to eat, and the big fish have to consume more calories than their little brothers and sisters. A fisherman can take confidence that the fish in Arena Lake are feeding most of the daylight hours, the exception being the heart of a hot summer season. Even then, deep submerged river channels, springs, and cool creek mouths can offer comfort and food all day long. With fish on the feed, it is then up to the fisherman to locate them, and choose the right fly and method to catch them.

While it is usually pleasant and renewing to fish alone in a beautiful stillwater setting, some of us welcome the challenge of competing with other anglers on a lake. I have my gladiator school; they have theirs. Today, if the fishing is difficult, there will be a contest between my gladiator flies and others' champions. Just like in the Roman arena, sometimes only one will prevail.

## Let the Games Begin

***April 8, 2011. Big Lake.***

Launched just before 2 p.m. A light, intermittent breeze made the afternoon seem cooler than the mid-50s air temperature. Three rods onboard my float tube—two floating lines for chironomids and Mini Leeches under an indicator, and a third with a clear sink-tip. Since the sink-tip was set up and ready to fish with an olive-with-black Flashabugger and a #12 Prince on the point, I stripped out line as I moved toward the far side of the 5-acre lake. I put out a dozen strips of fly line, allowing it to sink as I kicked the boat slowly. Once it had sunk a few feet and pulled tight with my movement, I slowly raised the rod tip about 3 feet, then dropped it again as I trolled, imparting additional movement to the flies.

There were three craft—two float tubes and a two-person pontoon—preceding me onto the lake, and another float tuber launching right behind me. One of the float tube anglers had landed a small trout as I was readying my boat. There was some hope, I thought.

Less than a minute into my initial troll, I got a strike. The hook held fast in the fish when I lifted for the set, and I quickly landed a 10-inch rainbow on the Flashabugger. Was it going to be one of those fish-on-every-cast sort of days? If so, that's both good and bad. Good from the standpoint of getting lots of fishing action photos; bad from the standpoint that no skill and thinking are involved, and any hack with a rod can catch fish. There's not much to be learned on a day the fish are suicidal.

After releasing my first fish, I was soon into my second. Another on the Bugger. And, a third struck the Prince, and was released. One of the tubers inquired about my fly. I indicated I was fishing a leech. A true statement, of course.

Champion fly designs usually employ a combination of fish-attracting materials. The Woolly Bugger pictured here has a lively marabou tail, an eye-catching Mylar chenille body, a soft feather spiraled over the body to create a soft, lively silhouette, and a metallic gold bead at the head.

Within the first five minutes on the lake I had landed three fish, so I was a bit baffled by my observation that no one else—now five other anglers total—was hooking anything. Some were apparently fishing chironomid pupae under an indicator, while others were trolling unknown flies. After a few more strikes on which I failed to keep the fish on the hook, the bite died. I trolled, I casted and retrieved. I moved to different locations and varied my retrieves. In the next half hour of fishing and watching the other anglers on the lake, I got a couple of light strikes. I saw one fish landed by the rest of the crew. Time for a switch.

One of my indicator rods was ready to cast, rigged with a red bead–red body chironomid pupa on the dropper and a black Beadhead Micro Leech on the point, I made my first cast near a partially submerged stump where the water was, perhaps, about 5 feet deep. Having charted the lake bottom last summer with my electronic depth finder, I had a good sense of the lake bottom topography. The trout liked the changeup. After my first cast with the new setup, my indicator soon went down with a fish on the Micro Leech. Then a second soon followed. The other anglers saw the commotion caused by my fish, but kept their distance. It's good that they did because I was not going to be engaged with conversation. If I sensed they wanted to move closer to chat, I would have kicked away to a different location.

Following the same pattern as my initial quick success with the Flashabugger, the action died after two fish on the Micro Leech. One of the float tube anglers landed a fish during my lull. So now I had seen a total of three fish landed by other anglers since I had arrived at the lake compared to my five fish landed.

I moved around the lake, probing the shallows toward the shore opposite the launch site, and the channels of deeper water that were up to 10 feet deep. Eventually I returned to the small "bay" rimmed by partially submerged stumps and wood debris. A couple more trout took the Micro Leech and came to hand. A larger fish grabbed the Leech and then hung the chironomid on a submerged branch, breaking off the Leech in the fight. I freed the chironomid and tied on another black Micro.

Leeches, leeches, leeches. In my cache of many stillwater fly boxes, my leech collection in all manner of sizes, colors, and designs is only outnumbered by one other pattern. This rainbow fell for a champion black Micro Leech. However, what is the single most numerous fly type I carry? Answer: the chironomid pupa.

Three more float-tubing anglers—a middle-aged-father and two sons—launched to join the fray. They were slowly heading toward me as they trolled the lake's perimeter. I was going to give them wide berth as chatty Dad led the flotilla in my direction. Before I began my retreat, the indicator went down again. The hook held. I soon realized I was into my best fish of the afternoon. As the battle continued, I watched to discover if anyone was heading my way to "assist" me and chat it up. Here comes Dad, his back to me, oblivious to me and my fish. When he does finally turn to see my splashing trout, Dad does not pull up to give me room. He continues on his path directly at me. Hmm. I decided to kick to a small island out of his path where I could tend the fish, pump its stomach, and release it after admiring the fish for a moment.

As I brought the 18-inch rainbow to hand I heard, "That fish is so big you might need a tag for it, boss!" I assured chatty Dad that the fish was to be released unharmed to fight another day. Boss? I think I definitely prefer this to Bub or Buddy.

When I pumped the trout's stomach, it was evident he had been dining enthusiastically on midge pupae. I watched the food items as they were drawn through the tube up into the bulb of the pump. As I let go of the fish I watched it jet away into the depths, no worse for the ordeal, except hungrier than when he had bit my red chironomid.

I laid the stomach pump on the apron of my float tube, and pulled out a white plastic yogurt container lid from the side pocket on my tube. The contents of the pump were gently squirted onto the rimmed lid revealing exactly what I expected—dozens of chironomid pupae. Most were still alive and wriggling. As I took photos of the pupae some continued the transformation from the pupa to adult. As I watched, some were splitting at the thorax where a head, wings, and legs were bursting through as the emerging adult struggled to be free to fly away, find a mate, and fulfill its prime directive of carrying on the species.

As I watched the chironomid pupae wiggling on the white lid, some of them underwent a color change! They became more silvery, shinier. It was from these shiny casings that adults emerged. Apparently, the trapped gas underneath the skin expanded (due to an increase in temperature, as I had exposed them to the warmer air, warmer than the water?). The expanding gas created space between the pupal skin and the adult inside this skin, making it easier for the adult to exit. This makes a good case for tying chironomid pupae flies with a silvery or shiny pearl body. The segmentation becomes clearly more pronounced, with the "ribbing" extending out instead of in. A larger diameter

Sometimes the day's champion fly does not closely resemble the preferred natural food items available to the fish. The Laser Beam has consistently proven itself in The Arena.

wire rib on a hard surface body (thread or tinsel) would create this effect.

To match the majority of these dozens of pupae on an appropriately sized hook, they would best be approximated with a thin pattern tied on a size 20 hook. My size 10 red chironomid fly was huge compared to these creatures. Obviously, the fish I was catching were not being too selective. With the water clarity not much greater than 30 inches, I wanted something big enough for the fish to see. The shiny glass bead on the pupa fly and the dark silhouette of the Micro Leech were easily seen, and that's why I had chosen them as my frontline soldiers. Neither remotely matched the available food source for the fish at this time, but they liked the flies and the way I was fishing them. On the other hand, the other eight anglers on the lake, plus one bank angler patrolling the shoreline with a spinning rod, fishing a vast array of food possibilities, were not catching fish. The trout were not being suicidal, no one's fools.

After landing my eleventh fish to a combined total of four scored by the other eight anglers in the course of three hours, it was time for me to head out. For me, the fishing had been a bit challenging and fun. Most of the fish were not big, but no matter. They reinforced the flies and methods I chose for the day. I am not convinced that the specific areas I chose to fish were particularly special, especially as I sensed the fish were not concentrated in any one particular area or areas. I fished where I did partly to stay out of the way of the other anglers. Having caught fish in many different locations on this lake, I took what was given to me. I deduce it was the right flies and the right method for the conditions.

## Keep It Simple? I Wish I Could!

When I guide rivers for trout or steelhead, my clients must catch fish. Chances are great I will not see them again if they do not. Even with a lot at stake when guiding moving waters, I can usually keep my fly selection to a reasonable number of fly patterns and sizes, able to fit what I need in a single fly box. However, in lakes and ponds I typically have a dozen fly boxes or more with me. If I am fishing unfamiliar stillwaters, I take a large zippered athletic bag that holds thirty fly boxes or more.

Even a few fly patterns can grow exponentially in number when varying the size color, color combination, and fly-tying materials. As an example, consider how many sizes, colors, color combinations, and different materials can be used to tie one of the staples in every stillwater fisherman's fly box: the Woolly Bugger. There are countless mix-and-match combinations. My Woolly Buggers and variations of them easily fill a dozen of my fly boxes.

It is a rare day when I don't change flies often on a lake. Among other things in a typical day on a lake, different aquatic organisms increase or decrease their activities or hatching hour to hour. Fish relocate to different depths and locations. Water temperatures, wind, light intensity, and barometric readings change, influencing the fish and their activities.

When the bite isn't happening, it can be hard to know if a switch to a different fly pattern is the answer. To expedite the discovery, I always have multiple rods with different flies tied on and ready to cast. If I am in my float tube or pontoon boat, I carry three rods, each having two different flies on the leader. Even with a minimum of six different flies on the three rods, I know I will be changing some of them. It behooves the fly angler who wishes to maximize his or her chances to be able to remove and tie on flies quickly. To compensate for poor eyesight or dim light, it is best to be so familiar with knots as to almost be able to tie on flies with your eyes closed.

Matters would be simpler if selecting the right fly were enough to change your luck; you must also fish it at the right depth, and with the proper retrieve. Darn it! So once you have decided on a new fly (or flies), it will take a while to experiment with where and how you fish the fly in order to be relatively sure this is, or is not, the fly to stay with.

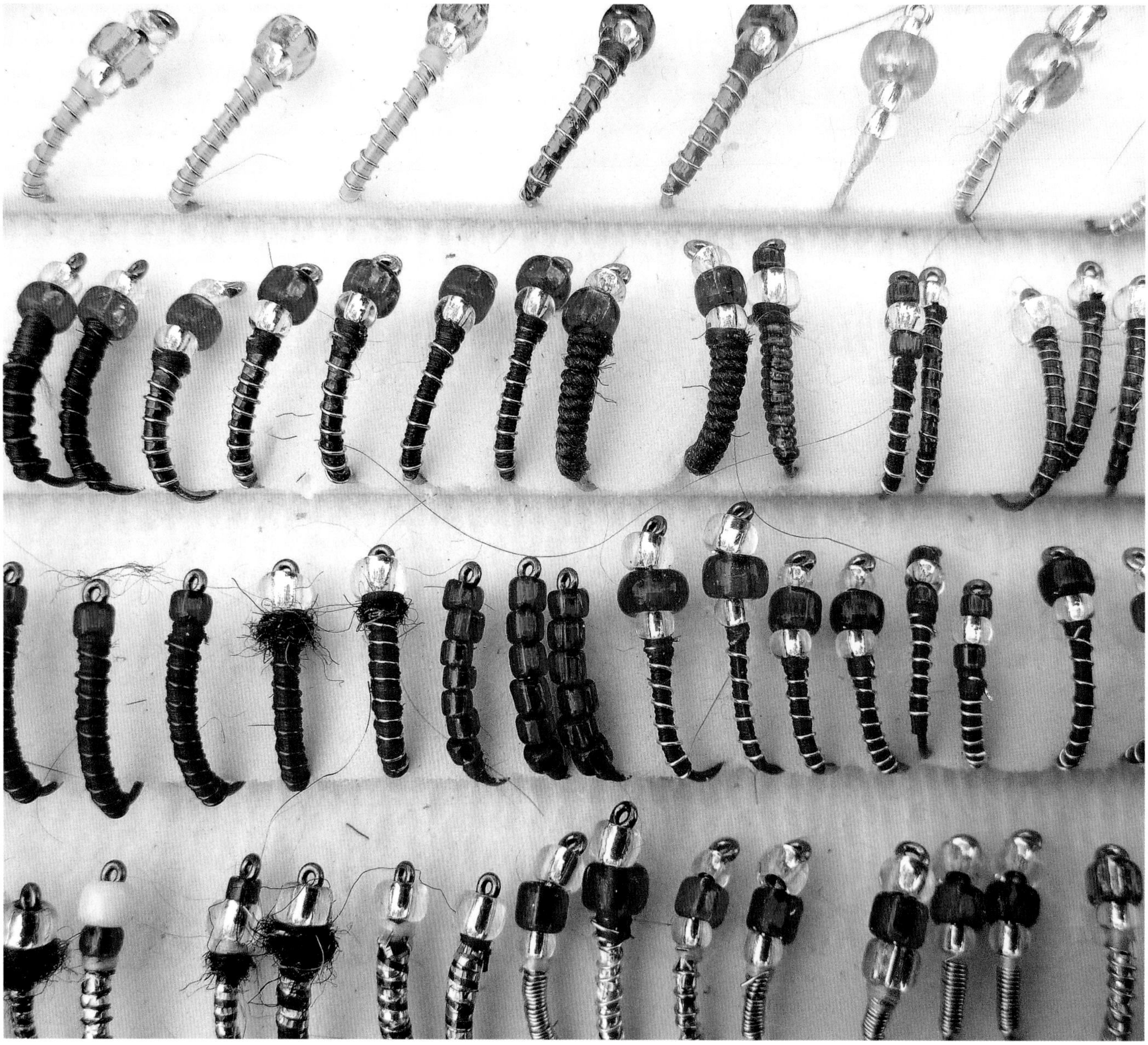

Pictured is a sampling of both champion and experimental chironomid flies.

## I Can See What You Are Up To!

Unlike streams and rivers where an artificial fly is propelled and tumbled by a speedy current, a fly retrieved or trolled in still-waters—often slowly—can be carefully scrutinized by a fish considering eating it. Lake fish demand a more convincing fly pattern of a convincing size, shape, and color. Closer scrutiny of a pattern in stillwater naturally results in the need for a greater variety and quantity of flies to meet the demands of selective fish at any given time.

The materials of which a fly is constructed and the way they are incorporated into the fly design are of paramount importance when picky fish in clear water may inspect closely everything they eat. The materials in the fly must work together to create the illusion of life. Soft feathers, furs, and synthetics that convey movement and life, even when the artificial is not being actively retrieved by the angler, have the potential to be solid building blocks out of which superior flies are created.

A visible feature of many aquatic insects when hatching activity begins is the gas bubble. To aid nymphs and pupae in their ascent to the surface, some will generate gas bubbles that inflate the skin or are trapped and held against the exterior of the body by tiny hairs. It naturally follows that fly patterns that are meant to mimic insects about to hatch can have enhanced effectiveness if materials that trap and hold gas bubbles are part of the fly.

For a natural bubble-trapping material, there is none better than the fur from a hare's mask or ears. The spiky guard hairs in the fur trap and hold air bubbles within the fly. This is one reason that the Gold-Ribbed Hare's Ear nymph has been in use since the 19th century. You would think that with the explosion of fly tiers, fly-tying materials, sophisticated methods and tools

A stillwater angler can never have too many flies. I carry an athletic bag full of stillwater fly boxes in my 4Runner so I have maximum choices when I arrive at my fishing destination. By contrast, I carry only one or two fly boxes when I fish rivers, even when guiding.

over the last hundred years that flies like the Hare's Ear would long ago have been pushed into obscurity by successive generations of ambitious young gun patterns each seeking to make a name for themselves. Such is not the case.

Hare's ear dubbing fur is available in a vast variety of dyed colors as well as the natural brown. It is also available mixed with a synthetic material that has an affinity for gas bubbles: Antron. Gas bubbles cling to this three-sided fiber. By itself, Antron can be an unruly material to work with, so if a tier applies it to a hook as a dubbing, it is best mixed with a more pliable natural fur such as rabbit. As yarn, Antron can be wrapped on the hook, but yarn bodies are usually not the most realistic when compared to a dubbed one, especially on small flies.

When I use Antron yarn for chironomid bodies, I twist it repeatedly to make it rope-like. As this tightly twisted Antron is wrapped on the hook, it creates an obviously segmented look. I have had good success with black, dark brown, olive, and claret imitations.

Another aquatic insect imitation where an exterior bubble representation is important is the water boatman. Because they are air-breathers—no gills—water boatmen carry a shiny air bubble on their abdomen. Pearl or silver tinsel are obvious choices for abdominal materials when tying flies to imitate these insects.

Another very effective class of fly-tying materials that can be incorporated into flies to create the illusion of gas or air bubbles is beads. I am particularly partial to silver metal beads and silver-lined clear glass beads when creating the bubble effect. Most patterns find the bead at the head of the fly. However, they can be used in the thorax or the abdomen, too. A silver or clear bead, or pearlescent tinsel, as the underbody of a water boatman fly is killer.

## Magic Beads

As I mentioned in my journal entry about the April day on Big Lake, there are times that the shine of a bead and maybe the color, too, are enough to intrigue fish. Though the trout on that day ate nothing but chironomids, they were obviously willing to consider other foods. I caught fish on four different flies, different sizes, shapes, and colors. The one thing they shared in common was a bead. The beads on the various flies were red, clear, silver, and gold. The one thing all the beads had in common: reflective shine. Though I saw none of their flies that day, I bet many of the other anglers were using beadhead patterns, just as I did. Besides my specific pattern choices, how, where, and at what depth my flies were fished all had some bearing on my success, and the other fishermen's lack of it. I won't know if I would have had success using their flies fished how and where I did. I think not. None was a standard, commercial-stock fly except the Bead Prince. Experience caused me to gravitate to the particular patterns I chose. They had been proven previously in the arena, and they proved themselves again.

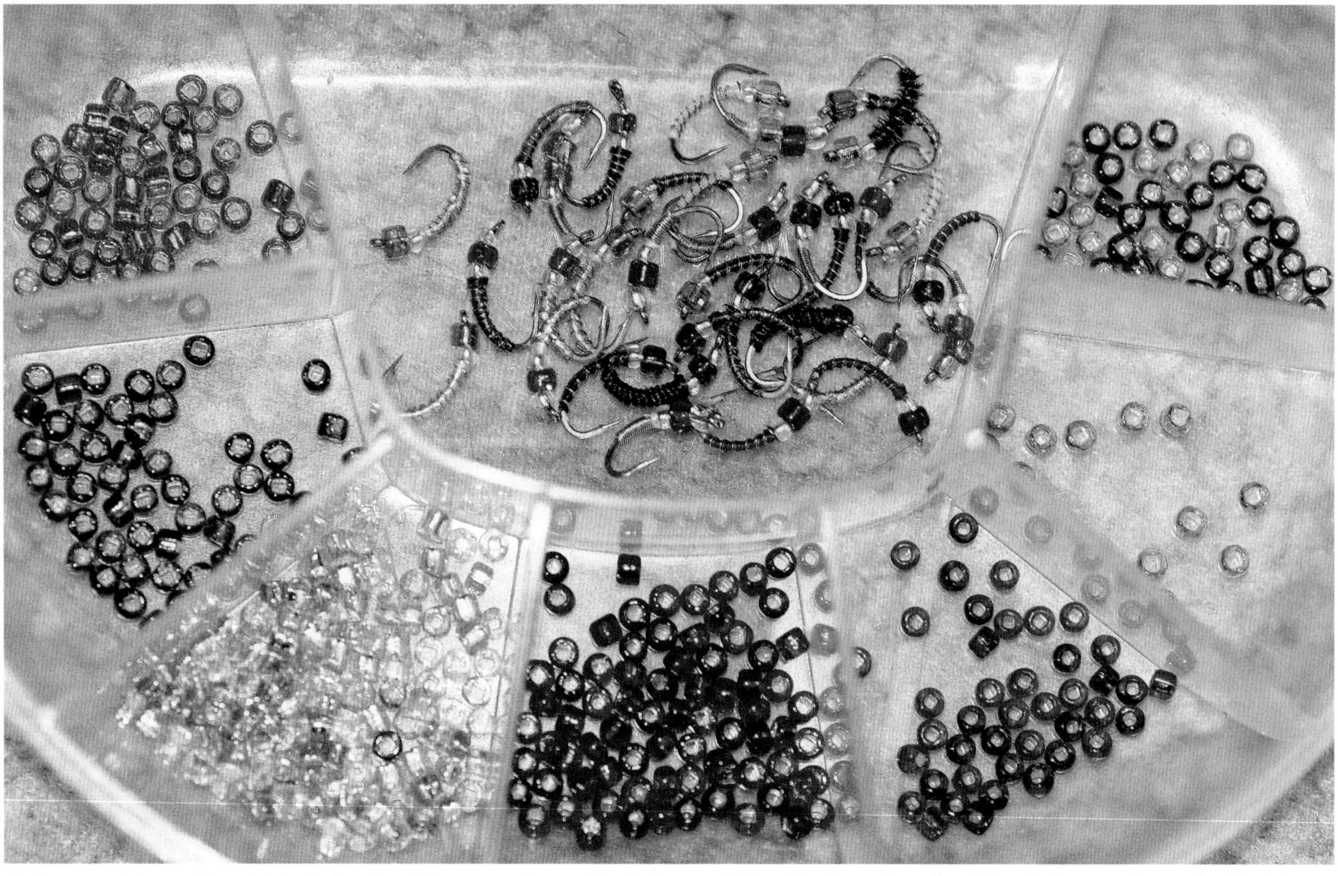

Various metal, crystal, and plastic beads will be part of every fly tier's materials collection. Silver-lined beads have enhanced reflectivity.

Over the last 30 years, no one fly-tying material has impacted subsurface fly patterns like beads, especially metal beads. Metal beads give a fly at least three potentially fish-attracting attributes: shine, enhanced sinkability, and, in some cases, swimming undulation. With any given fish, any number and any combinations of these attractive characteristics of metal beads may be at play. As for glass or plastic beads, I think it is mostly the visual attractiveness of the glimmer or shininess of the bead, since there is little weight to influence the sinkability or swimmability of the fly. Heavier than plastic, glass beads may influence sink rate and swimming action, but usually not to the degree of metal ones, especially tungsten metal beads.

Glimmer and enhanced sink rate are fairly straightforward. However, the swimming movement created as a bead at the head of a fly may not be obvious to all anglers. As a beadhead fly is retrieved, there is naturally a pause as the angler lets go of the fly line with his stripping hand to reach farther up the line to grab and pull the line again, making the fly commence swimming. During this pause, the fly will naturally drop and dive, headfirst. As the fisher pulls the line tight once more, the fly ascends and swims forward. Seen underwater from the side, the fly undulates and swims in little sinusoidal waves. It isn't hard to imagine how this vertical bobbing and weaving added to the horizontal swimming movement of the beadhead fly, might intrigue a fish looking for a living food item. An observant fly angler may note that at any given time fish may show a biting preference for the artificial as it descends during the pause between line strips. Or the fish may attack as the strip commences and the fly ascends.

When it comes to color variety, glass and plastic beads have the edge, as they are available in all colors imaginable. Red and clear crystal glass beads with silver linings are my favorite go-to beads, but I do use green, blue, purple, periwinkle, orange, green, olive, and pearl, too. If the hole in the bead is lined with silver, it greatly boosts the eye-catching shine of the bead. Besides enhanced fish-catching appeal, beads of any type add fun and creativity to fly tying. The mix-and-match possibilities of color, size, finish, combinations, and positioning placement on the fly pattern all stir enthusiasm to sit at the fly-tying vise to create something new and interesting.

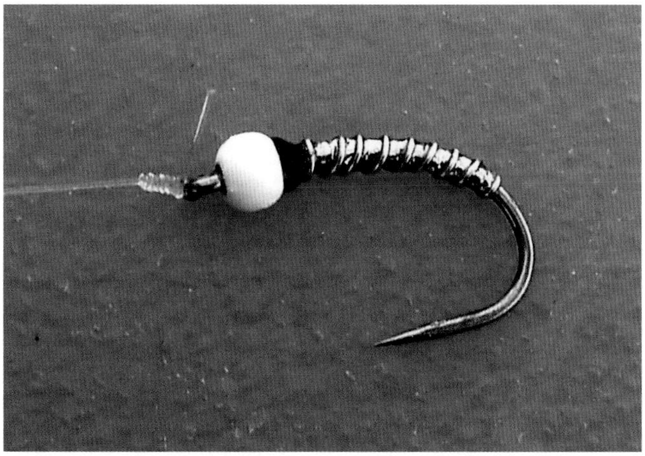

A gunmetal gray body simulates the silvery sheen of a chironomid pupa with gas-inflated skin. Pictured is a Gunmetal Ice Cream Cone.

## Pupal Gas

Gas trapped under the skin of chironomid pupae causes a change in the color and sheen of these insects as they ascend toward the surface, where they will shed their skins to emerge as adults. The pupae, which are normally some shade of olive, green, charcoal, black, brown, or red, will appear to the fish as shiny silver or shiny grayish tan. You can use Flashabou, a silver holographic tinsel, or antistatic bag packing material in creating the body of some chironomid pupa flies. I'm sure other materials could be used to mimic the color and sheen of hatching chironomid pupae. I continue to search, as do other innovative fly tiers. There are common household items, I'm sure, that, once tried, could be one of the ingredients in a new champion stillwater fly.

## Realistic . . . to a Degree

When lake fish are being quite selective, flies often need to look quite similar to the real thing. Some skilled artistic fly tiers can fashion artificial flies out of plastic, monofilament, foam, and balsa wood that are very convincing replicas of living aquatic organisms. I have seen many authentic look-alikes at public fishing shows and fly-tying exhibitions. However, such realistic patterns seem to fall far short in convincing lake fish that they are edible; they can lack lifelike movement in the water. Some of the realistic, motionless look must be sacrificed in order to incorporate fly tying materials such as lively fur and feathers to give the illusion of life, convincing a fish that would eat the fly that this is, indeed, the real thing.

At the other end of the extreme, there are patterns like one of my most dependable lake flies—the Prince—that does not appear a very close imitation of anything I can discern in lakes. It might be somewhat reminiscent of a beetle larva or water boatman, but how is its effectiveness sometimes enhanced by the placement of a shiny metal bead at the head of the Prince? The same holds true of other sinking lake patterns tied with a gold, silver, copper, black, or red bead secured at the head. I have caught fish on hooks adorned only with thread and a bead when the body and tail of the fly has been chewed off or unraveled. What were these fish thinking?

## The Right Feathers Can Add Life

Another important and attractive fly-tying material incorporated into flies like the Prince, Zug Bug, some leech and Carey patterns is peacock herl from the "eyed" feathers of the peacock. The iridescent shades of green and bronze attract fish. The herl is hairy and lively in the water, fooling many fish into believing that they are just about to eat a living organism, or at least something intriguing. Peacock is a magic material.

The peacock body of the Prince nymph is one of the features that contributes to the making of this champion fly. When in doubt, tie a Prince!

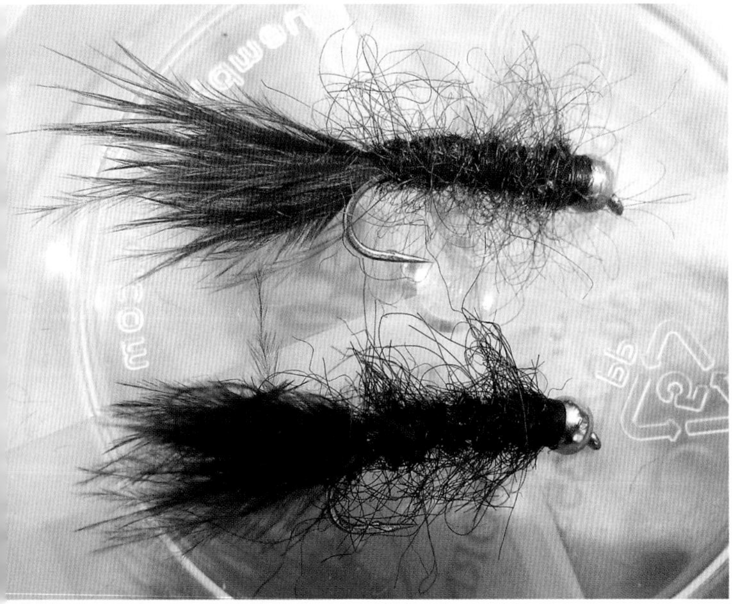

Picked out dubbing fur softens the silhouette and adds a bit of lively realism to the Halo Micro Leech. My top two colors are black and burgundy.

When it comes to lifelike, tantalizing swimming movement, marabou is unmatched. Marabou is the name given to the soft body feathers of a turkey. Did you ever wonder what happened to the bazillions of feathers plucked from all those turkeys who ended up on our holiday tables? Now you know. Nymphs, wet flies, and emergers tied with marabou are legion, and every experienced lake angler has patterns that incorporate this material.

Natural and synthetic dubbing furs can effectively add life and realism to lake flies. Besides movement as they are retrieved, properly applied dubbing can add a "halo" effect to flies. At the periphery of insects, crustaceans, and other aquatic organisms, light creates a halo, or lighter, softer outline, of the body where light passes through the very edge of the creature. Dubbing fur can simulate this softer, halo outline that the fish perceive in living food items. On my Halo Micro Leech patterns, I apply a synthetic fur over the very dense and opaque chenille body of the flies, thereby creating a softer, lighter-on-the-edges silhouette. This is a little touch of attractive realism, at least to me. As long as the fish agree, I continue to halo this fly. The same can be done with numerous standard lake patterns like Woolly Buggers and Carey Special-type flies.

The halo effect can be done on smaller patterns like chironomid pupae, the Cate's Turkey, and the standard Pheasant Tail Nymphs using pheasant tail fibers or sections from a dark, mottled turkey tail feather. Wound on a hook, pheasant and turkey tail fibers have a slightly hairy appearance, making the edge of the bodies softer and haloed. These fibers are also mottled, with various shades of dark and light colors and hues, mimicking the camouflaged appearance of many living naturals that depend on blending in their environment so as to not be easily discovered and eaten.

Many subsurface fly patterns utilize a soft, lively feather as a hackle or beard in their design. Effective feather fibers undulate and wiggle realistically with the slightest movement of the fly in the water. Indian hen back, hen neck, partridge, pheasant, grouse, soft rooster chicken saddle and hen chicken, and duck breast and flank feathers are all prime candidates to be incorporated into champion lake flies.

## Flash and Segmentation

The last materials I want to mention because of their importance in fly design are wires and tinsels. Insects and crustaceans are obviously segmented. Besides adding to the durability of a fly, wires and tinsels accentuate segmentation. These materials come in a vast array of diameters, widths, and colors. It never ceases to amaze me that on certain patterns like chironomid pupae, merely changing the wire color can be the magic touch that turns a slow fishing day into a memorable one.

The fly-tying materials I have mentioned here are surely not the only ones that add fish-catching attractiveness to lake fly patterns. However, these are some of the "must" materials every stillwater fly tier should have at his bench. The mix-and-match possibilities for fly designs and colors are endless. There's always one more combination left untried. Even tying for a lifetime, no fly tier will ever be able to claim her or she has tied and fished them all. New materials and new ways to use them come along all the time. This keeps the game fresh and interesting.

This could be as close as I could ever come to creating the Ultimate Lake Fly: a single pattern that incorporates a bead, pheasant tail, a section of turkey tail, hare's mask, Antron, peacock, marabou, an attractive dubbing fur, holographic tinsel, wire, and a soft, mottled feather hackle or beard. This is a lot of materials to incorporate onto a single hook, especially if it is a small one. Fly tiers, here's your challenge.

## More Considerations

There are some aquatic organisms that display very little movement. Examples would be snails, midge pupae, emerging insects in the surface film, and stationary adult insects as they dry their wings before taking flight. Flies that imitate immobile food items must be that much better in design since the curious fish can get an excellent look at them. Fly-tying materials that create the illusion of the real thing are an important component.

It's hard to get a fly much thinner than a bare hook!

A good fly creator will try to look through the fish's eyes. The closer he can come to replicating what the fish sees as it inspects a living food item—size, shape, color, translucence, subtle movement—the more effective the artificial imitation.

## One More Design Element

Many superior gladiator flies appear realistic . . . within reason. Get the size, shape, and color right, using lively materials, and you have a possible champion. Getting any one of these attributes not quite right can seriously detract from the fly's effectiveness with selective fish. In my fly creation endeavors, I am particularly conscious of shape: less is better. Give me thin—no stocky, muscle-bound flies for me. As an easy test for any given fly in your box, lay it next to a natural insect or other aquatic organism you seek to imitate with that fly. It's quite revealing.

## Mad Scientist

With an indelible felt-tip pen, I label my opaque fly boxes; at a glance I cannot see the flies inside these boxes as I sort through them, so I write on them. Since I have dozens of boxes filled with lake patterns, it's good to not need to open each to discover the contents. One box I always carry is labeled "D & E." Dangerous and Experimental. It's usually good for a chuckle when my fishing companions see it for the first time.

Much of my experimentation involves some crazy color combinations and, often, the incorporation of glass beads in the flies. Kelly green, orange, purple, blue, and yellow are fun colors. I have used cat hair and fuzz balls or "rug pills" that can be found on the surface of a freshly-laid carpet in some of my fly experiments. It is fun when some of my creations actually work, especially when the fishing is tough. When the fishing is easy, I have to consider that the fish are in a careless mood, willing to eat anything fished at the proper depth with the correct retrieve. Only further testing on future trips will reveal a new fly's potential effectiveness.

We see this as a purple and red fly, but, depending on the light conditions, the fish's eye may perceive these colors a little differently than we do. This variation of a Carey Special *does* catch fish.

Many of my experiments never or rarely draw strikes. Having spent time and effort to tie them, I am reluctant to discard these unproductive flies, especially if I deem them pretty. So, they may live in my fly box for years to come, maybe forever. There's always the chance they may be called into duty when the fishing gets silly just so I don't risk losing my better or more complicated flies. Glitzy experimental flies can look good in a close-up photo of an excellent fish when the fly is prominently featured in the picture.

## Take Advantage of the Fat Times

After I disparaged easy fishing earlier in this book, here I go backpedaling a bit. Most anglers naturally experiment with fly patterns when the fishing is tough. However, a good time to test new or experimental patterns is when fishing is good. If I have landed thirty or forty fish by noon, I am sated. I don't need to catch another fish. So now the game is: can I catch a fish on an untested experimental fly? The quickest way to try out an array of experimental flies is to fish two different patterns at once. As for method, I will fish the same manner in the same area that has produced for me already today. The only variables I have changed in the successful formula are the flies. The success of the experimental flies may move them to the forefront of your attention on subsequent trips. If an experimental model generates only mediocre interest from suicidal fish it can be sent to the minor leagues for rehabilitation, or left to languish in the fly box for eternity.

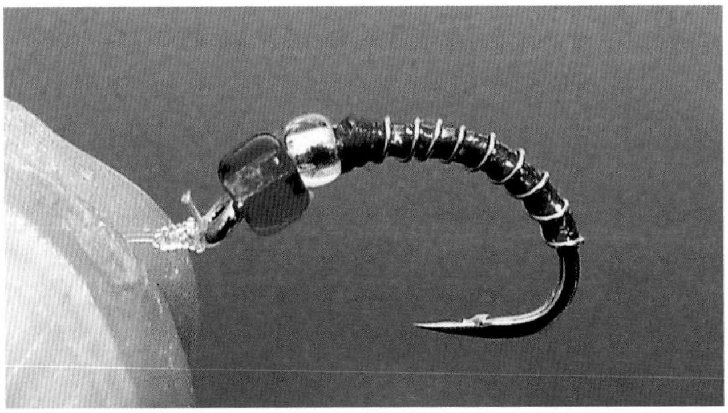

Be prepared to be surprised at some flies that can be effective fish-catchers on any given day, like this quirky Purple Laser Beam.

## Prepare to Be Surprised

Every now and then, a fly not given much hope—one created in some sort of Frankenstein moment—blossoms into a winner. Like the short skinny kid who finds a way to beat the brawny athletes in a foot race, an unlikely fly can become a winner.

My fishing partner for the day and I were trolling and casting on a busy lake. We were catching more than our share of fish, which, that day, was not a very big number. We had tallied perhaps ten fish between us in a little over an hour, significantly more than the total we saw hooked by the six or seven other anglers on the lake. When she decided upon a change of flies, I had my partner look into a chironomid box, which held a bunch of goofy experiments I had tied with a rainbow assortment of glass bead colors. She was immediately drawn to a chironomid tied with a light purple bead and a silver body. I had caught a few fish at another lake with the purple bead, but I assumed that the trout on that day were being too easy.

Once the purple-bead fly was dangled under her indicator, she put the hurt on the rainbow trout, including the biggest fish of the day, of course. Though this purple-bead misfit has not attained All-Star status, it has found a place in the playing lineup occasionally. It's a utility infielder, but it's still a player, not an observer perpetually doomed to sit in the bleachers.

## Simpleton Rule Breakers

After I have written here about the a large stable of wonderful furs and feathers for the creation of Wonder Flies—some of which can be a little complicated to tie—I have to address Plain Jane patterns that defy the rules of cool design and trickiest materials. Some effective lake flies are just bonehead simple: the San Juan Worm, Thread Body Chironomid Pupa, and the Mohair Leech are examples. The Worm is merely a length of red chenille secured by thread on a hook. The Thread Chironomid involves sliding a bead onto a hook, fashioning a skinny body of the thread used to tie the fly, and a barber pole spiral of wire over the body. The Mohair Leech uses a single strand of mohair yarn wrapped around a hook, then brushed back (yes, with a tiny brush or old toothbrush) to create a slender, hairy thing. For the beginning fly tier, these are good starting points to get acquainted with placing and securing materials on a hook, while at the same time creating something that will catch fish.

The Skinny Minnie is a simple fly with a slender peacock body and a couple turns of pheasant rump feather. Fast and easy to tie . . . and effective enough to make my All-Star Team.

I am going to circle back to remind you all of something I have already told you. As a teacher, I know my students sometimes need to be pounded with reminders. So here's a reminder, class. An angler may have a magic stillwater fly attached to the end of his leader. But he may not catch any fish today with it, so the fisherman may put the All-Star artificial back into his fly box where it will be forgotten for all eternity, sadly never called to duty ever again.

## Intrigue Lives!

Besides lively materials, an enticing design, and a proven pedigree, there is an "X" factor in play for effective stillwater flies. There is some unrealized attribute about a particular experimental pattern that fish—sometimes seemingly selective fish—will find enticing to the point they will attempt to eat it. For determined fly anglers and imaginative fly tiers, the intrigue of yet-to-be-discovered superior lake and pond flies adds much to the allure of fly fishing. There will always be one more All-Star fly to be discovered. This is quite fortunate for the sake of our enjoyable, endless pursuit of superior gladiator lake patterns. Yes, I'm truly glad the Holy Grail fly does not exist.

The Turbo Worm has aesthetic glitz for the angler and quirky attractiveness for the fish.

CHAPTER 14

# All-Star Nymphs

The Hare's Ear Nymph and variations like the Flashback Hare's Ear pictured here have spiky guard hairs that trap and hold air bubbles, simulating hatching insects that use gas bubbles to assist them in ascending to the surface during a hatch.

Of all my All-Star Team selections, my Nymph Team is probably the most stable lineup. I will always continue to seek out new and more effective nymph patterns, but I find myself fishing the same effective lineup year after year. If I had selected a Nymph All-Star Team ten years ago, I would have included the same flies you find here. These have truly stood the test of time for me. Although I have tried to tweak these patterns with glitzy Mylar strands, different color beads, glass beads instead of metal, and other furs or feathers on the body, I have been unable to improve the flies on this team. I am convinced my fly-tying experiments are better dedicated to chironomids and wet flies. My Nymph Team is solid year after year.

## FLASHBACK HARE'S EAR

The Hare's Ear nymph has stood the test of time, tracing its origin back into the 1800s. With the emergence of tens of thousands of fly patterns over the last hundred years, it's amazing to realize that this is still to be found in virtually every angler's trout fly box today. The magic is in the spiky guard hairs that trap air bubbles, simulating the silvery gas bubbles fish see clinging to the hairy little aquatic insect nymphs and pupae as they ascend in the water column during a hatch. The flashback model is just a slight variation on the original.

| | |
|---|---|
| Hook: | #10-20 TMC 3761BL |
| Thread: | Tan, olive brown, or wine 6/0 Danville |
| Bead (optional): | Gold |
| Tail: | Hare's mask guard hairs or mottled hen back fibers |
| Rib: | Fine gold Mylar tinsel |
| Body: | Dark hare's mask or hare's ear dubbing |
| Overbody: | Strip of pearlescent Mylar |
| Wing Case: | Wide strip of dark mottled turkey tail |

## PRINCE

With its brown biot tails and white biot wings, this fly does not closely resemble any aquatic insect I know, but fish of many stillwater species love this fly. As I said earlier in the book, when I fish a new lake or pond, or I am unsure of what other pattern I should tie on my leader, I reach for the Prince. I carry both the beadhead and standard types in my fly box. The Prince and Flashback Hare's Ear are my top two nymphs in both rivers and lakes.

| | |
|---|---|
| Hook: | #10-16 TMC 3761BL |
| Thread: | Black 6/0 Danville |
| Bead (optional): | Gold |
| Tail: | Medium brown biots |
| Rib: | Fine gold tinsel |
| Body: | Peacock |
| Wing Case: | Pair of white biots, the length of the body |
| Hackle: | Brown |

## STUBBY BUGGER NYMPH

Whenever the fish are interested in a Woolly Bugger but not enthused about eating it, I will often pinch back (not cut) the tail on a bugger. It could be that the fish are seeking out dragonfly nymphs or emerging caddis pupae, and the Stubby more closely resembles the food du jour. Shortening the tail also makes for fewer "short strikes," whereby an interested fish gets a mouthful of marabou tail feathers but not the hook. This pattern is quite similar, also, to a Woolly Worm, but it seems to have much more sex appeal.

| | |
|---|---|
| Hook: | #6-12 TMC 2302 |
| Thread: | Black, olive, or brown 6/0 Danville |
| Bead: | Copper, gold, black, or silver |
| Tail: | Marabou, pinched short equal to the hook gap |
| Rib: | Fine or medium gold or copper wire |
| Body: | Speckled crystal chenille or coarse dubbing |
| Hackle: | Dyed brown, black, or color of choice grizzly, palmered over the body |

## HARE SCUD

My good friend Matt Ramsey first showed me this fly for catching picky summer steelhead. Because its design looks very much like a scud, a prominent food source in many quality lakes and ponds, it's a logical choice where these crustaceans are found. I have had some days on stillwaters when this fly is absolute magic. As the fishing day ends—and the final individual catch totals are tallied, and I am top rod—I may have to fess up to my friends that I was fishing a Hare Scud. Hare's ear dubbing fur strikes again.

| | |
|---|---|
| Hook: | #10-16 TMC 2487BL or 2499SP BL |
| Thread: | Brown, tan, or olive 6/0 Danville |
| Bead: | Gold |
| Rib: | Fine gold wire |
| Body: | Dark hare's ear or hare's mask with guard hairs |
| Overbody: | Strip of pearlescent Mylar |

## MCU (MOST COMMONLY USED) SCUD

Canadian Phil Rowley published a pie chart of a typical trout's diet in quality lakes. It can be found on his website, Fly Angling with Phil Rowley. Based on his research, he contends that about 19 percent of a trout's diet may be composed of scuds. Every lake and pond angler's fly collection must include these. Scuds are active swimmers; fish your fly accordingly.

| | |
|---|---|
| Hook: | #10-16 TMC 3761BL, 2487BL, or 2499SP-BL |
| Thread: | Olive or olive-brown 6/0 Danville |
| Bead (optional): | Gold, silver, or olive glass |
| Tail: | Feather fibers matching body color |
| Rib: | Fine gold or silver wire |
| Body: | Coarse dubbing or dyed hare's ear dubbing with guard hair, picked out |
| Overbody: | Strip of pearlescent Mylar or Scud Back |

## PHEASANT TAIL

This is another nymph classic, an impressionistic fly that serves as an excellent mayfly nymph. Pinch the tail off completely and you have a very reasonable and effective caddis or chironomid pupa. The hairy pheasant tail fibers and the peacock thorax make for an enticing fish-catching combination. For variations, add a beadhead and/or flashback.

| | |
|---|---|
| Hook: | #10-18 TMC 3761BL |
| Thread: | Black 6/0 Danville |
| Bead (optional): | Gold or copper |
| Tail: | Pheasant tail fibers |
| Rib: | Fine gold tinsel |
| Body: | Pheasant tail fibers |
| Wingcase: | Wide strip of dark mottled turkey tail |
| Hackle: | Brown or brown partridge |

## GOAT/PHEASANT DAMSEL

Rick Coxen shared this fly with me back in the early 1980s. It quickly played its way onto the All-Star Team. It's a simple pattern. Vary the size and color, add water, then fish it. I have even simpler versions, also, in my damsel box. Eliminate the pheasant tail completely. To create a tail simply comb or brush some of the angora goat hair back beyond the hook bend before spiraling the tinsel over the body. Important: Keep the fly thin. As for retrieving this pattern effectively, remember the damsel nymph has a very distinctive swimming motion. Three short, medium-slow strips of the line, followed by a three-count pause. Strip – two – three; pause – two – three. Keep repeating this rhythm . . . and hold on tight.

| | |
|---|---|
| Hook: | #8-14 TMC 2302 |
| Thread: | Olive, brown, tan, or olive-brown 6/0 Danville |
| Eyes: | Olive, brown, or black plastic dumbbell |
| Tail: | Pheasant tail fibers |
| Rib: | Fine gold tinsel |
| Body: | Olive, olive-brown, gold, or tan angora goat dubbing |
| Overbody: | Natural, dyed olive, or dyed gold pheasant tail fibers |

## BIRD'S NEST NYMPH

I love flies that do double and triple duty. The Bird's Nest, created by the late Cal Bird, is such a pattern. Besides being a very good general searching pattern, when the *Callibaetis* mayflies are hatching or caddis pupae are swimming their way to the surface, the Bird's Nest will excel. When fish are feeding at the surface, I cast this fly to the rise and begin a very slow retrieve. In this situation I definitely prefer an unweighted version of this pattern. I like to pair this fly with a cripple or dry fly on the dropper.

| | |
|---|---|
| Hook: | #12-16 TMC 3761BL |
| Thread: | Tan 6/0 Danville |
| Bead (optional): | Gold or copper |
| Tail: | Lemon wood duck fibers |
| Rib: | Gold or copper wire |
| Body: | Brown, tan, or olive hare's ear dubbing |
| Collar: | Lemon wood duck fibers |
| Head/Thorax: | Brown, tan, or olive hare's ear dubbing |

## EPOXY-BACK CALLIBAETIS NYMPH

When selective fish demand a fairly realistic looking *Callibaetis* mayfly nymph, I tie on this fly. Swim it slowly just below the surface on a floating line, or troll it deep on a full sinker. Fish love it. This is most definitely an All-Star, year after year.

| | |
|---|---|
| Hook: | #14-16 TMC 3761BL |
| Thread: | Tan 6/0 Danville |
| Tail: | 3 pheasant tail fibers |
| Body: | Hare's mask dubbing |
| Thorax: | Hare's mask dubbing |
| Wing Case: | Mottled turkey feather covered with epoxy |

## TWO-TONE MARABOU DAMSEL NYMPH

Because of the very lively, lifelike movement of the marabou body and tail, this pattern can outshine the Goat Damsel. Some damsel nymphs have a slightly darker dorsal body color than the underside. Both the Goat and Two-Tone allow for easy simulation of this effect. If you want to play extra dirty, fish a tandem of the Goat and Two-Tone on the same leader.

| | |
|---|---|
| Hook: | #10-14 TMC 5262 |
| Thread: | Black 6/0 Danville |
| Eyes: | Black or green mono dumbbell |
| Tail: | Brownish marabou over olive or gold marabou |
| Rib: | Fine gold tinsel or wire |
| Body: | Brownish marabou over olive or gold marabou |
| Legs: | Pick out marabou strands behind head |

CHAPTER 15

# All-Star Wet Flies and Streamers

It's hard to know if the green glass bead and glitzy Mylar strands in the body of this leech pattern made a difference for the trout, but this fly adds some interesting aesthetics to the photo.

Trolling is the preferred method for many lake anglers. For some, it is their only method for stillwater fly fishing, and wet flies and streamers predominate their fly selections. When I am in searching mode on a new lake or experiencing a challenging day on familiar water, I will have at least one wet fly or streamer on my leader. Because these flies are fished with a tight line, I can feel the strike—I love to get that tug, or sometimes a hard pull. It's an adrenaline bounce. There are times I will choose to ignore all other methods and fly possibilities, fishing streamers and wet flies solely to feel the solid strike on a trolled or retrieved fly. Toward this end, I want flies that have a lot of movement in their design and materials. Rabbit, along with other soft dubbing furs, and "choice" marabou convey living movement. Flies with understated glitz can sometimes enhance a fly's effectiveness, so a bead and a *few* strands of pearlescent or metallic Mylar in the tail or along the body can draw more interest to the fly. In this chapter, you'll find some of my time-tested favorites.

## NEW AGE BUGGERS

No stillwater fly fisherman on earth goes without at least some variation of a Woolly Bugger in his fly boxes. If there is one pattern that all lake and pond fly anglers can agree on, this is the fly. Everyone has them for a reason: they catch fish year round. Whether the fish take it as a leech or a mystery morsel that looks alive and enticing, the fact is they will eat this fly. There are many ways to vary this pattern. Add a bead, flash on the body, flash in the tail, multiple colors of marabou in the tail, or whatever; this pattern commands a lot of variations, in an array of sizes and colors, and a lot of space in every angler's stillwater fly collection. Cast it, troll it, or fish it under an indicator.

| | |
|---|---|
| Hook: | #6-10 TMC 2302 |
| Thread: | Black, olive, claret, or brown 6/0 Danville |
| Bead (optional): | Gold, silver, copper, or black nickel |
| Tail: | Marabou, with 2–4 strands of Flashabou or Krystal Flash |
| Rib: | Fine wire, silver, gold, or copper |
| Body: | New Age or Speckled Crystal chenille |
| Hackle: | Soft, webby saddle hackle palmered over the body with fibers shorter than the hook gap distance |

## TRI-COLOR PEACOCK BUGGER

This is a very specific, very effective variation of a Woolly Bugger, so it commands a special stand-alone place on the All-Star Team. When I offer an angling companion a fly from my Bugger collection during our fishing day—their choice—it's interesting how often they gravitate to and choose this fly. On a given day, the fish can do the same thing.

| | |
|---|---|
| Hook: | #6-10 TMC 2302 |
| Thread: | Black, olive, or brown 6/0 Danville |
| Bead: | Copper, gold, or silver |
| Tail: | Marabou, black over brown over olive, with 2 strands of pearl Flashabou or Krystal Flash on each side of tail |
| Rib: | Fine or medium gold or copper wire |
| Body: | Peacock |
| Hackle: | Brown rooster saddle |

## O'KEEFE CAREY BUGGER

The Carey Special is a long-standing lake fly with a big following of anglers who fish them, especially when dragonfly nymphs are active. Add a marabou tail to a large soft-hackle fly design, and you end up with a Carey Bugger. I prefer this rather oddly matched combination of colors and materials, first shown to me by Brian O'Keefe, to the standard Carey Special. For lack of any other origin, I have always referred to this fly with Brian's name. There are many, many mix-and-match materials and color possibilities for this pattern. Besides mistaking this fly for a swimming dragonfly, it could be taken for a leech, or something that just looks very edible.

| | |
|---|---|
| Hook: | #6-10 TMC 2302 |
| Thread: | Black, olive, or brown 6/0 Danville |
| Tail: | Gold marabou |
| Rib: | Fine or medium gold or copper wire |
| Body: | Peacock |
| Hackle: | Partridge or duck flank |

## DOC SPRATLEY VARIATION WITH BEAD THORAX

Another old standard on Canadian waters, the Doc Spratley still accounts for epic numbers of fish fooled each season. I particularly like to pitch this fly along the shoreline and strip it toward deeper water. When dragonfly nymphs and caddis pupae are active, the shore-cruising fish will climb all over this fly.

I have my own variation here with my own touches, including a metal bead in the thorax. The bead does three things I like, and the fish seem to like. One, it adds some weight to the fly for some instant sinkability. Two, the bead adds some attractive eye-catching glimmer. Three, the bead causes the hackle to flare outward; as it is stripped through the water, the hackle alternately collapses and opens, adding lively movement to it. As with most All-Stars, vary the size and color.

| | |
|---|---|
| Hook: | #6-10 TMC 2302 |
| Thread: | Black, olive, claret, or brown 6/0 Danville |
| Tail: | Dyed saddle hackle peacock or guinea fibers |
| Rib: | Flat gold or silver tinsel |
| Body: | Dyed wool, dubbing, or pheasant tail fibers |
| Thorax: | Metal bead, copper, gold, or silver |
| Wing: | Pheasant tail fibers, natural or dyed |
| Hackle: | Dyed rooster saddle, pheasant rump, or guinea |
| Head (optional): | Peacock or dubbing |

## BIG BUNNY LEECH

Trophy fish have large mouths. Accommodate their ability to eat big morsels with a large fly. The rabbit strip body and tail, along with a soft, webby saddle hackle at the head, ooze the illusion of life as the Bunny wiggles and pulses through the water. Besides being an effective daytime fly, this is an excellent night-fishing All-Star. Use a stout tippet for safe casting and turnover. Use as short a leader as the fish will allow. This is the kind of clumsy-flying pattern that can—especially when waterlogged—knock the glasses right off your face!

| | |
|---|---|
| Hook: | #4-10 TMC 5263 |
| Thread: | Black, olive, or brown 6/0 Danville |
| Bead: | Red metallic, or color of choice |
| Tail: | Rabbit strip as long as hook |
| Body: | Crosscut rabbit strip wound around the hook shank |
| Hackle: | Large saddle hackle matching body color |

## HALO MICRO LEECH

Another variation on a theme, my Halo Micro Leech gets lots of room in my stable of All-Star flies. The standard Micro Leech has a dubbing fur or wrapped marabou body. Because I often use the variegated, glimmering effect of a fine-diameter New Age chenille, I will spiral a light layer of dubbing which I then brush out to form the halo. Besides a little lifelike movement, the halo softens the silhouette of the body of the fly. Though I often fish this pattern suspended under an indicator, it can be equally effective cast and stripped, or trolled.

| | |
|---|---|
| Hook: | #12 TMC 2302 |
| Thread: | Black, olive, claret, or brown 6/0 Danville |
| Bead: | Copper, gold, red, brown, green, or silver |
| Tail: | Marabou with a strand of Krystal Flash or holographic tinsel on each side of tail |
| Body: | Fine New Age chenille, overwrapped with spiky dubbing. The dubbing is teased out to create a halo. |

## LASER BEAM MICRO LEECH

Mark Severson is credited with this specific color combination of the Micro Leech. Though I sometimes substitute a copper or brown bead at the head, the red glass bead is usually the best producer. Also, I may put a light halo of matching dubbing fur over the marabou body.

| | |
|---|---|
| Hook: | #12 TMC 2302 |
| Thread: | Tan, rust, or olive-brown 6/0 Danville |
| Bead: | Red glass |
| Tail: | Rusty reddish brown marabou with a strand of copper or metallic red Krystal Flash on each side of tail |
| Body: | Spiky rusty brown dubbing or marabou wrapped around the hook shank. The dubbing is teased out a bit. |

## BALANCED HALO MICRO LEECH

When a fly is tied to the leader or dropper line, and suspended passively underneath an indicator, the fly hangs vertically. In the real world most insects and leeches swim or rest in a horizontal orientation. It only stands to reason that most artificial flies would appear more natural situated parallel to the horizon. One method for moving the hook eye to a position more toward the center of the hook shank is detailed below. Jerry McBride designed and popularized the horizontal fly. In addition to leech imitations, any nymph pattern to be fished with little or no movement under an indicator can be tied in this "balanced" style. The hook point will sit above the "upside down" fly.

| | |
|---|---|
| Hook: | #12 TMC 2302 |
| Thread: | Black, olive, or brown 6/0 Danville |
| Bead: | Tiny clear glass or plastic bead and 1/8" copper, gold, or silver bead |
| Body Extension: | Straight (or satin) pin |
| Tail: | Marabou with 1–2 strands of Krystal Flash or holographic tinsel on each side of tail |
| Body: | Fine New Age chenille, overwrapped with spiky dubbing |

Slip the glass or plastic bead onto a straight (or satin) pin. Then slip the copper, gold, or silver bead onto the pin. The glass or plastic bead acts a stopper for the larger bead, which would otherwise slip off the head of the straight pin.

Use a wire cutter and reduce the length of the straight pin by a third to half before tying it to the hook shank. Tease out the dubbing on the body to create a halo.

## PUMPKINHEAD

This oddball fly distinguishes itself from zillions of other patterns different enough with its prominent orange glass-beadhead. It was originated by John Kent as a damselfly imitation on Tunkwa Lake, BC. Swim it like you would any other damsel nymph, or fish it under an indicator. On popular lakes when the fish can get picky seeing the same old damsel artificials day after day, show them something different.

| | |
|---|---|
| Hook: | #8-10 TMC 2302 |
| Thread: | Olive 6/0 Danville |
| Bead: | Orange glass |
| Tail: | Olive marabou |
| Rib: | Fine gold, red, or copper wire |
| Body: | Fine olive New Age chenille or medium olive fur |
| Hackle: | Grizzly dyed orange saddle feather |

## HARE'S EAR SOFT HACKLE

This is another effective generic pattern that imitates nothing in particular, but a lot of things in general. This proven design pulsates enticingly when fish are looking for swimming or hatching aquatic insects. The pattern is so convincing it was voted to the All-Star Team.

| | |
|---|---|
| Hook: | #12-16 TMC 3761BL |
| Thread: | Black, olive, or brown 6/0 Danville |
| Bead (optional): | Copper, gold, or silver |
| Tail: | Partridge or mottled hen back fibers |
| Rib: | Fine or medium gold tinsel |
| Body: | Brown, gray, tan, or olive hare's ear dubbing |
| Hackle: | Mottled hen back or partridge |

## PHEASANT TAIL SOFT HACKLE

Again, the finely haired pheasant tail feather fibers on the body and the variegated partridge feathers for tail and hackle are a combination fish like. I usually fish the beadhead version of the fly, with the added sinkability and flash provided by the bead. A non-bead model is preferable when the fish want a fly near or on the surface.

| | |
|---|---|
| Hook: | #6-10 TMC 2302 |
| Thread: | Black or brown 6/0 Danville |
| Bead (optional): | Copper or gold |
| Tail: | Gray or brown partridge fibers |
| Rib: | Fine gold or copper wire |
| Body: | Pheasant tail fibers |
| Hackle: | Gray or brown partridge |

## SKINNY MINNIE

Another simple fly with magic properties, the Minnie (or my rendition of it) has proven itself a very dependable fish catcher. This pattern is the epitome of versatility: it can be trolled, cast and slowly stripped, or fished under an indicator. It may imitate a swimming nymph or pupa, or merely something delectable to sample. In particular situations, fished in the right size, this fly may imitate a mayfly, a caddis, a dragonfly, or a chironomid. When I find myself experimenting with fly patterns trying to catch fish that are refusing more traditional fare, I tie on a Skinny Minnie. It is not always the answer, but it has been often enough to make my All-Star Team.

| | |
|---|---|
| Hook: | #6-16 TMC 2302 |
| Thread: | Black or olive 6/0 Danville |
| Rib: | Fine or medium gold wire |
| Body: | One strand of peacock herl |
| Hackle: | One turn of pheasant rump or partridge feather |

## CHAPTER 16

# All-Star Dry Flies and Emergers

When damselflies sometimes crash land flying back to the water to lay their eggs, alert fish think of these as sputtering, skittering candy.

Frankly, I don't fish dry flies and emergers as much as I should, which doesn't make sense in light of all the rising fish encounters I have in my fishing travels. What fly angler is not absolutely thrilled to witness a good fish rise to engulf a surface fly? It used to be that the only floating fly line rod I carried with me had an indicator and chironomids secured on the leader. There was a natural inertia to my taking the time to remove the indicator and flies to tie on dry flies or emergers. In recent years, I carry an additional floating line rod rigged with a dry fly and emerger on the leader, my usual two-fly combination, knowing that many rising fish are actually taking the hatching insect helplessly struggling to free itself from its pupal or nymphal skin. The team members which follow have been, like my nymph All-Stars, a fairly stable lineup for years. If I thoughtfully select the right flies in the right sizes from this team when the fish are rising, catching surface-feeders is almost a certainty.

## FILOPLUME CRIPPLE/EMERGER

This fly is a Hall of Fame performer whenever aquatic insects are hatching and the fish are drawn to the surface. In the right color and size, fish get foolish for it. I usually pair it with a dry or another cripple or emerger. If the fish show little interest as the fly sits stationary, I will give it a slight twitch, or skate it a little. Don't be fooled. This pattern does not look very exciting, but it draws a lot of excitement. Once you try it, I am confident enough to say the Filoplume Cripple/Emerger will make your All-Star Team, too.

| | |
|---|---|
| Hook: | #12-16 TMC 100BL |
| Thread: | Gray, olive, or tan 6/0 Danville |
| Tail: | Small clump of gray, tan, or olive filoplume or marabou |
| Body: | Gray, tan, or olive filoplume or marabou dubbing |
| Wing Post: | Elk |
| Hackle: | Grizzly |

## SPARKLE DUN

A simple tie with a realistic silhouette, when the *Callibaetis* mayflies are hatching the Sparkle Dun will draw their interest. When there is a simultaneous mayfly and chironomid hatch happening spring and early summer, I will tie a Sparkle Dun as my dropper/indicator. Two to three feet below it, I knot on a chironomid pupa. Most often I cast this to the shoreline and wait for bank cruisers to find the flies. Some will prefer the Dun, while others will pull the Dun underwater as they suck in the chironomid pupa. The realistic silhouette of the Sparkle Dun can fool selective trout. This is especially important when the lake goes flat, no hint of a breeze. Under such conditions, the fish get a very close examination of your fly.

| | |
|---|---|
| Hook: | #12-18 TMC 100BL |
| Thread: | Gray, olive, or tan 6/0 Danville |
| Tail: | Olive Antron yarn |
| Body: | Tan, hare's ear, or olive-tan dubbing |
| Wing: | Elk hair tied as a fan |

## PARACHUTE ADAMS

Whether in moving water or stillwater, this is a "must" pattern. It will forever reign as my all-time favorite dry fly. The Para Adams has a great silhouette, attractive color combination, and high visibility on the water. Adjust the size and fish this as an imitation of an adult caddis, mayfly, or midge. This is a "007" pattern, carrying a license to kill! Figuratively speaking, of course.

| | |
|---|---|
| Hook: | #12-20 TMC 100BL |
| Thread: | Gray 6/0 Danville |
| Tail: | A mix of grizzly and brown hackle fibers |
| Body: | Fine gray dubbing |
| Post: | White calf body hair, calf tail, or Antron yarn |
| Hackle: | Grizzly and brown wound together |

## TIED-DOWN CADDIS

Those patterns that look like nothing exactly, but many things in general, can be used in many situations. With the right color and size combination, the old Tied-Down Caddis can be mistaken for hatching mayflies, caddis, and midges. Fished on a sinking line to pull it subsurface, I have caught fish looking for scuds. This is a versatile pattern.

| | |
|---|---|
| Hook: | #12-18 TMC 100BL |
| Thread: | Black, olive, or tan 6/0 Danville |
| Tail: | Fine tips of elk- or deer-hair wing tied at rear of hook shank |
| Body: | Olive, yellow, or orange dubbing, or peacock herl |
| Wing: | Elk or deer hair |
| Hackle: | Brown, palmered over the body |

## MIJCADMAY

I created the name by combining midge, caddisfly, and mayfly. Sometimes when the Filoplume Cripple needs a teammate to help fool picky fish, I will pair these two flies. The proverbial one-two punch. Like the Cripple, this fly tends to sit somewhat vertically in the surface film, tail sunken and the elk post pointing toward the sky, kind of like many hatching naturals do. The spiky hare's ear–dubbed body traps those attractive gas bubbles for a little one-upmanship on the Filoplume fly.

| | |
|---|---|
| Hook: | #12-20 TMC 100BL |
| Thread: | Gray, olive, or tan 6/0 Danville |
| Tail: | Gray, olive, or tan Antron yarn |
| Rib: | Tying thread |
| Body: | Gray, olive, or tan hare's ear dubbing to match the natural |
| Wing Case: | Elk |
| Post: | Elk |
| Hackle: | Grizzly |

## ANT

Ants taste good . . . apparently. If winged ants start crash landing on the surface, the fish can lose focus on whatever else they might be doing, or eating, and cruise the surface for ants. You had better have a few in your box, or you will be sorry you missed it.

| | |
|---|---|
| Hook: | #12-20 TMC 100BL |
| Thread: | Black or brown 6/0 Danville |
| Body: | Two rounded clumps of black or brown dubbing, simulating the body and the thorax |
| Wing (optional): | Black, gray, or brown hackle tips |
| Hackle: | Black or brown, tied between body and thorax |

## BRAIDED MONO DAMSEL ADULT

Know how to spell "fun"? Here it is: a-d-u-l-t d-a-m-s-e-l-f-l-i-e-s. When these insects are either crash landing onto the lake surface because of pilot error on breezy days, or the females are returning to deposit their fertilized eggs on the lake, the fish can go bonkers as they chase these insects. Because damselflies can fly both fast and erratically, the fish have to strike fast and hard, all-out committed. The water can literally blow up when a trout makes a sprint to catch your fly before it "flies" away. This can definitely be some of the most memorable fly fishing of the year. I know anglers who plan their annual lake fishing trips specifically timed to the damselfly egg-laying event. They have been behaviorally conditioned by surface fishing excitement when fish are on the prowl for these big and tasty insects.

| | |
|---|---|
| Hook: | #8-10 TMC 100BL |
| Thread: | Black or blue 6/0 Danville |
| Eyes: | Mono dumbbell |
| Tail/Body: | Extension of blue braided monofilament, banded with a black indelible felt tip marker |
| Post/Wing Case: | Blue pearlescent Krystal Flash |
| Hackle: | Grizzly, wound parachute style |

## CDC BIOT COMPARA-DUN

When *Callibaetis* mayflies are hatching, this fly pattern can be the best choice, especially when there is no hint of a breeze and the fish can very closely inspect the fly. The CDC edges of the CDC wing sit flat on the water and have a rather "ragged" appearance, simulating a helpless dun trying to fully extricate itself from its nymphal skin. Naturally impregnated with oil, the CDC feather is water repellant and floats quite nicely without the addition of fly floatant. A soggy fly is quickly returned to a nice floating position with a couple of false casts. This is a go-to fly when the conditions are challenging and the fish are being picky.

| | |
|---|---|
| Hook: | #12-16 TMC 100BL |
| Thread: | Black, olive, or brown 6/0 Danville |
| Tail: | Microfibbets or hackle fibers, brown or dun, tied in as a "V" |
| Body: | Brown or olive goose biot |
| Wing: | Brown CDC feather clump, situated on top of the hook, then fanned out Compara-dun style, in a semicircle, followed by a small clump of mallard flank feather tied into the center of the CDC clump |
| Thorax and Head: | Hare's Ear dubbing, two wraps behind the wing and two wraps in front of the wing |

## STIMULATOR

This is a very versatile, high-floating fly that can be skated without easily sinking. When caddisflies are hatching, this is as good as any dry fly to tempt surface-oriented trout. I like to pair this fly with a Pheasant Tail Soft Hackle or a Hare's Ear Soft Hackle fly on the point. If the surface is rippled by the wind, an angler can fish a fairly short line to accomplish an easy skate of the fly with a high rod tip; the twitched fly is less likely to sink when pulled at the low angle of a longer line on the water. Sometimes cruising fish do not require any movement of the fly. In this case, the soft hackle fly will sit suspended under the Stimulator, and the Stimulator can then act as a strike indicator.

| | |
|---|---|
| Hook: | #10-14 TMC 200 |
| Thread: | Orange, olive, or yellow 6/0 Danville |
| Tail: | Small clump of elk hair |
| Rib: | Fine gold wire |
| Abdomen: | Fine orange, olive, tan, or brown dubbing |
| Thorax: | Fine yellow dubbing |
| Hackle #1: | Brown, palmered over the abdomen |
| Hackle #2: | Grizzly, palmered over the thorax |
| Wing: | Elk hair, tied onto the hook before dubbing and palmering the thorax |

CHAPTER 17

# All-Star Chironomids

It's always amazing to fly fishing beginners that such small fare, like this red midge larva, can be of interest to fish. My experience has shown me that tiny hooks are much more difficult for a fish to dislodge during a fight than larger ones.

The difficulty in selecting a Chironomid All-Star Team is that there are so many "players," particularly when selecting the midge pupae patterns. With so many variations on the same general pupal fly design, there are hundreds—-if not a thousand—-of choices, and new variations spring up constantly. I have more stillwater fly box space dedicated to chironomid pupae than to all my other flies combined, with the exception of leech patterns. Leeches command much of the space because they are large flies. In terms of the actual *number* of stillwater flies that I carry, chironomids win. Despite the ever-changing chironomid pupae fly population, I have selected my current go-to favorites. I will continue to experiment and mix and match materials and colors, with the hope that I can find more additions to the team you find in this chapter. What a great excuse to go fishing! So many experiments, so little time . . .

## GLASS BEAD TURKEY TAIL/PHEASANT TAIL

Some flies have "the look." This is one of those flies. Turkey and pheasant tail feather fibers have a slightly hairy, haloed appearance that adds a touch of realism to this fly. The appearance of the pattern can be altered merely by changing the color of the body and the wire. There are no rules about changing the bead color, either.

| | |
|---|---|
| Hook: | #12-18 TMC 2499SP-BL or TMC 2487 |
| Thread: | Any color 6/0 Danville |
| Bead: | Clear glass, appropriate for the hook size |
| Tail (optional): | White Antron yarn |
| Rib: | "Brassie" size or fine silver wire |
| Body: | Turkey or pheasant tail fibers, natural, dyed green, gold, black, olive, or red |
| Thorax: | Peacock herl or black dubbing |

## GILL HAT CHIRONOMID

When I was teaching my sister Joann (a most excellent fly angler) to tie these flies, she kept referring to them as those with a "gill hat." The name has stuck, and it makes me smile every time I reach for a Gill Hat Chironomid to tie on my leader. And I smile every time I hook another fish on one of these.

This pattern is simple, fast to tie, durable, effective, and has endless mix-and-match possibilities. How can any single fly have such a list of magnificent attributes? The body of this fly can be kept quite slim, as the bodies of living chironomids are very slender.

| | |
|---|---|
| Hook: | #12-18 TMC 2499SP-BL or TMC 2487 |
| Thread: | Green, olive, gold, black, brown, gray, or red 6/0 Danville |
| Bead: | White, silver, gold, nickel black, copper, red, or clear glass |
| Head gill filaments: | White Antron yarn |
| Rib: | "Brassie" size or fine wire, silver, gold, black, copper, red, or orange |
| Body: | Tying thread |

## LASER BEAM

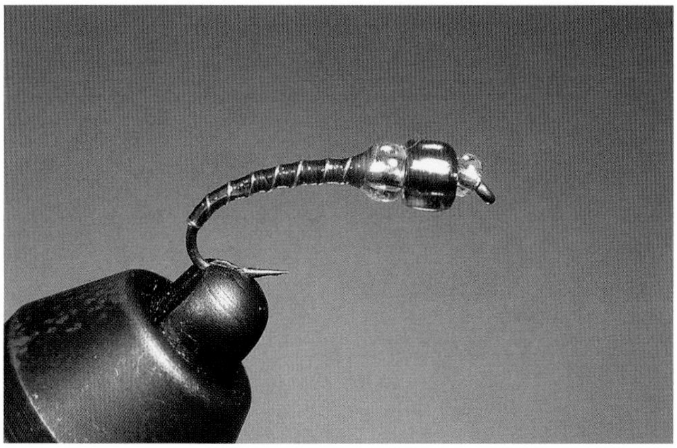

When the fish are receptive to something out of the ordinary—you would be surprised—this is a go-to fly for me. The key element is the red glass bead, the laser beam color.

| | |
|---|---|
| Hook: | #12-18 TMC 2499SP-BL or TMC 2487 |
| Thread: | Red 6/0 Danville |
| Bead: | Red glass, sandwiched between two smaller clear glass beads |
| Wire: | "Brassie" size or fine silver |
| Body: | Red holographic tinsel or red thread |

## SON OF LASER BEAM

The attraction of the color red, combined with the convincing sheen of an ascending midge pupa with trapped gas under its skin, can be deadly. When the fish get conditioned to the same flies day after day, the Son can be the one. When stuck in a fish's jaw, this fly makes for a striking macro photo.

| | |
|---|---|
| Hook: | #12-18 TMC 2499SP-BL or TMC 2487 |
| Thread: | Red 6/0 Danville |
| Bead: | Red glass or metal, usually paired with a smaller clear glass bead |
| Wire: | Red "Brassie" size or medium |
| Body: | Gunmetal Flashabou |

## ICE CREAM CONE

When the water is a bit murky, and an extra bit of visibility is helpful, the white bead on top of the Ice Cream Cone beckons the fish to take a bite. Sometimes it can be the fact that the white bead offers the fish a fly with a different look. During a hatch of a species of chironomid that have very prominent white gill tufts protruding from the top portion of the insect, the white bead approximates that feature.

| | |
|---|---|
| Hook: | #12-18 TMC 2499SP-BL or TMC 2487 |
| Thread: | Black, red, brown, gray, olive, green, lime, or gray 6/0 Danville |
| Bead: | White |
| Tail (optional): | White Antron yarn |
| Wire: | Black, red, silver, copper, or gold "Brassie" size or fine |
| Body: | Tying thread |
| Thorax: | Peacock herl or Spirit River Black Squirrel blend dubbing fur |

## GUNMETAL NOID

This pattern specifically emulates the shimmering grayish tan body color of a chironomid pupa swelled and changed by gasses trapped underneath the skin. The sheen of the body and its color can be key visual triggers when the fish are being selective as they feed on ascending midge pupae. Anti-static bag material wrapped over gray or tan thread can be used to also simulate the sheen and desired color.

| | |
|---|---|
| Hook: | #12-18 TMC 2499SP-BL or TMC 2487 |
| Thread: | Black 6/0 Danville |
| Bead: | Nickel black |
| Head gill filaments: | White Antron yarn |
| Tail (optional): | White Antron yarn |
| Rib: | Red, orange, black, or copper "Brassie" size or fine wire |
| Body: | Gunmetal Flashabou |
| Thorax: | Spirit River black Squirrel Blend dubbing or peacock |

## KRAZY CHROMIE CONE CHIRONOMID

Of British Columbia origin, this fly has caught fish for me on several occasions when nothing else would entice the fish. I'm thinking specifically of Roche and Horseshoe Lakes, near Kamloops, BC. I always have these in my lake fly box . . . just in case.

| | |
|---|---|
| Hook: | #12-18 TMC 2499SP-BL or TMC 2487 |
| Thread: | Red 6/0 Danville |
| Bead: | White |
| Rib: | Red holographic tinsel |
| Body: | Silver holographic tinsel |
| Thorax: | Peacock herl or Spirit River black Squirrel Blend dubbing |

## TURKEY/PHEASANT NOID

When I sense that picky fish want an old school chironomid, I reach for a no-bead type. My favorite two body materials are turkey tail and pheasant tail fibers. These have a hairy, buggy look that fish like—me, too. The tier's challenge is to keep the body thin. Pheasant is a little harder to work with in keeping the body of the fly very slender, but it is readily available in dyed colors. In addition to natural brown, other colors like gold, olive, black, and insect green are particularly useful.

| | |
|---|---|
| Hook: | #12-18 TMC 2499SP-BL or TMC 2487 |
| Thread: | Black 6/0 Danville |
| Head gill filaments: | White Antron yarn |
| Tail (optional): | White Antron yarn |
| Rib: | Fine silver wire |
| Body: | Natural, dyed insect green, olive, gold, or black turkey tail or pheasant tail fibers |
| Thorax: | Peacock herl or black dubbing |

## SAN JUAN WORM

Fly patterns don't get much simpler than a strand of chenille lashed onto a hook. The Worm supposedly mimics the blood worm larval stage of a chironomid, but the real insect is über skinny and not nearly as long as most of the common-size artificials used to catch fish. The proven effectiveness of this fly will always be a bit of a mystery to me. On any given day it can be a killer.

| | |
|---|---|
| Hook: | #10-14 Red Dai-Riki 1273 or TMC 3761BL |
| Thread: | Red 6/0 Danville |
| Rib: | Red 6/0 Danville |
| Body: | Red Ultra Chenille or Vernille (medium) |

## ANOREXIC WORM

When designing a fly, I cannot create a body much thinner than the diameter of a hook. On this fly there is nothing covering the anodized red hook except the silver wire that is spiraled onto it to create a segmented appearance. Red is an attractive color to fish, and the red glass bead looks neon in clear water and creates an attraction for fish like the matador's scarlet cape to a bull.

| | |
|---|---|
| Hook: | #14-20 Red Dai-Riki 1273 |
| Thread: | Red 6/0 Danville |
| Bead: | Small metal or glass bead matching body color |
| Rib: | Fine silver or red wire |
| Finish: | To bond the wire to the hook, coat with super glue for the final step. |

## LARVAL LACE LARVA (A.K.A. THE LALALA)

This is another simple chironomid blood worm imitation passed along to me by a former student at OSU, Pat Allen. You don't even need thread to tie it. It's merely a hollow brilliant red section of Larva Lace threaded onto a hook. If you are concerned it does not qualify as a fly, add an inconsequential tail of red Krystal Flash and a dab of red dubbing at the thorax, like the fly pictured. Voila! It now certainly qualifies officially as a fly.

| | |
|---|---|
| Hook: | #10-14 Red Dai-Riki 1273 or TMC 3761BL |
| Body: | Hollow, red Larva Lace. Slip a piece of Larva Lace onto the hook. Warming the lace can make it a little easier to work with. |
| Thoxax: | Red dubbing |

## FILOPLUME CRIPPLE

This All-Star pattern is often my first choice when fish are rising actively to hatching *Callibaetis* mayflies or hatching midges. Fish often prefer a very vulnerable, immobile emerging insect to a winged adult, which can be a moving target that zigs or flies off, causing the fish to miss its intended target. The color theme can be altered. Light brown and olive are excellent alternatives to the gray.

| | |
|---|---|
| Hook: | #14-20 TMC 100BL |
| Thread: | Gray, olive, or tan 6/0 Danville |
| Tail: | Small clump of gray, tan, or olive filoplume or marabou |
| Body: | Gray, tan or olive filoplume or marabou used as dubbing |
| Wing Post: | Elk |
| Hackle: | Grizzly |

## GRIFFITH'S GNAT

This fuzzy, little nondescript fly is a good generic choice when midges are hatching and the fish are feed in or on the surface. Putting a little movement can often add to its effectiveness.

| | |
|---|---|
| Hook: | #16-20 TMC 100BL |
| Thread: | Black 6/0 Danville |
| Rib: | Fine gold or silver wire |
| Body: | Peacock |
| Hackle: | Grizzly, palmered the length of the body |

## PARACHUTE ADAMS

*Callibaetis* mayfly imitation, the Parachute Adams in the appropriate size can be effective in fooling the fish when midges and caddisflies are on the water. No action? Twitch or slowly skate it. The white post "wing" makes this fly very visible to the angler. The standard Adams with feather tip wings is also an excellent fly.

| | |
|---|---|
| Hook: | #14-20 TMC 100BL |
| Thread: | Gray 6/0 Danville |
| Tail: | A mix of grizzly and brown hackle fibers |
| Body: | Fine gray dubbing |
| Post: | White calf body hair, calf tail, or Antron yarn |
| Hackle: | Grizzly and brown wound together |

## MIJCADMAY

This is my rendition of an emerging midge, mayfly, and caddis. If a touch more realism is required for selective fish, I would choose this emerger/dry fly over the filoplume Cripple. Gray, olive, and tan cover the vast majority of color themes.

| | |
|---|---|
| Hook: | #16-20 TMC 100BL |
| Thread: | Gray, olive, or tan 6/0 Danville |
| Tail: | Gray, olive, or tan Antron yarn |
| Rib: | Gray, olive, or tan 6/0 Danville |
| Body: | Gray, olive, or tan dubbing to match the natural |
| Wing Case: | Elk |
| Post: | Elk |
| Hackle: | Grizzly |

## LADY MCCONNELL

Originated by British Columbia chironomid guru Brian Chan, this fly has a good look on the water to the fish and is easily seen by the angler. It has excellent floatation.

| | |
|---|---|
| Hook: | #14-20 TMC 100BL |
| Thread: | Black 6/0 Danville |
| Tail/Trailing Shuck: | Grizzly hackle tip over white Antron yarn |
| Body: | Fine black or gray dubbing |
| Overbody/Shellback: | Natural deer or elk |
| Wing: | Grizzly hackle tips |
| Hackle: | Grizzly |

Plan, implement, and adjust. John Gorman put all the puzzle pieces in place to hook, and eventually land, this feisty rainbow.

Many chironomid pupae patterns are a simple matter of mixing and matching many of the same materials, with different color combos, in a broad range of hook sizes.

# CONCLUSION

Even those not living in the American West, as I do, can find at least a bit of fascination with the stereotypical image of the American cowboy of the late 1800s: resourceful, self-reliant, independent, and adaptable. Whatever the day's challenges—unruly cattle, swollen rivers, or rattlesnakes—our hero managed to meet all trials and tribulations head on. He coped, survived, and maybe even thrived. If you will indulge me, this image and these same characteristics may combine into an excellent metaphor for the successful lake fly angler.

Compared to the constantly changing challenges of stillwater angling, fishing streams and rivers is a cakewalk, as I alluded to in chapter 1. Instead of a few simple pieces to discover and correctly place in moving waters, there may be an intricate twenty-piece puzzle to be assembled on a successful stillwater fishing outing.

Like the American cowboy (or cowgirl), the successful lake angler needs to not only meet the challenges, but also welcome and embrace them. That is, you may need to "cowboy up" sometimes, to use a Western colloquialism. Such challenges are opportunities to learn, adapt, and tap into your resourceful, creative core. Adopt the attitude that you are not defeated by a tough day of fishing when few fish (or none) were caught. Just like the cowboy, bandage (or lick) your wounds, reflect on the day's events, ponder possibilities "outside the box," determine what you would do differently next time, and formulate a game plan. Then, on your next outing, implement the game plan and make adjustments as needed.

What's a little snow or ice in the guides to a determined fly fisher? Absolutely nothing.

I have mentioned Roche Lake, BC, numerous times in this book. This famous productive lake was one of my all-time best teachers. It was only on my third British Columbia trip that I finally experienced some of the fish-catching potential I knew this lake held. I fish many locations, both rivers and lakes, in a given year. But since I fished Roche Lake for the first time in 2010, it was the single body of water I pondered and planned for more than any other. What this lake taught me, or summoned from my memory banks, can obviously be applied to every other lake and pond I fish, and adopting the outlook of a cowboy was invaluable. When I was figuratively bitten by a rattlesnake and stomped by stampeding cattle at Roche Lake, I was determined to successfully rebound, learn, and succeed. My second trip in 2011 was a minor success—I caught some fish and hooked others—but I was not able to assemble all the puzzle pieces in my allotted time. It only made me more determined. The game plan of 2011 had to be torn apart, fine-tuned with additions and deletions, and then rebuilt. The effort was worth it. The plan produced excellent results the following year, and I became a better stillwater fly fisher as a result.

Some of us anglers are much more motivated to return to the scenes of our defeats than to the waters of our major successes. I was much more determined to fish Roche Lake than any of the other ten Canadian lakes where I had experienced good to excellent fishing. Roche presented my greatest opportunity to think, learn, and adapt. This again reminded me that fly fishing is not merely about catching fish, and not merely about running up the tally on my score card. Instead, fly fishing is more about being challenged to solve the puzzle, especially when previously defeated, and especially when others, too, cannot solve the same puzzle. The satisfaction that results when adversity is met head on (at high speed) may be unequaled in the realm of fly fishing. I may not ever again fish Roche Lake when there are many others in western North America waiting to challenge me . . . and you. For now, it's on to the next challenge.

If this final bit of encouragement strikes a chord with you, I think you have the potential to add not only to your fish-catching success, but also to your enjoyment of stillwater fishing. Fruitless or disappointing lake-fishing days are as certain as death and taxes. It's how we react to such "defeats" that have the chance to make us much better anglers— resourceful, creative, more satisfied, and proud of ourselves as we create and implement successful fishing game plans. It is specifically the never-ending challenges of stillwaters that provide such vast opportunities.

Cowboy up, my friends.

# INDEX